IMAGES OF COMMUNITY

*This book is dedicated to the memory and intellectual heritage
of Basil Bernstein (1925-2000), sociologist*

Images of Community

Durkheim, social systems and the sociology of art

JOHN A. SMITH
CHRIS JENKS
Goldsmiths College, University of London

Ashgate

Aldershot • Burlington USA • Singapore • Sydney

Published by
Ashgate Publishing Ltd
Gower House
Croft Road
Aldershot
Hants GU11 3HR
England

Ashgate Publishing Company
131 Main Street
Burlington,VT 05401-5600 USA

Ashgate website: http://www.ashgate.com

British Library Cataloguing in Publication Data
Smith, John A.
  Images of community : Durkheim, social systems and the
  sociology of art
  1.Durkheim, Emile, 1858-1917 2.Sociology - Philosophy
  3.Durkheimian school of sociology - Influence 4.Visual
  communication 5.Art and society
  I.Title II.Jenks, Chris
  301'.01

Library of Congress Control Number: 00-134508

ISBN 1 84014 518 8

Printed and bound by Athenaeum Press, Ltd.,
Gateshead, Tyne & Wear.

Contents

1 The Need for Paradigm Change

This study began in opposition to the predominance of notions of *wording* in the study of human culture and society. Of course we cannot, as writers and as 'members' in the general sense, sidestep this predominance but we can at least *try* (with our words) to give greater weight to the distinction between verbal and visual 'images' and, in particular, the *different* social processes and possibilities inherent in visual and verbal praxis. We said that the study *began* in this way. As such it would have been compatible with the current and fashionable stress on 'heterotopia' - the pluralism, difference and incommensurability that are said to characterise postmodern society. It might have been seen as, we *saw* it as, a kind of theoretical-political intervention in which the everyday dominion of words (especially in universities) is placed in question.

What emerged, however, was altogether more radical. Along with the growing conviction that the burgeoning literature of postmodern 'heterology' was in fact describing something with actually quite strict but *unmentioned* limits - came the gradual emergence of a quite different paradigm that showed itself as necessary to our original intent. Consequently, the exploration of the different social processes of visual and verbal praxis also entailed the task of elucidating the paradigm that makes it feasible. That, of course, also involves the general critique of the paradigm it seeks to replace.

Dissatisfaction with one's 'home' paradigm (we can call it 'postmodern critical aesthetics' for now) encourages the prospector's instinct and, predictably (thankfully) we found we were not alone in our misgivings – although much of what is now accessible was not so at the outset. But of course, the prospecting instinct introduces new lands, new cultures, new heroes and villains very different from those of the home paradigm. We were, then, faced by what might in other circumstances be called a choice but in fact was a necessity. We *could not* abandon the study and analyses of 'our' heroes and villains (mainly philosophers and artists) and say: here's an account of complexity or chaos theory and this is how it relates to art. For a start, that approach would have more or less precluded the analyses of 'our' heroes and villains and therefore the detailed account of *why* their strengths and weaknesses pointed to the need for a 'new' paradigm in which complexity is a central issue. Instead we wrote precisely that critique in the knowledge that its outcomes would (or should) propel postmodern critical aesthetics towards a common ontology that is concurrently emerging from a number of other disciplines.

Consequently, our analyses begin from the influential figures in the qualitative relationships between epistemology, aesthetics and society (such as Plato, Michelangelo, Kant, David, Durkheim, Manet, Lyotard) rather than the more usual quantitative applications of complexity/chaos theory whose influential figures are often mathematicians.[1] Also we are in several senses closer to the systems theory of Niklas Luhmann and in particular with the transformations or discontinuities within and between verbal and visual orders. We shall clarify that shortly. At this stage, however, let us emphasize our interest in qualitative rather than quantitative transformations and consequently the reader is likely to meet the more familiar figures of aesthetics than the 'strange attractors' of more quantitative descriptions. 'Our' field, then, if related to is also somewhat different in its focus, concerns and consequences. Hence both our title: *Images of Community*; and also what we see as a distinct advantage: we shall not be presenting a altered paradigm and its altered epistemology as a *fait accompli* (as usually happens in quantitative applications) but attempting to deduce its detailed relationships, differences and transformations *vis à vis* the traditional corpus of critical aesthetics.

We shall argue that much writing that currently passes for, to use a catch-all, postmodern 'critical theory' (that claims heterogeny and plurality as its truth) is both uncritical and homogeneous rather than heterogeneous. As such it *represses* both difference and our understanding of the social processes of differentiation.

That in turn implies that the paradigm we seek to elucidate is *necessary* to the limited study we first proposed, namely the *differentiation* of verbal and visual social processes, and more generally to the understanding of *all* social heterogeny.

At first glance there are (at least) two ways we might set about this. The first would be to construct an extremely formal argument about all sorts of ways of wording set against all sorts of ways of visualising. But to bracket, for example, painting, photography, film, printmaking all together as 'the same sort of thing' is a typically reductive *verbal* strategy; just the kind of 'linguistic imperialism' we seek to avoid.[2] We have instead chosen to focus more specifically on how *sociology* as a verbal discipline approaches *painting* as a visual discipline. Notice that we begin with this equality of 'discipline' and specifically reject the currency of 'theory' and

2

'practice' as hierarchical, demeaning, politically 'incorrect' or more importantly, *misleading*. That is to say that the conventional distinction between theory and practice is not just 'politically' but *plainly* incorrect. And that, amongst many other issues is a *general* consequence that is not limited to our specialised study.

That, however, is not quite the full story since it is quite clear that the paradigm shift we propose will inevitably alter what we mean by painting and (more importantly at this stage) what we mean by *sociology*. That, of course, is a matter for the whole text rather than these introductory remarks but we can offer some indications. Our changes involve a degree of interdisciplinary cross-fertilisation mainly from systems theory, chaos/complexity theory and the currently-renewed interest in Darwin. This will of course alienate some readers! (There will be those who put the book down right here.) But that would be on the basis of an expectation we are, emphatically, *not* going to fulfil. Suffice to say at this stage that 'our' version of systems theory should not connote notions of elegant, harmonic homeostasis nor 'right-wing' conceptions of function. Just as systems in nature are 'messy' - implying alliances, competition, interdependence, predation, reproductions and extinctions - so our notion of systems in social settings can be equally patterned or chaotic, emancipatory or coercive. What we propose is not, then, a functionalism like that of Parsons, nor another attempt to assimilate Darwin in the legitimisation of power, but simply an *ecology*[3] of social phenomena open to inter-dependent relationships of construction and de-construction, like any other ecosystem. And crucially, this system is active and open, not alone in splendid isolation, but *inter*active with and *inter*dependent upon the other ecosystems of the planet. In that sense, the conventional reader, we admit, has something to fear but not the old and failed claims of functionalism or social Darwinism. It is rather that an implicit shift has taken place - some would say none too soon - in which humans cannot any longer claim to occupy the stage alone, nor even centre stage as the dominant phenomena of the Earth and the dominant phenomena *of* or *for* understanding. Put simply, 'our' sociology is not inspired by or grounded in the long history of humanism and *this* is the decisive change.

This is not, however, an especially original idea. It is foreshadowed by a number of writers, Darwin included, but most importantly for sociology, by Durkheim (so far as we are concerned).[4] Indeed it is reasonable to argue that Durkheim's whole approach to the distinctness of *sui-generic* (self-generating) *social* phenomena as opposed to the phenomena of 'individual' human consciousness constitutes an explicit rejection of humanism, or more broadly, human-*centred* analysis for *socio*logy. Our contention is twofold: the rejection of humanism may be demonstrable but its detailed analytic implications and consequences are scant in Durkheim - and that specification is part of our task. Second, it is now clear (from systems-theory) that social phenomena are by no means the only *sui-generic* or 'autopoietic' (self-structuring) phenomena and that, therefore autopoiesis in social and non-social systems cannot be assumed as a sort of random free-wheeling. On the contrary autopoiesis - as anything but a formal principle - presupposes an ecological context in which it can be realised. Our arguments will, then, turn as much on material drawn from cognitive systems-theory, in particular the work of Maturana and Varela (who coined the term 'autopoiesis') as it will from the similarly-influenced social systems-theory of Luhmann, or the notions of evolved consciousness in Dennet's philosophy.[5] We can now turn to a first critical sketch of the paradigm we oppose.

This cannot be yet another book on postmodern aesthetics. Nor is it the place for any remotely comprehensive survey of the enormously extensive and varied literature that could be assembled under that heading. But in describing the different standpoint we take, we must engage postmodernity, or theories of the 'heterotopia' of contemporary culture. We have chosen to focus on Lyotard in this opening chapter partly because of his generally-recognised influence in defining postmodernism but more importantly because of the explicit relationships he proposes between politics, ethics and aesthetics. In other words, for us, his imagery of community is important because it combines elements of narrative and aesthetics and as a place to focus critical opposition.

Lyotard's defintions of the modern and postmodern can be abbreviated as follows:

> I will use the term modern to designate any science that legitimates itself with reference to a metadiscourse ....making an explicit appeal to some grand narrative such as the dialectics of Spirit, the emancipation of the rational or working subject or the creation of wealth.[6]

Appropriate substitutes for 'metadiscourse' or 'grand narrative' would be 'worldview' or 'paradigm' or 'ideology' or 'belief system' or 'religion'. Note that each carries with it a series of quite different connotations and social requirements: no religious fundamentalist would tolerate the reduction of his creed to the status of 'paradigm' and even though Hawking might aspire to 'know the mind of God' it is doubtful that science would tolerate more than a metaphoric intent, so that the paradigm (like all paradigms) would remain *not* elevated, incomplete, a series of *effective* postulates, unlike God, open to criticism. Lyotard's choice of examples of grand narrative are equally ironic in their difference: the colossal theoretic ambition of Hegel's totalising Spirit, the 'subject' of Marx's and Sciences' drive for moral and rational emancipation, the utter pragmatism of the 'creation of wealth'. We can be reasonably sure that Lyotard's irony, or better, *indifference,* is quite deliberate. The *postmodern* on the other hand is defined as:

> incredulity toward metanarratives. This incredulity is undoubtedly a product of progress in the sciences: but that progress in turn presupposes it. To the obsolescence of the metanarrative apparatus of legitimation corresponds...the crisis in metaphysical philosophy and the university institution which relied on it. The narrative function is losing its..... great goal. It is being dispersed in clouds of ....language elements. Conveyed within each cloud are pragmatics valencies, [relations, connections] specific to its kind. Each of us lives at intersections of many of these. However we do not necessarily establish stable language combinations...[7]

The decisive sense here is that we are already and irretrievably 'postmodern': we *disbelieve already* so that the 'truth' as it may have been manifest to earlier marxists or liberal democrats or political economists or scientists is already, openly and *only* a 'narrative apparatus of legitimation'. All that remains is pragmatism, efficacy. This has, however, its positives and its negatives:

> the society of the future falls less within the province of a Newtonian anthropology (such as structuralism or systems theory) than a pragmatics of language particles. There are many different language games - a heterogeneity of elements. They only give rise to institutions in patches - local determinism.
> ...consensus does violence to the heterogeneity of language games. And invention is always born of dissension. Postmodern knowledge is not simply a tool of the authorities; it refines out sensitivity to differences and reinforces our ability to tolerate the incommensurable. Its principle is not the expert's homology but the inventor's parology.[8]

The law of pragmatics, then, appears self-regulating. On the one hand it says that *effective* power will eventually succeed, become the very mark of success, the performance criterion. On the other, *heterogeneity* acts against the accumulation of power in one place and for its dispersal within the differentiated and *un*collectable elements of the community. The incredibility of metanarratives is then both the means of dispersal (because heterogeneity is then 'all right') and, ostensibly, the guarantee that no totalising or totalitarian re-collection is feasible or credible.

What then of Lyotard's conception of aesthetic praxis?

> The answer is: Let us wage war on totality; let us be witness to the unpresentable; let us activate the differences and save the honour of the name.[9]

So ends Lyotard's answer to the question, 'What is Postmodernism?' - He speaks of 'the answer', of war waged against totality, of the dissolution of the 'nostalgic' modern aesthetics, of the sublime, as:

> ...that which denies itself the solace of good forms, the consensus of a taste which would make it possible to share collectively the nostalgia for the unattainable; of that which searches for new presentations...in order to impart a stronger sense of the unpresentable.[10]

Or again:

> We have paid a high enough price for the nostalgia of the whole and the one, for the reconciliation of the concept and the sensible...[11]

These sentiments, the denial of the solace of good forms and 'we have paid a high enough price', mark out the complex relationship in Lyotard's thought between the aesthetic and the political. Both are destined

> to have to furnish a presentation of the unrepresentable... The aesthetic supplements the historical-political and the theoretical in general....as a means of pushing the theoretical beyond itself in pursuit of what it cannot capture or present, [or] conceptualise.[12]

The aesthetic, in effect, models an image of how the theoretical-political *ought* to function: in contrast to totalising and totalitarian impulses, the aesthetic shows how the task, the 'destination', is not consensus - whether imposed or 'freely' elected - but rather that of keeping the critical tasks unresolved; 'finding ways to phrase *differends*'.[13]

The problem now begins to insinuate itself. The description of authentic aesthetic practice is too unified and in several senses. There is the vexed problem (we called it linguistic imperialism) of 'aesthetics' being for all 'practical' (i.e. theoretical) purposes 'the same'. In other words the *category* - 'aesthetics' will *do* whether we are talking of music or painting or poetry or film. Well, try telling Barbara Cartland she is a soulmate of, say, Jackson Pollock. Or perhaps Ingres and Pollock? It is obvious what Lyotard will *make* happen: Cartland never was a genuine aesthete and Ingres only appeared to be until Pollock came along. And Pollock can now be 'safely' regarded as nostalgic (along with every other modernist from Cezanne to Robert Morris to Stravinski to Fowles to Matisse to Manet to Epstein; it really doesn't matter!) Why? Because in Lyotard's caricatured prescriptions for aesthetics, uncannily like dadaesque notions of the *modernist* avant-garde, its functions are too simply *disruptive*.

Lyotard's aesthetic is not bound, for example by what we might think as the many desires or many disciplines of its own traditions, its own manifold versions of the 'solace of good forms', the relationship to a collectivity of practice (and its audience) - which Lyotard thinks as 'nostalgic'. And so the call to 'activate the differences' actually falls by virtue of its own caricatures: neither discipline nor tradition is seen as *inaugural* but instead prejudicially - as the obstacle, the nostalgic object, the consensus that *substitutes for* the unpresentable.

The desire to paint, for example, is fundamentally ungroundable by the Lyotard represented by these selections. Certainly it is rather more groundable in the Lyotard who speaks of micronarratives, of a community living at the intersection of many such language games, of painting as 'libidinal machine'. But so far as the mean *orthodoxy* of disruption takes precedence over the radically more varied *discipline* of, painting - the difference represented by all of its characteristic terms is not at all *activated* but is rather *dissolved*.

Let us be clear: we are not arguing for any kind of return to tradition and consensus. Discipline and consensus are not the same thing; but neither are discipline and disruption. We are not proposing any kind of visual or aesthetic retreat or retrenchment. We *are* saying that Lyotard's *wordings* are insufficient to the task of respecting heterogeneity - his own ostensible requirement. But we can go further: his conception of heterogeny is itself *ludicrous*. Or, to put it another way he *cannot* mean it.[14]

If the university audience is a significant indicator we would guess that most readers regard pluralism, 'heterotopia' as preferable to a more prescriptive political or intellectual regime (and we agree). Lyotard's critical influence is sufficient evidence of this tendency. At the same time, of course, we could not allow a Hitler fan club to flourish openly on campus. The example is extreme but unfortunately the extreme is also very flexible. Let us say that as supporters of heterotopia we cannot at the same time support its opponents. Included under that definition would be many others beside Hitler; others we could not label as pathological without looking

7

unacceptably intolerant and sounding very much like supporters of eugenics. We could waste endless hours debating the margins of acceptability: for the university population there would be little doubt where to place Margaret Thatcher or Ronald Reagan *despite* the contradiction of their electoral success. Where does that place the electorate? In the line for sterilization? And how do we feel about Tony Blair's *Christian* socialism? There would be many points scored, many a career improved, and so much embarrassment caused (many a career ruined) by pursuing a line of the kind; a line that showed how quickly Academe ditched democracy for the sake of its own so-obvious supremacy! Apart from the possibility of headlines and sales, however, all of that is beside the point. For anyone but the academic hack the point really at stake is this: Lyotard's, our, *your* preference for the heterogeneous is so much nonsense. We are all guilty by habit not so much of formalism but *bad* formalism. There is *nothing* preferable about heterogeneity. Of itself it makes no such claim: it means only *difference*. It says nothing about the *value* of Margaret Thatcher or Fred West or the Kray Twins or Mother Theresa - except that their priorities are different. If you, (we, Lyotard, academe), apparently preferred 'heterotopia' it is because it had no genuinely formal meaning at all. It really meant: diversity that *we* could *accept*; the actions of people not too unlike *us;* difference that does not threaten our interests. That is the real analytic point - the paradigmatic essential. And concretely it is far less important to establish whether Margaret was blessed or damned and far more important to realise how bad we are at thinking and how easily we gloss our own prejudices; Margaret Blair and Tony Thatcher after all have limited tenure - but 'we' are always with us.

We concede that it *is* important to choose between a far-right-of-centre, post-Thatcherite agenda and a right-of-centre New Labour agenda. We concede that our interest in 'analytic' or paradigmatic questions might be thought over-specialist, and 'academic' in the insular sense. But that is to miss the point and to lose the really important concrete issue. This can be shown by example. The well-aired question of Rushdie's *right* to publish *The Satanic Verses* is no doubt significant. In our terms it is far more significant that Rushdie *thought* his enemy was Margaret Thatcher (her again!) and the objections from Iran and elsewhere - not to mention their scale and outrage - were *completely unexpected;* not just by Rushdie but by *all* of 'us'.

Or again: who in the seventies would have predicted the rise of nationalism in Europe? Who would have thought that an apparently defunct force would become the focus of so much conflict? What is meant by 'us' and 'who' in this context? They mean: 'people like us'; people who *could*

8

not even imagine ethnicity being the most burning issue in others' social lives.

Those who have had the mixed fortune to sit through lectures and seminars in what currently represents sociology or cultural studies will have heard Derrida's dictum, 'Il n'ya pas de hors texte' [15] construed as: 'There is nothing outside text'. Or, statements that assert the *social* world, not to mention *the world*, is 'brought forth' by culture, location, technology, the media and that its perception is *primarily* constituted in language - and is by implication both conventional and contingent - are commonplace. But when the queer world brought forth in the lecture theatre and the seminar room has reached its timetabled ending *everybody* will be trying to get something to eat or drink. And that night everyone who is capable and lucky will be having sex. It is amazing that no one (to our knowledge) has ever waved a condom in a lecture asserting 'there is nothing outside text' and asked: 'You mean I don't really need this?' You can imagine the splitting of hairs over sexual mores that would follow - and thoroughly miss the point. In case it remains missed let us spell it out.

It is an *absurd* simplification [16] to say that 'the' or 'my' or 'our' world is *primarily* constituted in language, text or anything else. Worlds, emphatically plural, are indeed constituted by language, and texts, *but also* by images, food supplies, animal populations, sexuality, disease, nervous systems, death, climate, soil erosion, rainfall, chemical environments, thermal environments, gravity, the slope of the land, the tides. Worlds are *ecologically* constituted. So, you see we must reject the charge of 'academic insularity' and earnestly point out instead that the crass insularity of much current sociology and cultural studies is merely what one would expect from so insular a culture as the one we unfortunately share. In *practical* terms, then, we are unprepared for and cannot imagine the unexpected because it differs from ourselves and that is both politically very dull and very dangerous. If we say that the cause of our insularity is the old humanistic habit of putting the human being in the centre of the stage as the paradigm of and for understanding, we are mouthing only a half-truth: the 'human' at the centre of humanism is reduced from the complex living being to 'thinker' (in Descartes) to 'speaker'-or better, 'hearer' (in Heidegger) and to 'writer' (in Derrida). In Lyotard, in common with most of our shared 'postmodern' perspectives, the human is reduced to a fatuous heterogeny which, taken literally, has no character at all, other than the sentimentalised urge to disrupt - but *nicely* of course!

That is the current (and terminal) corruption of the academy so far as it ostensibly teaches cultural and social studies – when, for the most part, it

9

actually teaches western, liberal 'good manners' of concealed self-interest. Crucially, we conceal our mannered interests from *ourselves*. No one else is fooled for a second by our moral 'neutrality' our ostensible pluralism; everyone *else* can see that postmodern heterotopia is just another name for 'our' kind of political economy, 'our' kind of market place, defended by 'our' kind of tolerances and 'our' armed forces. *This is not a criticism of that choice.* Indeed, we argue that liberal democracy is central to our theoretic position and that 'heterotopia' is a structural requirement with its own ecological advantages and dangers. Our point is that we do not adequately understand our own position and that under current standpoints we cannot really begin to do so. For more critical readers, let us underline that a more rigorous understanding is indispensable for more rigorous critique. We are not, then, defending a status quo but rather arguing that it is to a significant degree unknown.

If Lyotard's, or 'our', concepts of heterotopia and aesthetic praxis are flawed, what of his concept of postmodern science and knowledge? Recall that the distinction turns on the disbelief in metanarratives of legitimation. Again, this conceals as much as it reveals. It is perfectly true that *for us* the question of performance, of efficacy, of economic development has eclipsed ethical grand narratives, for example, of the marxist kind and that the non-moral action of the market is seen by New Labour as the better way to deliver 'the goods' (pun intended) than the moralities of sufficiency, excess and redistribution. But that is not to say that grand 'narratives' do not exist nor that they are disbelieved. It is rather that the *moral* dimension has come to look redundant set against the dimensions of effectivity and preference. This *is* uncomfortable (it is no more than a slightly franker version of Lyotard) but *must* be faced.

It is also true that many grand narratives are incomplete and possibly incompletable. That is why we have not changed the term from narrative to 'explanation'. One could say that an 'explanation' is definable as a fully-unified and complete 'narrative'. But again the problem of elasticity haunts us. Physics still strives for a final or unified theory and to that extent its 'explanations' still contain narrative elements. In the case of systems theory, which holds the best explanation of ecological forces that shape the planet's 'life', there exists a striking inter-dependence of mathematical tautology and speculated relationships that the texture of narrative and explanation might be described as 'marbled'. The one great field which we know to have *once* been speculative in its origin, i.e. narrative, is now overwhelmingly explanatory since its implicit mechanisms have been increasingly discovered. We are of course speaking of the counter-'narrative' to humanism, the theory of evolution and the *subsequent* discovery of its genetic bases. One cannot imagine grander 'narratives' than these; we find Lyotard's talk of *clusters* and institutions in *patches* and *local* determinism a long way from the mark. Differently put, when truths of this magnitude confront us without *any* alternative it is understandable but plain stupid, plain humanistic, to ask about legitimation. Morality is a *subsequent* possibility.

It is possible, indeed routine, to draw two false conclusions from this position. We shall not attribute it to any writer or grouping at this stage though instances will follow in due course. The argument runs like this.

Generally, we are at the beginning of science; attempts to produce 'final' or 'unified' theories are absurd. All such accounts are partial in the same and ordinary sense that 'first attempts' are generally less successful, less well rooted, less well understood, than subsequent developments. This, then, is a fairly simple 'progress' theory.

Put more specifically, and with a *little* more sophistication, post-Darwinian theory may have *some* validity, indeed it may be dominant (like Newtonian physics once was) but what we might call 'the manifold history of human error' shows that persuasiveness is not identical with truth; (though how we recognise *genuine* error is analytically indistinguishable from recognising *genuine* truth). This has been formalised by Kant's famous criterion and worked to death ever since: 'Experience teaches that a thing is [appears] so and so but not that it cannot be otherwise.'[17] The problems associated with this statement will be analysed at length below For the moment let us say that it is used routinely to justify what is called 'pluralism' or 'heterodoxy' on the grounds that (in this case) if we, on the basis of our experience, find neo-Darwinism convincing that does not necessarily hold for any cultural 'other'; and so competing views are also 'valid'. This, then, is not a progress theory and as such appeals to the politics of inclusiveness.

Of course it *is* appealing, who would not prefer tolerance to violent or demeaning exclusion? The trouble is again (as any cultural other will tell you): *we don't mean it, even if we'd like to*. It does *not* imply that 'any argument goes' but only ones that we euphemistically call 'reasonable' or 'feasible'. We still think *real* cultural others – religious fundamentalists, creationists, flat Earthers - are potty and they think we're bastards. They are certainly not interested in being *tolerated* by us. The uncomfortable but inevitable conclusion is that we are not actually interested in heterodoxy but, however implicitly, in some sort of 'progress' and this is precisely because we *correctly* see that neither we nor Kant nor his (post)modern descendents have *yet* offered any justification or ground for heterodoxy.

We could sum this up by saying that despite many postmodern attempts to call into question the 'project of the Enlightenment' *it,* rationalism, still has not done with *us.* Critical readers will say: what can 'us' mean here? A pair of academics and their readers? So what? But that only underscores the first error by implying that rationalism, the Enlightenment project, was primarily or wholly a matter of cultural *preference.* Neither the ideological influence nor the pragmatic success of 'enlightenment' are grounded in preference but on the contrary are forged out of the human relationship with Being. That is an ecological argument whereas 'preference' is just humanism in consumerist guise.

In that sense Lyotard is truly mistaken: it is not that the pragmatic success of science has discredited metanarratives and promoted heterodoxy. On the contrary, the practical success of science has instead specifically displaced narratives of *legitimation* from the first rank to a place somewhere well below pragmatism, or even more bluntly, effective power. This no more nor less than saying, as before, that morality is a subsequent possibility. Put differently, the interaction of humans and Being (or for that matter any other species) will put a *practical* ontology (literally, a way of being) far before *any* preference, ethical or otherwise. A practical 'ontology' - whether it is constructed by humans or a plant responding to gravity and sunlight - is a condition of first existence and future survival. Or again, practical 'enlightenment' is not a *preference* owned and exercised by humans any more than it is by plants. That is the first false conclusion, painfully rectified; now the second.

Gloom has descended: Lyotard's pleasant heterotopia has dissolved in the acidic current of scientific progress. But our earlier analysis showed this heterodoxy to be a concealed orthodoxy. That is still thoroughly negative but a positive possibility can be discerned. We still *desire* variety as opposed to uniformity; there is little evidence, despite our concerns in the West - crime, pollution, others' poverty - that we believe a new totalitarianism of religious or political form is desirable or likely to be effective. Perhaps the desire for heterotopia is well-founded; a good instinct, so to speak. Given our analysis above, if heterogeny is anything but an illusion founded in a second-order morality with virtually no authority, then heterogeny and its desirability must arise out of (our) interaction with Being itself. Heterogeny, if at all authentic, must be understood as an ontological *requirement* and not as a second-order ethical *preference.* This will be the subject of our next chapter.

Before we embark on the *ontological* grounding of heterogeny and heterodoxy let us be clear what is at stake. If heterogeny-heterodoxy can be shown to be an *ontological* requirement its *ethical* desirability will follow. That would decisively place orthodoxy of whatever kind in an *inferior* moral place. If we fail, the reverse is necessarily the case.

Notes

1. See, for example, Eve, Horsfall & Lee (eds.) 1997.
2. The phrase is from Mitchell (1986). Our analysis of his position occurs in Ch.9.
3. Or 'human choosing…is only the most complex and most articulated member of a class of free, orderly events with many examples throughout the physical world.' Eve, Horsfall & Lee op. cit.
4. Homans is the preferred candidate for Eve et al. His grounds for social units appear more 'elementary' than Durkheim's *sui generis*. That criticism is fair but we shall take it rather differently in the following chapters.
5. Maturana & Varela's key text is *Autopoiesis and Consciousness* (1980), Luhmann's is *Social Systems* (1995) and Dennet's *Consciousness Explained* (1993) and *Darwin's Dangerous Idea* (1995).
6. Lyotard, J-F. (1984) p.xxiii.
7. ibid. p.xxiv.
8. ibid. p.xxiv-v.
9. ibid p.81.
10. ibid. pp.81-2.
11. ibid. pp.81-2.
12. Carroll, D. (1989) p.182.
13. ibid. p.169.
14. Lyotard acknowledges precisely this difficulty in 'Discussions, or Phrasing after Auschwitz' in Andrew Benjamin ed. (1989).
15. Derrida, J. (1976). For a discussion of the meaning(s) of this assertion see Jay, M. (1993) Ch. 9 and especially pp. 515-6. See also Carrol, D. (1987) especially Chs. 4 & 6.
16. Note that we do not thereby *diminish* the importance of the world 'brought forth' in human linguistic understanding – especially for humans. Rather we place it in a competitive environment where the ostensible superiority of that understanding or even the survival of the species cannot be taken for granted. The discipline markers that normally surround the analyses of culture, however, allow such matters to be ignored.
17. Kant, E. Kemp Smith trans. (1973) p.43.

2 Durkheim's Dangerous Idea

Chapter One argued for an ecology in which social phenomena are interactive with other classes of phenomena. Amongst the obstacles to an ecological understanding we identified the general, persistent legacy of human-centred explanations and in particular its contemporary manifestation in an unworkable, incredible and actually unintended heterodoxy. We argued that any 'heterotopia' based on *human* (western) *preferences* was irrelevant and trivial unless the preference reflected sound ontological requirements.

This chapter will examine instances, from Darwin and Durkheim, of non-humanistic paradigms of complexity and inter-dependence. We formulate sociology as a science of complexity and not an ideology of either heterogeny or homogeny. The title is taken from Dennett's book *Darwin's Dangerous Idea* [1] and in the several instances (in our view) the 'danger' is parallel, but in others divergent. Dennet sums up his first chapter as follows:

> Before Darwin, a "Mind-first" view of the universe reigned unchallenged; an intelligent God was seen as the ultimate source of all Design, the ultimate answer to any chain of "Why?" questions. [2]

And his second chapter:

> Darwin conclusively demonstrated that...species are not eternal and immutable; they evolve... Darwin introduced an idea of how this evolutionary process took place: via a mindless, mechanical - algorithmic - process he called 'natural selection' This idea, that all the fruits of evolution can be explained as the products of an algorithmic process is Darwin's dangerous idea. [3]

Durkheim writes:

> That the substance of social life cannot be explained by purely psychological factors, i.e., by the states of individual consciousness, seems to us most evident. Indeed, what the collective representations convey is the way in which the group conceives itself in its relation to objects which affect it. The group differs from the individual in its constitution and the things that affect it are therefore of a different nature. [4]

In the dense little passage above Durkheim raises a number of issues central to the very possibility of sociology. A paragraph earlier, he prepares his position: 'Social facts do not differ from psychological facts in quality only: they have a different substratum; they evolve in a different milieu; and they depend on different conditions.' [5]

The first explicit parallel, then, is this: whether we speak of natural 'facts' (the outcomes of evolution) or social 'facts' (intelligible social behaviours and structures), they are not, for either writer, derivatives of a designing mind. Neither subscribes to a mind-first ontology; for both writers their primary phenomena are *sui-generic*. Both sets of phenomena are 'evolved' within specific *melieux* and 'depend', indeed *inter*depend, on specific conditions.

We take it that given a contemporary readership and our remarks above that by 'evolution' we do not intend any sense of 'progress' from lower to higher states but rather a homeodynamic with specific characteristics over a certain period. In the case of evolutionary biology, the case is reasonably clear: even that loaded expression 'survival of the *fittest*' is properly taken to mean the fittest *for a certain environment* and not simply, unequivocally, 'better'. Recent literature points away from harmony and superiority and towards models of inter-dependent homeodynamics with periodic instability and extinctions. With 'evolving' societies there are greater problems. However much we now distance ourselves from classifications of the type simple/complex or primitive/advanced, it remains the case that 'complex', technologically-'advanced' societies do tend to have greater power *and exercise it*. Moreover, the origin of this type of inquiry is inevitably, not simply 'developed' societies but the idioms of post-industrial society. Can we, then, portray our 'analysis' as anything more than one ethnographic account substituting for another? Is our *sociological* reasoning in all or in part a narrative in arbitrary competition with other narratives, perhaps of the 'mind-first' persuasion? Before addressing this directly, we can consider the issue in a related sense.

Returning to Durkheim's social facts, let us formulate two extreme positions. **Reading One:** no doubt there exists an entire complex of relationships between (say) individual mental or physical ability, desire or opportunity and the various courses of strictly *social* action. But the issue for *sociology* is not some concrete dispute concerning the *degree* of relation, or *reducibility* of some specific social phenomenon to individual human attributes. The point is rather that, analytically, sociology would rapidly become a biology or a psychology operating within a specific (social) sphere

16

whose phenomena would assume greater or lesser importance. Durkheim's socio-phenomenology only *begins* to operate when the contingency is entirely reversed: when the *social* setting becomes the irreducible determination of that which *appeared* to precede and generate it. The situation is familiar to writers concerned with gender: biological attributes are the fundamental substrate of all social determinations of gender but the *social* determination of gender is a *sui-generic* phenomenon, independent of its originating causes, except, perhaps, as retrospective myth.

It is essential to see that this is not just a question of either an 'extreme' or a 'moderate' socio-phenomenology: if the social determination of any aspect of gender were genuinely tied to biological attributes (let us say child-bearing & rearing) it is properly analysable precisely under the terms of a biology operating in a contingent social setting and so would be *improperly* taken as a topic for sociology. Conversely, if the social determination of gender has nothing but socio-phenomenological status, it is absolutely and only a proper topic for sociology.

Placed rather more sharply: *sociology* can properly *only* be concerned with a set of *sui-generic* phenomena whose re-presentation in an organised social milieu operates in such a way as to make their 'original' or 'immediate' presence fundamentally irrevocable, except, perhaps, as a reflexive dimension of their subsequent mediate, social manifestation. We must presuppose, then, that all such phenomena and their retrospective representations - in order to have entered the unique sphere of sociological enquiry at all - will be 'organised' or capable of demonstrating something of the rules of its intelligibility for other members.

The unfortunate consequence of this extreme but analytically plausible position is that '*sui-generic* phenomena' taken in their most fundamental sense appear to have no formal limit and are free to invent themselves at will, subject only to the condition that they can demonstrate their various, contingent rules for other members (or they would not *be* social phenomena; they would not 'present'. In this, **Reading One,** Durkheim seems to have formulated the *difference* between social phenomena (with some of their conditions) and natural phenomena but showed nothing of their *relationships*. This is Durkheim's dangerous idea: it places social phenomena in a space without limit and sociology therefore in a place without *reasonable* limit; that is, sociology cannot appeal to reason.

Now Reading Two. This is a hybrid, distilled from various 'extreme' or mechanistic neo-Darwinisms but the summary is ours. This reading asserts that whilst *homo sapiens* is characterised by a high degree of post-natal mental plasticity, the ability to learn and adapt, the primary forces of both individual and social development are genetic and these include social propensities such as the acquisition of language. Under this reading, the modernisation of Durkheim consists in a critique of his distinction between individual and social - if Cartesian only in an inverted and perverse sense, it is certainly dualistic. In this sense, strictly *social* phenomena are explained as evolved adjuncts to more commonly recognised survival strategies and explained in terms of probability. The better adapted are likeliest to survive, to reproduce and to predominate, whether the advantage is: physical strength; better eyesight; greater intelligence; the ability to master languages or software codes etc., set against the 'costs' of maintaining each of these attributes. In this sense, the position of higher/lower forms, whether of organism or society, is set against costs, so that reversals and extinctions are not surprising - if the balance is disadvantageous. This paradigm would have no difficulty in explaining the reversal of apparent progress, (the cost is too high), and therefore has absolutely nothing to do with the eugenic forms of social Darwinism. They are analytic opposites. This dangerous idea, more Darwinian than Durkheimian, also excludes sociology from reason through the primacy, not of market forces but of the outcomes of probability, of which the market is just a specific case.

We are now in a position to consider the value of sociological analysis compared with other, ostensibly available narratives. The unconditional availability of other narratives belongs to the outcomes of **Reading One** - the presumption of *general* unconditionality. It is painfully easy to see, however, that this model also tacitly depends on assumptions that belong to the ideology of free markets, such as perfectly free, equal access. In the context of academic writing that is ironic. Moreover, the differential availability of academic writing (amongst other phenomena) is structured by both the presence and the absence of choice: we are not religious fundamentalists *by choice* and not because our cultural backgrounds *denied* us the choice.

Put more generally, **Reading One** and the unconditional availability of alternative narratives are not incorrect but *inadequate* modellings. We may employ the analogy of the chocolate box to model apparently unconditional alternatives. First, we all have preferences. Second, the box has to go round in some sort of order: here the box itself conditions the availability of access. We take it that alternative strategies like throwing them all in the air or fighting for them or melting them all down and stirring them up (or something like that) have been 'considered' during the evolution of our social history and the box itself is, of course, a social construct (and not simply that: a *viable* social construct) the sort of phenomenon **Reading Two** proposes.

This is the crucial absence in all models of unconditional alternatives: *unconditionality* is already a caricature that suppresses complexity. One cannot describe every factor that determines access or preference or ownership or access to information but one can insist that the conditions will increase in complexity with every influencing factor. It is through general knowledge of this principle and the assessment of local conditions that *reason* enters the situation. And it enters not as a privileged or sacrosanct spirit but as pragmatic, tactical, languaged, interested, informed, aged, lustful, complex and fallible.

Reading Two as an exercise in modelling has a little more going for it: at least there is a dynamic of sorts involving costs, benefits and probabilities. But again the order of complexity is not adequate to the phenomena in question. If **Reading One** is a caricature that suppresses complexity, **Reading Two** is a caricature of determinism: something of a one-way street, an infinite reduction to first cause, a model with its feedback loops missing. Rose provides a more compelling critique of reductive determinism and a statement of the *necessity* of interaction:

> It is the organism in interaction with its environment....that determines which of its available genes are to be active at any one time. [6]

> Like 'gene', the term 'environment' is .... complex and multi-layered. For individual gene-sized sequences of DNA, the environment is constituted by the rest of the genome and the cellular machinery in which it is embedded; for the cell it is the buffered milieu in which it floats; for the organism, it is the external physical, living and social worlds. ...Which features of the external world constitute 'the environment' differs from species to species...no environment is constant over time. [7]

This modification makes clear the complexity the needs to be modelled as a feature of our analysis. The existence of the genome denotes certain possibilities and probabilities. Let us say a sketch of a possible 'lifeline' (to borrow Rose's words) is made but the 'decisions' and 'reasons' for what is delineated, developed, made prominent or erased at any one time is decided out of the interactions of genetic materials and environmental conditions, not forgetting that what counts as 'environment' is itself a complex variable. In the case of humans in social formations, that environment *may* include at any one time 'plastic' reflective capacities, or incapacities, cultural and linguistic codings, metabolic responses, the actions and inactions of others, orders of representation, and so on, in any order of importance.

19

Like the conditions that impinge upon 'preference' in **Reading One** the list of similar, more complex or extensive factors cannot be specified. That, in our terms, is the *solution,* not the problem. In other words, we grasp sociology as a science of complexity, an inquiry that *accepts* complexity as its first condition. Instead, in our view, sociology's *problem* is the marked tendency to simplify that characterises all-too common decent into ideologies of the kind: 'there is nothing outside text', *arche*-writing; heterodoxy is good, orthodoxy bad; economic, technological or any other determinism, any overarching primacy of language, genes, progress, moral orders, intellectual orders, mind-first, human-first or anything-*first* reductionism. More explicitly, we argue that our text should be taken more seriously - it is more *reasonable* - than those kinds of ideological reduction precisely because it recognises and admits the level of complexity we all address and therefore our own *in*adequacy. That, in a strong sense, is our 'image of community'.

We formulate sociology as a science of *complexity* and not an ideology of either heterogeny or homogeny. This becomes necessary *immediately* the cause of 'design', structure, recognisable patterns, organisms, natural and symbolic orders is *not* mind-first or human-like but on the contrary is the result of interactive processes resulting in probable, possible and realisable, that is, *autopoietic* phenomena. In place of a heterotopic field - which should by definition, be called random and relation-less - or a homogeny of either a static or progressive type, we formulate the objects of sociology's study to be homoedynamic complexes. Where that is the case, where 'strictly' social and other kinds of phenomena *inter*act, sociology will necessarily tend toward *inter*-disciplinarity.

It may be helpful to reconsider these questions (in a preliminary way) in more explicit 'systems' terms and to review something of the terminology and its history. As we explained, corresponding roughly to Durkheim's *'sui-generic* phenomena' is the concept of *autopoiesis*. This was coined by Maturana and Varela in relation to the systems of the living cell and means 'self-making' or self structuring or self-maintaining.[8] This, then, has no similar origin and should not invoke the old, and mistaken, left/right sociological divide corresponding to dynamics and stasis: system theory is less concerned with fixed structures and rather more with self-organising dynamic processes or 'homeodynamics'. Elsewhere it is stressed that tends to take place in the context of high levels of surrounding *dis*equilibrium.[9] This view was put forward by Lovelock as a characteristic of 'Gaia', literally an Earth Goddess, and a name for the Gaia hypothesis: 'I now see the systems of the material Earth and the living organisms on it evolving so that self-regulation is an emergent property.'[10] For a systems-led approach to other

20

phenomena (whether social or not), the key point is that the 'network' is 'produced by its components and in turn produces its components' and 'the product of its operation is its own organisation'.[11] 'Network', and 'component' then, are generalised shorthand for (for example) the interdependence of environment and organism we discussed above, whether the context is a bio or social 'sphere'. Luhmann's *Social Systems* [12] assimilates general systems theory for sociology with considerable criticism of the latter's conventions. For the moment we must attend to the following *sociological* consequences.

First: To formulate 'a sociology of', rather than a social biology or psychology, is to presume that the social phenomena in question are independent *social* systems and not subsystems of bodily or mental processes. This cannot be taken for granted and must be argued in each and every case.

Second: The independence of social systems must be *possible* vis à vis their non-social environment. Social phenomena are *not* therefore 'independent' in the sense of infinitely inventable or infinitely variable. Nor can they be *fundamentally* arbitrary. [13]

Third: The static or dynamic quality of any 'enclosed' social network or subsystem partly depends upon itself and is therefore determined by itself and partly depends upon its viable co-existence with other neighbouring systems. Put simply, the *possible* ways in which such social phenomena can manifest themselves depends on their inner possibilities and the possibilities of their environment. Such phenomena are both independent and (or but) specific -*because of* their place within an 'ecology' of distinct phenomena. Stasis or dynamic change are therefore *possible*, so are creation and extinction. None of these are in themselves *necessary*.

Fourth: The persistent characterisation of social phenomena in ordinary sociology and philosophy as 'merely' matters of culture, taste and convention that 'could be otherwise' without limit is patently ridiculous, not to say destructive. It corresponds to environmental analyses and actions that ignore or suspend ecological perspectives, usually because of the persistence - and arrogance - of humanism.

Fifth: The apparent 'randomness' of social phenomena only says that the analyst does not perceive a pattern and not that a patterned process does not exists. Where authors assert chaos, randomness and at every claim to unfettered deconstruction it would be at least prudent to read: 'we do not know'.

Sixth: For every moral claim about standards, tradition, revolution, modernisation, dynamism, the ends or the people to be served, and so on, read: the author would like to exert some control over the system of phenomena. This is to be expected: social phenomena and interested parties presuppose each other

Seventh: Never trust disinterest! It usually implies that the (dis)interested party thinks the phenomena in question are random and so valueless. On the other hand, they may be right. We shall insist that the question is rarely absolute - the value neither random and so worthless or 'universal' and so to be preserved. Questions and answers of value always presume an interacting ecology of systems and functions.

Notes

1.   Dennett, D. (1995).
2.   ibid. pp.33-4.
3.   ibid.
4.   Durkheim, E. (1964) p.xlix).
5.   ibid. p.31.
6.   Rose, S. (1990) p.139.
7.   ibid. p.140.
8.   Capra, F. (1996) pp. 95-8 and Maturana, H. & Varela, F. (1980).
9.   Lovelock, J. (1995).
10.   ibid. pp.19-20.
11.   Capra (1996) pp.95-8.
12.   Luhmann, N. (1995).
13.   Runciman, W. (1998) argues a similar position in his opening chapters. However, he far more concerned with the old debates on the superiority of science and the doctrines of positivism. He is certainly not interested in complexity in the senses we describe. His index, then, shows no mention of Luhmann or of systems theory, except the dismissal of Parsons as a 'platitude merchant'. Neither does his attachment to positivism square with either the philosophy or the practices of contemporary science. See for example, Weinberg, S. (1993).

3   Kinds of Representing

Chapter Two was concerned with complexity. A critic might argue that all we have said is that phenomena are complex, interdependent and fuzzy at the edges. Quite right! But that still has important methodological and analytic consequences. This chapter will employ that methodology in the context of the difference between iconography and narrative in a generalised social setting. We insist that iconography is not narrative; both exist as complexes amongst many classes of (re)presentation.

A minor cottage industry is active in criticism, sociology, philosophy and what has come to be known as 'art theory', attempting to 'show' in various *narratives* that 'visual art' (we shall shorthand this as 'iconography' for reasons we shall discuss in due course) is either something like a 'reflection' of a wider set of social phenomena or is really another kind of narrative.

The first asserts that art is 'determined' by its social context and is consequently called 'determinism'. This is actually rather coy, because what determinists *mean* is that visual art is determined by its *original* conditions of production. They do not usually question current conditions of 'reception' - rather a passive metaphor when you consider how we graciously 'receive' (i.e. steal) work such as the Egyptian collection in the British Museum. Nor can it tackle the vexing fact that many 'receivers' (active artists included) often have very scant knowledge of 'original' conditions but this does not stop them doing lots of eclectic 'receiving'. This, we think, is not so much a doctrinal position as a failure of imagination on the part of determinists, who are generally a dull lot; they dismiss the status of 'eclectic receivers' as ill-informed and so analytically trivial. Since, by definition, determinists are those who research and explicate 'original' conditions, codings, contexts. etc. the 'ill-informed' are everyone other than themselves and their readers. Artists, by and large are not often included. If you think this an unhealthy situation remember it has been the dominant modern tradition especially in the sociology of art - and so is at least 'viable' in the sense that it produces jobs, publications, status and money for its practitioners, not to mention their control over university departments.

The second group, also determinists of a kind, focus rather more on the tight relationships, at times amounting to virtual identity, between the narratives that sustain cultural reproduction and an iconography (the visual arts) that, in *their* analyses, does more or less the same job. They too have a bias toward 'originating' dialogues and, therefore, all of the points above also apply. An extra twist is given in the relationship between the coder (the artist) and the decoder (the critical theorist). It is true that ordinary determinism exhibits the same kind of structural relation but in that case all manner of conditions 'conspire' to 'overdetermine' the work of art. In the latter case the coder, inexplicably, makes icons but the decoder knows what they *say* and this is their *essence*. Since social dialogues and narratives are rarely innocent and are usually about exerting power, the artist tends to end up as the icon-making dupe (whose function is to dupe in turn) and the analyst does the remedial work of exposure.

Later chapters will detail such relationships and their effects on both art 'practice' and art 'theory'. (These are detestable terms but serve their purpose for the moment in accurately describing an equally detestable social relationship.) For the moment we want to focus on the paradoxes of determinism, which in essence says that certain classes of social phenomena (art, culture) are dependent upon *other* social phenomena (the economy, political narratives, gender, technology, religion) in an almost causal way. That is, as we said last chapter, the process is taken to run primarily in *one* way. The paradox, then, of both sorts of determinism is the recognition of dependence, but not of inter-dependence. Therefore, to use the terms of the previous chapter, the determining conditions are seen as autopoietic but not the phenomena of art: *they* are both determined and *dependent*. In this sense, the difference between narrative and iconography, which we see as an autopoietic complex, tends to be reduced by determinists to a question of 'coding' or of signification in the simplest sense: the iconography is a sign that can be surpassed; it is 'surplus' once the 'meaning' has been narrated. The work would be a sociology of (say) political relationships at best *illustrated* by art.

Before moving on to thinking the difference between narrative and iconography as an autopoietic complex, let us briefly consider a further, current objection to their conflation. Summers offers this:

> ... I now wish to state a second major theme of this paper: the rejection of what W.J.T. Mitchell has called linguistic imperialism, which I understand to be the assumption that the paradigm of language is adequate to the explanation of art, or, more simply that art is a kind of language. Although what we mean by art and what we mean by language are in various instances continuous, parallel or overlapping relative to one another I wish to argue that in crucial respects they are, to use a strong term, absolutely different

from one another, and that at the deepest levels the significance of art is to be found in an area of prelinguistic certainty. [1]

This, emphatically, is *not* our direction and is no part of our purpose. Of course we agree with the objections to 'linguistic imperialism' - it could be taken as shorthand for some of our arguments above. But 'absolutely' different does not easily square with the inter-penetration of homeodynamics; and prelinguistic 'certainties' tend to suffer from extreme turbulence in autopoietic fields.

The prejudice so characteristic of the sociology of art [2] - that 'individual' artists be shown or explicated or restored by reference to a social context that is at once both 'theirs' and yet somehow distant or obscured by the very fact that they are artists - rests on the positions described above. On the other hand, forms of determinism and 'linguistic imperialism' are not-unreasonable responses to types of 'prelinguistic certainty'. If 'certainty' is not quite the stuff of Mitchell's or Summers' writing, it is present (if somewhat discredited) in the literature in two forms: as the traditional presumption of artistic genius; [3] and its more modern manifestations which range from Merleau-Ponty's phenomenology, [4] arguably in entrenched Modernistic conceptions of the avant-garde, and the earlier work of writers now showing more ostensibly sociological and certainly more semiological orientations.[5]

We want to argue that this opposition between preliguistic, or better, presocial origins and semiology or cruder determinism is misconceived. Instead, the making of art is an *inherently* social act; it is not an act to be redeemed, as it were, from some peculiar isolation, whether actual or illusory. This can best be understood by reference back to Durkheim. In the same way that he asserts the analytic necessity of the irreducibility of social phenomena as that which differentiates a genuine *sociology* from a biology or psychology operating within a social context for purely circumstantial reasons, the irreducibility of works of art (to other social phenomena) in turn stands as the absolute requirement for a genuine sociology of art.

Now this looks rather hard-edged compared to our approach in Chapter Two and it is admittedly a rather 'old' Durkheimian formulation. 'Our' Durkheimian formulation, then, despite the tendency to interdisciplinarity says: *the difference* - between iconographies, narratives and other ostensible determinants - is *itself* irreducible. Or to put it another way the *difference* is the social act, constituted in the homeodynamics of social structures; the *difference* is the key autopoietic phenomenon. Notice that no asocial genius arises in this space, but an artist-as-member: it is in the social *difference* that the artist *per se* becomes intelligible. It is then ironic that conventional sociology should break its heart, mind and integrity and collapse into the mode of illustration in the attempt to undo or remedy the difference itself.

Such 'illustrated' sociologies, or even those that *analyse* illustration, can unquestionably point to *depicted* social circumstance or ideology. Think, perhaps, of feminist reinterpretations of art history. But what such sociologies fail to do is confront the existential fact of these depictions and re-presentations. For all their *political* strengths, they do not yet ask why it is, how it is, that artists chose to portray or depict rather than engage in other more 'determinant' forms of socio-economic action, except by the tautological assumption that they 'already were' artists (an eminently alterable status in many ways). More radically put: doing art looks like a humanistic *choice* in which political realities get coded, presented, perhaps avoided, but in our model it is not *preference* but *auto*poiesis that constitutes visual art as a distinct category. Seen in those terms, political critique can certainly find evidence of political influence in art but it also operates to *define* in such a way as to preclude attention to other kinds of evidence. The same is true, of course, for other forms of determinism. This 'other' evidence will be summoned in later chapters. For the moment let us concentrate on the difference as such between iconography and narrative.

We formulate the difference as one distinction between *kinds* of representation. This raises a number of analytic issues centred on the word 'representation'. It is part of the usage of our discipline; certainly part of the perceived history of art; and certainly part of the commonsense understanding of signification. But it has all sorts of connotations in various disciplines that we expressly do not want. It would be a tedious exercise to present and 'adjust' these and in some senses it would be easier to use another term: as you will see 'presentation' is at times more apt. Perverse as we may be, we *want* it! We like it! We *need* all those senses like the 'change' in *re*-presentation and the 'activity' of (re)*presentation* and the existential thrust of the unignorable re*present*ation. So, we shall sketch 'our' sense with as few 'nots' as possible and we ask the reader to *leave behind any of those prejudicial meanings* that connote mimesis, correspondence, the processing of fixed units of information, realities 'out there', technological control, and the activities of academic painters.

Representation is often associated with analyses of framing. Thus Heidegger [6] treats enframing as involved with what he calls 'representational thinking' that seeks to order and control; the technological enterprise. Derrida[7] is interested in the definitions that the frame *tries* to impose and the instabilities that arise in the tension between representations of what lies inside and outside. By contrast, the icon on the computer screen represents a specifically-designated meaning and task and that is its *only* function.

Consider this position advanced by Marin:

> .... to represent first means to substitute something present for something absent (which is, by the way, the most general structure of the sign). This substitution is ruled by a mimetic economy: the postulated similarity of the present and the absent authorise this substitution. Yet to represent can also mean to display, to exhibit something that is present. Here it is the very act of presenting that constructs the identity of that which is represented that identifies it as such. On the one hand, then, a mimetic operation between presence and absence enables its functioning and authorises the present to function in the place of what is absent. On the other it is a performative operation that constitutes identity and propriety by assigning it legitimacy. [8]

Let us soften this complexity with some examples. The paradigm case must be Goya's etching. Surely there can be no greater nor more forceful collision of subject matter and the *act* of re-presenting than *The Disasters of War*? There is a *most* problematic difference between the 'political' position of Goya *as an artist* and that of a more practical reformist. To put the matter in more general terms: to see art as an illustration of socio-political reality is fair enough, but 'to illustrate' is itself a socio-political act which crucially elaborates and diversifies the meaning of the simple verb in a way that differs sharply from all simple notions of causation and correspondence. To say the least, there is a question of intention and responsibility here, which does not end with Goya, but with every moment of influence, every act of collection, criticism, every viewing. Neither can it be the case that the concept of re-presentation is only an issue in the narrow sense of 'representative art', making pictures *of* things. Indeed making pictures of things, making art of things, such as: Rauschenberg's assemblages; Johns' flags; Noland's colour-saturated canvases; such, even, as R. Mutt's urinal; [9] *especially* the urinal - is an act of diversion from one possible social presence to another. It is a re-presentation inextricably implicated in every such act of fashioning. Every *modernist* abstract painting is caught in the tension between the refusal to represent in the more conventional sense and the presence (or lack) of some other kind of representative project. Every *postmodern* painting is implicated in a reflexive denial of a former project and the affirmation (however ironic) of another.

What do these examples show? That the 'mimetic economy' is by no means the controlling factor; that representation is both selective and transformative; above all, *active* and *complicit* and *professionally* so. This

27

can hardly be explained either as 'mimetic' or as 'determined' by other social phenomena unless as a subterfuge to exempt artists and their institutions from responsibility. Unfortunately, we also meet an echo of the extreme **Reading One** of absolutely *sui-generic* social phenomena: the artist seems entirely free to invent; those inventions are arbitrary, worth everything and/or nothing and artists' professional or institutional responsibility is as grave as it is insubstantial. Hence the influence of Duchamp. What do these examples also show? That examples are at best anecdotal and that Marin's complexity is not quite complex enough.

Marin, Heidegger, Duchamp, Derrida, computer icon-makers, our paragraph above, concentrate on what Marin calls 'assigning legitimacy' or more broadly on what certain humans *do*, certain sorts of project, certain sorts of sovereignty, acts of *will*. None of these are compatible with homeodynamics and all of them are narrowly humanistic. Taken in a more fundamental sense, *re*-presentation is not necessarily a matter of signs and symbols. Taken as an action upon a 'present' in much the same way that Marx defines *labour*, re-presentation is as rudimentary as re-shaping: re-shaping a shelter, or a food-source to aid productivity, using fire for safety and demarcation, emphasising gender, self-decoration (or mutilation), signalled concessions of dominance and subordination. In this sense, signs and symbols of the pictorial or written or spoken forms are only one amongst many productive instances of *re*presentation. Moreover, to the extent that we concede forms of signalling through bodily gesture or sound as 'representative', then representation is by no means confined to our own species. This is not to invite a regress through the rudimentary forms of representation and the proto-sign but to underscore that there is no underlying 'neutral' form by which to identify or gauge the veracity of mimesis. Put differently Marin's 'seen' original is a consequence of human stereoscopic-perspectival sight. And 'perspective' is a consequence of the manner of perception and not of the thing perceived. As we argued earlier: what counts as environment, in this case visual environment, is a variable part of the homeodynamic that sustains various species in relation to their surroundings. In that sense, every organism's environment is already a representation: not an act of will, not signification in the various human senses but nevertheless an autopoietic structuring of an essential and varying relationship.

This is not a hair-splitting distinction of the kind: do we really see what we see and how would we know? The answer to that sort of nonsense is, 'Check it out!' by looking again, touching etc. Quite the reverse is intended: we insist that sight is as virtual and as real as the dolphin's sonar or the cat's sense of smell. Our sight is, then, not 'privileged' nor objective but ecologically viable, (for the moment) along with our language, along with some of our institutions, along with the senses, practices, groupings and societies of many other species. The same applies to artists, writers, speakers, workers in the field: the question is not one of human *will* (even if your surname is Nietzsche or Duchamp) but of *viability*. Can the proposed views, actions, programmes be socially sustained? An artist or writer, a Nietzsche or Duchamp, *may* have more flexibility than a colony of bats, or even their recent human ancestors but their ecological viability does not turn on some massive act of will on their part any more than the bats can *will* to survive. Instead it turns on the other elements in the homeodynamic, the society, competitors, economic and climatic conditions. Moreover, the success of Duchamp and his descendants or the bat colony in maintaining that particular niche as 'theirs', literally keeping possession, will inevitably limit the ostensible free will of those seeking similar territory. The completely free artist, like the completely indeterminate species is a relic of Creation theory, even when God is dead. The autopoietic requirement is *structured* variation.

The autopoietic complex with which we begin, then, is not the reduction of visual representing to one particular type of work, nor the assimilation of the visual to the verbal or any other ostensible determinant, nor yet some prelinguistic or previsual or presocial core or centre; nor some act of will *ex nihilo*. We begin in the evolved and evolving difference between iconographic and narrative representations as a socio-ecological feature that exhibits dynamic continuity with the actions of other species.

These points are both complex and essential to our enterprise, so it is worth reworking (representing) this ground in another way. Marin's 'complexity' consists in mutual substitutions: presence for absence; absence for presence. But the 'representation' turns on a kind of causality which begins with an 'original' that is in turn supplanted by its representation - and so questions turn on how 'we' assign, question, reconstruct - or deconstruct - the legitimacy of that action. Whether we concentrate on the individual, the class, the gender, or the politico-linguistic *regime* controlling the substitution, the *will* of the act is crucial and is usually presented as conventional - in the strict sense of 'could have been otherwise'. These are the characteristic parameters of contemporary critical theory.

At the same time, any contemporary critic worth his salt will quickly include the 'original' - and hence the whole ostensibly memetic process - within overlapping regimes of representation. Foucault's analysis of *Las Meninas* is a classic of this kind: the 'original' is already represented politically as the King's family, who commissions but also 'concedes' the *next layer* of representation to Velasquez and so on. Looked at in this way, the 'complex' of presence/absence starts to look decidedly thin. Hence Derrida's denial of 'outside-text' or 'presence', and we are back to the primacy of the trace, the will, the political will, the representative convention. Derrida's 'originals', then, are often the portrayed as 'ruins' [10] of an earlier inscription: ruined because no origin, no outside-text, sustains or reinvigorates them.

Drawing on other disciplinary sources, decidedly more radical and less morose scenarios appear. We are not presented with a human-centred (and so exclusive) perspective, but characteristically, with an inclusive homeodynamic; in place of 'no outside' we find: 'Living systems are cognitive systems and living as a process is a cognitive process.' [11] The radicalisation, then consists in the inclusion of *all* living systems in cognitive processing: 'Even bacteria perceive certain characteristics of their environment. [for example] They... swim towards sugar and away from acid.' [12]. The conclusion is *not* that simple forms can 'correspond' to equally simple components of their environment (whilst 'text' as cognitive process '*substitutes* for') but rather:

> Since cognition is traditionally defined as the process of knowing we must be able to describe it in terms of an organism's interactions with its environment.....The specific phenomenon underlying the process of cognition is structural coupling......[A]n autopoietic system undergoes continual structural changes whilst preserving its web-like pattern of organisation. It couples to its environment *structurally* i.e. through recurrent interactions, each of which triggers structural changes in the system. The living system is autonomous, however. The environment only triggers the changes; it does not specify them.... [Here is the break with 'representation'] By specifying which peturbations from the environment trigger its changes the system 'brings forth a world'...Cognition, then, is not a representation of an independently existing world but a continual *bringing forth*....to live is to know...cognition is embodied action. [13]

As you can see, the rejection of 'representation' here is a denial of autocorrespondence. Our sense of representation, however, coincides roughly with 'embodied action' and more precisely with embodied-encultured action. Neither, however, does the denial of correspondence lead to no outside-text or outside world: the autonomy of the organism in 'its' environment (the world it 'brings forth') must be ecologically *viable*. If to 'live is to know' its cognitions cannot be *despite* embodied action in which the 'body' is understood as a viable autopoietic 'closure' that regulates the relationship between 'outside' and 'inside'. [14]

Now, in the simplicities of the *frame* Derrida and his followers see this interpenetration of inside/outside only too clearly: one might call it 'enframed' action; they see it as an *attempt* to 'specify the triggers'. But in the complexity of *text*, the insight is lost: text is seen as limit and closure, *not* as structural coupling, *not* as a complex boundary phenomenon that structures the relation of inside/outside or one that 'brings forth *authentic* worlds' rather than so much tragic insularity. Moreover, the *authentic* difference between narratives and iconography, which we all experience at some level, is 'analytically' lost (or losable) because 'text' is seen to regulate merely its own 'interior', *conventionally*.

Limits - closures, 'causes', *determinisms* - operate like Venn diagrams where the 'limited' set of phenomena is merely a dependent subset which, through its difference, through its 'deviance', serves to illustrate the dominant (or normative) phenomena. If, however, we take sociology as a science of complexity and choose to focus its attention on the mutual determination of different spheres of phenomena, then it is clear that the difference, in this case narrative/iconography, is neither a matter of simple *in*clusion or *ex*clusion. In other words, neither the relationship, nor the difference is absolute; both are features of a homeodynamic whose manifestations are themselves differentiated, for different people, for different genders, for different interest groups, for different classes, for different economic purposes. In the case of visual art, the paradigms of its relation to text has differed radically in the past 150 years: a simplified scheme might point to the rule of the French *Academie* , the 'modernism' of Manet and the quite different modernisms of the Bauhaus and post-war American painting. Moreover, even this fractured coherence has disappeared in the apparent pluralisms of postmodernity. All this, of course, is from the academic point of view - the academic's 'bringing forth'. For a considerable section of the public, very little has been 'brought forth' since Impressionism.

Conventional sociology of art finds this fracturing and differentiation threatening. Many sociologists, then, find it difficult to handle what *they* call *individual* artist as a consequence of principle. Thus Wolff argues, '...to reject the Sociology of Art on the ground that the focus is not on individuals seems to prefer a Psychology of Art to a Sociology of Art.' [15]

Precisely so, though the truth of the objection lies not in concretised preference but is instead both implicit and wholly analytic. In the first place an *individual* is always unquestionably and immediately so - in an absolutely formal, indeed purely mathematical sense - whereas *an artist* carries with it explicit notions of initiation, recognition, confirmation and rejection; that is, a structured negotiation of a specific kind of membership. This must apply even in the most pluralistic of contexts: the problem is not concrete policy but analytic identity.

In the second, the practice of art is manifestly a category developed and recognised as such within the complexities of the division of labour and not a description of processes within 'the state of individual consciousness' (not to mention the complex structures of its 'reception'). Consequently, whilst the objection to a discourse whose locus is the *formal* individual is thoroughly sustainable on the grounds that it lacks the mediating principles by which any such formal capacity might be socially organised (and so realised or recognised) the objection to a focus on individual artists, individual pictures, or for that matter, influential movements, is a spurious, trivial prejudice characterised by exactly the same absence: the lack of recognition that the name *artist* already indicates a mediating principle qua form of membership. The conventional sociologist has the key but not, apparently, the means to recognise it.

The specific identity of the discipline 'painting' is compounded by the high value traditionally placed within it upon creative originality, at least in post-Renaissance Europe. It is undoubtedly this challenge that sociologists find so threatening, so much so as to banish all questions of singular quality or at least urge their subordination to collectivity. But everyone else can see that the truly outstanding practitioner is the essential point and that the problem wouldn't even arise if the explanation of the *outstanding* in terms of the mundane were in any way credible. All of this does not threaten the outstanding practitioner's *social* status at all (a point many sociologists at least imply) but rather increases it. The historically significant artist is much more surely an artist, much more essential to art's traditions and social cohesion than any number of mediocre artists. Perhaps this indicates, by contrast, a certain tendency in *sociological* usage to emphasise, even require, a high degree of cohesion, or at worst, uniformity in social action. Consequently, it is arguable that we may be losing sight - though ironically it is the very thing we are looking at - of the potential for a high degree of differentiation as a characteristic of complex social structures. We would thus be guilty of the most commonsensical inability to see that *social* action is not necessarily *conventional* action in the narrow sense. This simply points to the distinctive absence of well-reasoned accounts of the processes of 'individuation' at the level of both practice and practitioner, (whether or not our topic is art). It would appear, then, that sociology may justly be accused of failing to grasp that its own practices and those of its subjects are consequent upon homeodynamic differentiation, for neither the professional sociologist nor the professional artist is conceivable as a sort of undifferentiated 'constant', external to the idioms that sustain them.

Sociology must shed its dislike of the 'individual' artist on account of the priority of membership. This is roughly the same point as we made before: 'free' (formal) individuals whether artists, members of some other social collectivity, or members of some indeterminate species are speech-relics of Creationism. On the other hand, 'individual' artists who get their work noticed (the same applies to academics) are precisely those in a strategic position to influence for good or ill what 'counts' (what is brought forth) as art, and its relation to other modes of (re)presenting.

Notes

1.   Summers, D. (1992) p.234.
2.   Choose your man or woman: G. Pollock, J.Wolff, T.J.Clark, practically anyone from Modernism who asserts that figuration is 'now' impossible. On the other hand there are more interesting versions of artist-as-member in French poststructuralism and hopefully, in this text. The degree of submission or determination set against the responsibilities and powers of membership is the crucial issue in what follows.
3.   The concepts of grace and artistic genius will be extensively discussed in our next chapter.
4.   See Merleau-Ponty *Cezanne's Doubt* in Johnson, G.A. ed. (1994) p.64 See also Smith, J.A. 'The Denigration of Vision and the Renewal of Painting' in Heywood & Sandywell (eds.) (1998).
5.   Compare the Bryson of *Visual Theory* (1991) to the Bryson of *Tradition and Desire* (1984).
6.   See Heidegger, M. (1993) *The Question Concerning Technology.*
7.   Derrida makes considerable use of 'framing' and in particular the regulation (by the frame) of *ergon* and *parergon* (main and subsidiary work). In a characteristically deconstructive flourish he describes this as a *parasitized* economy. See Jay (1993) p 516 also Smith op. cit.
8.   Marin, L. 'The Frame of Representation and some of its Figures' in Duro, P. (1996) pp.79-96.
9.   Marcel Duchamp's *Fountain* is the subject of Chapter 7.
10.   See Jay (1993) p.522.
11.   Capra (1996) p.260.
12.   ibid. pp.260-1.
13.   ibid.
14.   This point will be extensively developed with particular reference to Luhmann's notion of adaptive orders. See Ch.9. For a history and analysis of the three 'waves' of development of cognition, cybernetics and information theory (with Maturana and Varela in the second wave) see Hayles, N. K. (1999).
15.   Wolff, J. (1983) p.30.

4 The Dream of Human Life: Platonic, Sophistic and Christian Imagery in Michelangelo's Art

> if art can be transferred ontologically to the sphere of secondary and derivative entities - shadows, illusions, delusions, dreams, mere appearances, and sheer reflections - well, this is a brilliant way to put art out of harm's way if we can get people to accept a picture of the world in which the place of art is outside it. And since Plato's theory of art is his philosophy, and since philosophy down the ages has consisted in placing codicils to the platonic testament, philosophy itself may just be the disenfranchisement of art - so the problem of separating art from philosophy may be matched by the problem of asking what philosophy would be without art. [1]

Previous chapters were concerned with a generalised modelling of a sufficient degree of complexity that would allow social phenomena to structure and present themselves for cognition in an environment to which they responded in controlled ways and which in turn responded to them. We characterised this as both a *difference*, indicating the specificness of social phenomena (close to Durkheim's sense), but we also stressed a number of relationships to other kinds of *sui-generic* but non-social phenomena acting together in an 'ecological' or homeodynamic way. Neither of those terms is intended to connote value, especially *moral* value, in the human-centred sense. Both are no more nor less than descriptive generalities.

We indicated that it is now time to consider a more concrete set of relationships between social phenomena, or, our first explicit image of community. We choose Michelangelo's drawing *The Dream Of Human Life* and its relationship to Christian and neo-Platonic influences in the Florence of his time. A 'more concrete set of relationships' might be translated here as 'what people do' - and what they do in this instance is, in our eyes, truly strange. Let us begin by outlining two very real problems.

35

According to Danto, Plato persists as, so to speak, the 'normal' authority in matters of art. This can be disputed in many ways but he is undoubtedly important to the philosophy of art. In short - you *have* to take account of him *if* certain philosophers of art are present. Contemporary art students might not feel that requirement too keenly but we are inclined to agree with Danto that the influence is important and that it suffuses the way we speak and think about visual art. Danto ends with a neat twist: what would philosophy be without art? But he also sidesteps the main question: disenfranchisement. So let's spell that out really clearly

For doctrinal reasons Plato (through the voice of Socrates) wants to expel artists, along with poets and other degenerates and 'second-raters' (the sense of those terms will become clear shortly) from the Republic he theorises (in the book of the same name) and which he proposes, will operate under the guardianship of 'philosophers'. By this he clearly means not *philosophers* in the critical or the plural sense but the political *philosophy* he puts forward in the text. We shall examine those doctrines shortly but for the moment, can you see the urbane, cultured and lettered Mr. Danto going along with this *in any way*? Can you see him leading a 'close down the galleries' campaign? Of course not - and neither is Danto an apologist. But then why on Earth does Plato remain central to his concerns as a philosopher and indeed as a philosopher of *art*? Why isn't Plato simply best forgotten? After all if these political proposals make Plato the front-runner in the philosophy of art then Hitler, Stalin and a few other insane despots would be runners-up. And no one takes *that* seriously! So never mind Danto's sidestep: 'disenfranchisement' means prevention, abolition, expulsion and outside of the narcissistic world of Socratic *talk*, that means enforced political repression.

If that were not strange enough it is manifestly clear that political repression is not an unintended consequence of a decent doctrinal position. Rather the doctrine itself is rank nonsense and has been criticised many times and absolutely comprehensively detail by no less than Hegel. Now Danto *knows* this and he's a smart professional and he knows that *every other philosopher of art* knows this but he also knows - and this is what he's setting out to say *and we agree* - that despite all this Plato remains the front runner theory-wise. So has philosophy got it wrong?

A 'conventional' sociology of art with Michelangelo as its subject might run as follows. Michelangelo claimed 'genius' as an unsought privilege, literally a gift of grace from God, which carried with it certain duties and imperatives. He also drew on neo-Platonic sources that contrasted the 'original' or 'perfect' forms he sought to represent with the degenerate and secondary representations of everyday life. On the basis of this dual ideological foundation, he invented a powerful visual idiom that was of great use to the social order in which he worked. First it drew upon religious and philosophical roots and so generated a sense of continuity. Second, by constant contrasts between 'higher' and 'lower' (in the image, in the ability to understand or make the image) he reinforced an already-stratified social order. Third, since this stratification now had available to it tradable images and commodities, his work, rather than simpler forms of deference and submission, wove his imagery into the everyday *business* of the social order as both its aspiration and its higher quality products.

Part of the force of this account lies in description - but rather more in the fact that its ostensible author *wouldn't be fooled for a moment*. It is, above all, a descriptive *rejection*. We generally agree. It is not a solidarity we can share. The problem is, it misses a huge number of subtle differences between the work as art and the order it serves (as not-art); it also misses the entirely obvious ones as well, like Plato's hatred of painting, Michelangelo's rejection of mimesis, the peculiar twists that have to be woven into the social fabric of Christian neo-Platonism to make Michelangelo's art even remotely possible. And last, the uncomfortable fact that Michelangelo is still valued. Now those who *do* value him (the conventional author being self-excluded) must be nostalgic apologists, ideologues, dopes. As admirers of Michelangelo we are inclined to think that sort of sociology has got it, that is, *us,* wrong.

Put this way, the Maturana-Varela concept of 'bringing forth worlds' begins to look decidedly 'soft' in the context of 'hard' environments - in this case 'hard' but *social* environments. Can these oppositions be reconciled? We offer this emphasis. The premise, 'the living system is autonomous...the environment only triggers the changes; it does not specify them' (op.cit.) describes an autonomous, that is, an ecologically *viable* living system. In the case of *non*-viability and therefore eventual extinction, the environment holds *all* the cards - no matter what the living system may 'want'.

The same applies analogously to social 'systems' (please take the term loosely) in this sense: suppose we take Derrida's 'there is no outside-text' (our translation) to mean that there is no *deciding* text or that we as social actors are confined within a *textual* horizon in much the same way that Maturana-Varela's living organism is self-enclosed and autonomous. Both, of course, remain subject to possible extinction. Notice how sharp the polarity becomes: the 'trigger' (in the fundamental sense) is held by the *viable* organism *or* by the environment. A middle-ground looks decidedly fragile. One might say that the viable organism, social or not, is enclosed within the horizon it 'specifies', text or not, unless and until the environment overwhelms it. In that sense 'there is no outside-text' but, at the same time, the 'outside' may invade and utterly invalidate the text. We appear to be threatened by a 'reality' we 'sense' but cannot define, except by the platitude 'undefinable'. We shall return to the obvious resemblance to the Kantian 'thing in itself' in due course. For this chapter, our concerns are rather more concrete.

We may not be able to define our (social) environment fully, or, to put it another way, every 'outside-text' is provisional upon a certain kind of horizon. That does not prevent but rather *requires* the constant generation of provisional, 'fuzzy' definitions as an integral part of the organism's or the social phenomenon's viability. We, and you, are engaged in that task right now and at every moment of conscious or unconscious existence. It is essential to our argument to see how far this sense of ecological viability differs from the traditional philosophical conception of 'truth'. For the traditional conception, 'strictly speaking' in order to truly know something, we must know everything - or a truthful definition of x is dependent upon a truthful definition of non-x.[2] This is clearly a wholly formal proposition and a practical impossibility. What matters in the context of ecological *viability,* as opposed to *truth,* is practical sustainability. The 'truth' of the organism or of the proposition is decided by its interactions with its environment, social or not, and *not* by the individual member or any single collectivity. 'Truth' here is not an absolute quality *of* certain phenomena or propositions but is instead *another* phenomenon. Differently put, ecologically framed, truth (or viability) is finite; capable of birth, competition, evolution and extinction.

These considerations are crucial in the context of our formulation of Michelangelo. In the first case, there are several insistent 'outside texts' or non-art that demand his attention as an artist. There is no *a priori* way to delimit and catalogue these influences; this is not a surreptitious determinism. For our purposes ('true' or not) we want to confront the interplay between several kinds of idiomatic representing: the 'philosophical' style of Socrates; Plato's dramatic form; the visual traditions and their media; and the theological, ritual and political manifestations of Christianity and neo-Platonism in Michelangelo's Florence.

Given the blatant hostility of Socrates to Art and its singular lack of interest for Christian theology (we shall cite Augustine) our intention is to dramatise not the correspondences but the *subterfuges* that make a critical version of art possible within those confines. We do not want to suggest that Art - or Michelangelo's art - is, a priori, an inherently desirable social practice. So our account of these subterfuges or our own hostility to the limits of Platonism is not a tacit reference to some external standard by which religion is seen as dysfunctional; it is rather intended to illuminate the modifications to Platonic-Christian utterance that become necessary when we *desire* to make visual art. That *desire*, the determination, as opposed to the 'truth' of determin*ism*, is ecologically crucial. Our focus will be the image and convictions implied in *The Dream of Human Life* [3] which both titles one of Michelangelo's most famous drawings and invokes, gathers and through its association with the drawing, gives an explicit form - an explicitly vivid and volatile transformation - to neo-Platonic doctrine. *The Dream of Human Life* as an image and in its textual resonances seeks to shape the relations of discourse, visual practice and community. We are not, then, about to tell the old, old story of the distinction (in art) between theory and practice but rather to engage a specific evolution of the socio-political relationships between theory, image, solidarity and language. It is crucial to our approach that any socio-ecological action is only conceivable in the context of concretely-structured interaction and conversely, that there is no place in our paradigm for the formal individual or the random act. More of that in the next chapter; for the moment our context contains both 'normal' features (in the Durkheimian sense) and concerted attempts to make changes.

Despite the paradoxes we set out above, we are inclined to agree with Danto that the influence of Plato is important and that it suffuses the way we speak and think about visual art. In this sense Plato is both a specific historical individual and one who embodies or codifies a certain set of ideas that, for good or ill, we find, literally, compelling. How, to use Lyotard's term, is that authority 'narrated'? How does it persist?

Let us look first at the relationship between Plato and Socrates. Socrates derives his authority (in an inverted sense as we shall see) from the non-human agency of the Oracle. The Socrates that Plato represent (or 'bring forth') is utterly absolved, then, from the limitations placed upon *all other* human speech. Plato reports Socratic dialogues in the form of a series of dramas whose 'necessity' and doctrinal content flow from this source.

According to the Socratic account, the pronouncement of the Oracle meant:

> Human Wisdom is worth little or nothing... he amongst you is the wisest who, like Socrates, knows that this wisdom is worth nothing at all. [4]...His wisdom is the knowledge of the negativity of all finite content. [5]

We may view this in one of two ways. *Either:* this perverse enclosure of wisdom within the limited frame of 'Socrates' operates as an intelligible device but one in which we suspend belief. Then all our readings must be provisional: *if* a, *then* b. More importantly, neither that reading, nor the text nor the discourse, nor any interest whatever *need* follow. The 'election' of Socrates on this basis makes no social claim and has *no sociological significance whatever*; except perhaps as a branch of the sociology of caprice - which a less forgiving reading can immediately identify as the characteristic position of the Modernist Enlightenment, assimilating the 'less sophisticated' to its own banal version of 'fiction as fiction' (Hegelian totality; camouflaged but unmistakable). The apparent, continuing appeal of Socrates, then, has all the falsehood, self-deception and cynicism, or plain stupidity, of other postmodern pretensions of pluralism in the face of others' assumed totalitarian instincts. We should underline, as in the case of Lyotard, that *if* 'his wisdom is the knowledge of the negativity of *all* finite content' (our emphasis) that is not the liberal position it is often taken to be. It is an unsubtle nihilism that could 'justify' or better, 'equalise' literally *all* finite content. Which equals would you choose? Hitler and, say, Roosevelt? Baron Frankenstein and Louis Pasteur? Darwin and Lamarck?

Or: we may take the election of Socrates not simply as the *willing* suspension of disbelief but as the *compelling conviction* of the discourse. What charisma that now affords him! He must become the absolutely unique and proper subject, the very source, of representation and the proper manner of representation is to faithfully re-produce His words and not Plato's own; for Socrates was chosen and the best Plato can hope for is the status of the good disciple. Hence the willingness to risk the dramatic form, to risk writing at all: the tension of Platonic drama is irresolvably present as the difference between the unavoidably chosen and the compulsions of the witness. And the irredeemable condition of Platonism is that because, despite, its apparent concrete sense, analytically it is without *further* voice and it counsels you also to be mute. Its concept of reason and its discursive effort is directed toward a massive silence that begins immediately beyond its original, limited, uniquely excused, documentation. In this sense, the relationships between original and copy and all of the dimensions of mimesis, the logics of the supplementary, the status of writing, the 'father-disciple' relationship [6] are so much semantic excess, for He is chosen and others are not. He may - he should - be documented; others may not; other documents are not *sanctioned*.

To reiterate, of course there *is* space to disbelieve the words of the Oracle, but that converts Socrates into a sort of rhetorician, *another* Sophist. Perhaps again we hear Socrates' ghost's laughter, but crucially, not Plato's; for he would then find his subject disposed, reappropriated - if not as another Sophist then (as the tradition to Derrida would have us believe) as a *philosopher*; not without problems of consistency. Ironically, then, it is not philosophic analysis, nor the Socratic standpoint of irony that so crucially requires the fundamentally different and unique Socrates, but his mundane dramatist-supporter, disseminators, reporters and apologists: those properly named 'disciples' who seek to appropriate doctrine as discipline in forging a kind of social order.

So much for Socrates' authority and Plato's 'discipline'. What of the doctrine that follows from the curious conflation of all wisdom and all ignorance? Consider now the sheer volatility of Platonic discourse:

> We know this about the man who professes to be able, by a single....skill, to produce all things, that when he creates with his pencil representations bearing the same name as real things, he will be able to deceive....children, if he shows them his drawings at a distance into thinking he is capable of creating in full reality anything he chooses .....must we not expect to find a corresponding form of skill in the region of discourse...? [7]

The reference to the visual arts is in one sense 'unmistakable' and yet the intrinsic volatility of Platonic discourse immediately emerges when we re-read the phrase, 'creates with his pencil representations bearing the same name as real things', for the 'man' who utters this speech can be precisely described as a representation bearing the same name as the real Socrates. And yet in what sense does Socrates 'really' exist except in and through the palpable ambiguity of a series of representations or 'namings' which straightaway reduces the concept of a 'mis-take' to nonsense? Moreover, to the extent that Platonic discourse takes place in the 'space' between the real and its representation, if this space turns out to be in every sense imaginary, then so does the apparent sense of the discourse; it becomes an aural illusion, which 'will be able to deceive....'

The space of contradiction itself forms a site to negotiate a productive version of re-presentation: to let the matter rest here, say, in some conception of the primacy of language so that Socrates and his representation achieve a certain identity, is to *violate* that primacy, that ambiguity, that richness.

Language itself insists upon the reinstatement of the difference between Socrates and his representation even though in *speaking* the difference there is only a tension between moods of representation. One might make the same point by saying that Socrates cannot really exist in a world in which language does not really exist. Or, more mundanely, but with at least as important consequences, the persistent, 'privileged' reality of Socrates is crucially, ironically dependent on the 'actual' dependence of Plato, his disciple, or better, his betrayer (since he abandons the purity of Socratic discourse and resorts to the secondary form of *drama* which Socrates also despised).

Yet what else is a *disciple* to do? The crucial point is that Plato, the disciple, inevitably violates Socratic doctrine in the very act of reporting. Of course Socrates is also party to this act, partly through the claims in his own 'speech-performances' and partly through being the very subject of the dramas. The essential point, in contradiction to the traditional notion of 'truth' discussed above, is that the contradiction of Socratic 'doctrine' is an *unintended consequence* of Platonic drama. This 'truth' is not decided nor controlled by human action but by the relationships between kinds of representing. With horrible irony, then, it is patently clear that even Socrates' death did not absolve him from complicity in either his own fame or Plato's dramatological 'compromise'. By that time *his* actions had become irrelevant.

Plato reports Socrates constantly distinguishing between the original and its (partial) representations:

> and yet there is a sense in which the painter creates a bed....he produces an appearance of one.....And what about the carpenter?...what he produces is not the form of bed which according to us is what a bed really is, but a particular bed...(Their products are)....something which resembles "what is" without being it... [8]

Or again:

> There is an object called "circle". Its name is the word I have just uttered. Next comes its definition,...compounded of nouns and verbs,...Third, there is the representation, which can be later...rubbed out or destroyed: none of these things can happen to the real circle. Fourth there is knowledge and understanding...which comes closest to the fifth...

> ..and the actual entity which is the object of knowledge and understanding is the fifth..[9]

Yet despite this reasonably firm position which constantly contrasts the ontological priority of what 'truly is' over resemblance, a doctrine collected necessarily in words, we find this reservation: '....no intelligent man will ever dare commit his thoughts to words, still less to words that cannot be changed as is the case with written characters.' Or: '..a writing cannot distinguish between suitable and unsuitable readers.' [10]

Derrida cites precisely this passage [11] in drawing attention to the privilege Socrates accords to the relationship between presence and speech whilst citing his complex dependence both literally upon writing, or if you will, upon Plato and on the constant invocation of metaphors of inscription:

> And when we say that Plato writes *from out of* the father's death we are not only thinking of the event entitled "*the death of Socrates*"...but primarily of the sterility of the Socratic seed left to its own devices. [12]

He further describes the relationship of instruction and dependence of master to pupil that writing (as the *mediate*, rather than the mythologised 'living' *originary* relation of logos and phenomenon) - threatens to displace; or better, to *re*place. In this sense, Platonism represents the destiny of ostensibly revealed 'truth' having become *commun*icated doctrine and so fascinates Derrida on account of its instabilities:

> The disappearance of truth as presence, is the condition of all (manifestation of) truth. Nontruth is the truth. Nonpresence is presence. Differance, the disappearance of every originary presence is *at once* the condition of possibility and the condition of impossibility of truth. [13]

But (and we charge Danto with this too) - this is scholarship rather than thinking; or, thinking that has stayed too long within the confines of philosophy in which 'discipline' Plato is concretely important and which shares his sterility. Can Plato stand up to a more inter-disciplinary or perhaps a simply less reverent analysis? What are his doctrinal proposals? Well, he is amongst the first to appearance from essence: 'something which resembles what is without being it'.

Now in the case of the circle, it is quite a nice piece of reasoning to figure out the *definition* of a circle - the locus of all points at a given distance from a fixed point - and to place it 'above' its various examples. But these aboves and belows are humanistic things: circles are circles, named or not, human-made or not; circles and their definitions belong together. But what about the bed? What an *extraordinary* choice! What is the common form of a cot, a double bed, a single bed, a bed made of straw upon the floor, an animals bed...? Something you sleep in? So: a day bed, a hospital bed, a nest, a burrow? If that were not enough there is also the doctrine of anamnesis which asserts that these forms are not *derived* definitions (remember the negativity of *all* finite content) but are *true* forms from some other existence which we have half forgotten (hence 'anamnesis') now that we live in the everyday, corrupt world of genesis and decay. The language is prettier, you can read it up if you are so inclined and of course the 'other world' explains why he is so dismissive of this one, to the point of acquiescing in his own absurd trial and death sentence. The language is prettier, but as a doctrine it is absolute nonsense and *we all already know that*. This doctrine of other worlds, this anamnesis, this inability to choose between what appears to be right and wrong even if we are not certain, this inability to choose life over death - this 'platonic testament' - and 'philosophy down the ages has consisted in placing codicils to the platonic testament' - is *utterly pathological*. To say then, that 'philosophy itself may just be the disenfranchisement of art' is, to say the least, an understatement. That sort of philosophical pathology is the potential disenfranchisement of everything, or, should we say of everything *finite*. Despite the twists in the tail Danto would be better off twisting it the other way. Not: what is philosophy as the disefranchisement of art? Instead: what is *art* in opposition to philosophy?

By contrast, in *Michelangelo and the Language of Art,* Summers cites this statement, associated with Giorgias: 'He who practices deception is more just than he who does not, and he who has yielded to deception is wiser than he who has not.' [14]

The aptness of this notion of deception, or 'ornament', at the very least, is manifest in the sphere of visual representation, whose 'deception' occurs at the twofold level of the establishment of the image and the consequent 'ornamental' destabilisation of the real or actual materials of its construction. Whilst the latter may appear fairly innocuous, (though not unimportant, especially for Modernism), or to a rationality modelled after a strict version political economy, superfluous or extravagant, the former appears much more potentially sinister. No doubt its corrosive power rests upon the re-presentation of a material-as-an-image capable of influencing, for good or ill, one's perception of that to which it refers. Upon this irresolvably dangerous ground stands advertising, propaganda, the visual arts, in short, every form of representation, *including* writing and speech.

The proper use of ornament was 'to instruct or convince through delight'[15]; the characteristic requirement of classicism thus emerges, namely, restraint; but occurs as the need to subjugate invention to the demands of reason. However, this limitation cannot be analytically satisfactory unless reason is somehow severed from the 'destructive' potential of representation, that is, from image, writing and speech. One can see, then, the interest of

Classicism in a mathematical conception of order or correct proportion, but one can also see that such a form cannot hope to offer any adequate discipline for the content of either visual or verbal representing; it merely indicates some rules of a convention and the possibilities of variation. At first sight it appears, then, that a then-current affirmation, a sentiment that indeed bears a twofold affirmation: a compulsion toward ornament and a delight in its reception - lacked, so to speak, realisable conventions, a framework of discipline that could ensure that it did not simply destroy itself in its own virtuosity.

Christian theology is at least less perverse than Platonism. In Platonism there is an assertion about essential form but, unless you think anamnesis holds water, there is no reasonable account of the deteriorated presence or shapes of the mundane world. For Christianity, there is at least the doctrine of Creation, a metaphor that at least lets the everyday world have some connection, however tenuous with the 'essential'. That metaphor is also permeated, however, by Original Sin. St. Augustine, then, is doctrinally somewhat more open to the *equivocal* status of visual representation:

> It is one thing to be false; it is quite different to be unable to be true.....A man in painting cannot be true even though he tends towards the appearance of a man....Such things do not choose to be false, nor are they false through their desire to be so but they are compelled by a kind of necessity to conform as much as they are able to the artist's will....all these things are in some respects true precisely because they are in other respects false......To the end that we may be true to our nature we should not become false by copying and likening ourselves to the nature of another.....We should instead seek that truth which is not self-contradictory and two-faced so that it is true on one side and false on another. [16]

The paradox is, no doubt, ingenious and yet is not interested in its genius, far less in its genius as a kind of grace. But think of the potency of this idea in the context of Platonic irony: in a phenomenal domain where whatever human perception earns for itself constitutes a being which appears to be but 'is not', then grace, 'calling', is the one explosive resource that transcends the condemnation of speech to an analytic status indistinguishable from silence, of sight to synonymity with blindness. (It is precisely the resource employed but discarded by Socrates). In such terms, the artist who finds genius persuasive, and moreover, can affirm an essentially Sophistic tradition of compelling performance (skilful performance being in large measure both source and confirmation of his pretensions) can beautifully resolve the self-contradictory truth which is 'false on its other side'. Whilst agreeing that the finite particular bears intrinsic limitation and so 'is not' the painter can also argue that the flawless, unlimited being his genius can imagine 'is not' in quite the reverse sense: *it lacks an image*. Hence the painter can ground his project of representing with exactly the plausibility, dignity and paradox that Platonism affords to definitions, understandings and representations of 'the real circle'.

Thus it falls to Cennini to formulate this *brilliant* subterfuge that makes the commitment to making representative images a duty within the *neo*Platonic republic, indeed a task laid upon a distinct category of practitioners by reason of their skill and imagination, in short, their *calling*. He thus applies to a *community* of practitioners exactly the status that Socrates claims for *himself alone* and actually discards. Between the suffocating implications of the gross distinction between the master and the disciple, the one and the many, Heaven and Earth, there now potentially stands a principled duty, a calling, to re-present :

> It is the task of painting.... 'to find things not seen, to seek them beneath the shadows of the natural....to fix them with the hand, showing that which is not as if it were....' [17]

He is, then, able to deploy a close approximation to Giorgias' notion of deception which its Platonic opponents would find infinitely more difficult to dispute since both its authority and project lay perilously close to those invoked by Socrates. How different this appears from a simple notion of reflection; how crucially difficult a claim for a sociology whose practices tend to institute 'structure' as the ground of a corresponding and so conventional imagination, if we re-word 'shadows of the natural' as 'shadows of the social'.

Let's summarise the chapter so far. Socrates' position, his 'wisdom', in not so much *showing* but *knowing* that human opinion is 'worth little or nothing'. Kierkegaard calls this the standpoint of irony. It is taken, in our view falsely as we said above and will argue again, as one of the first and instigating instances of a critical standpoint. This, for us, is the essential error: it is not critical in any specific or focused sense; it has no argued *preferences* (except for itself) and instead operates as 'blanket' irony set against all finite content. It takes *nothing,* literally no finite thing, seriously. We shall return to the political implications of irony in the context of Socrates' trial. For the moment we shall stay with the ontology and its representation.

Platonic representing, the substance of his dramas, *has* to have an ironic character *because of Socrates*, or, so far as it believes in the ontology or the doctrine of its master. That is, the concept of anamnesis and so the relation

46

between original and derivative - or the grounds of representing and its particulars - is *not* intended ironically or as a negotiable metaphor. Plato has the *duty* to represent irony and this is a social duty in which we are also implicated; our solidarity is sought. But then Plato has a problem: Socrates matters but no one else does, or at least not much. And it its singularly hard to generate communal solidarity around that kind of exclusivity. Christianity, as Augustine's paradox demonstrates, has a similar problem and offers only the prospect of salvation through attending to 'that truth which is not self-contradictory and two-faced so that it is true on one side and false on another.' (op. cit.)

This is the point to raise a controversial and very unfashionable statement by Durkheim: '...society... is a part of Nature and indeed its highest representation'.[18]

Let us leave aside questions of higher and lower; nor can we get away with 'most complete' representation. Human representation is the most complete *for humans;* but the same is true for every other species. The salient point is the 'belonging together' of nature, society, and human representations, or 'culture'. Whilst for Plato and for Christianity 'wisdom is the knowledge of the negativity of all finite content' for Durkheim, 'culture' is a proper and an *authentic* aspiration. In this sense, where Platonic-Christian positions urge a denial of solidarity gathered around the institutions of 'this' world (a rejection of mundane culture) Durkheim urges that the same mundane culture is not simply a contingent feature of societies, but an autopoietic feature of the relationship between nature and society.

Our reading of Durkheim's notion of representation points to the genuineness of this relationship between Being (nature) and semblance. Crucially, for us, immediate semblance is wrenched from contingency precisely through the mediation of organised representation. For Cennini's, 'It is the task of painting..', Durkheim clearly substitutes, 'It is the task of sociology...'; and in case that falls to an ear dominated by what passes for contemporary critical philosophy, and comes out something like 'jointly recognised conventionality' let us draw the point to its maximum salience.

If the task of painting or of sociology is not intended as pure irony but instead as a kind of calling, then that calling can only issue from human interaction in the nature of being. The implicit claim, *made overt* is this: it belongs to the differentiated nature of being to have itself re-presented in these traditional, or better, 'disciplined' forms - painting, sociology and so on. This, as it were, is not the conceit, not the device, nor the posture, but the *belief* that gathers the discipline. And it is only in the context of that *belief* that the ecology of social and natural phenomena becomes a topic of authentic critical consideration.

Of course, it may be that the calling is subsequently modified, ended, even completed (as some readings of modernist painting might suggest). But then the point is to be argued, not decided *a priori*. Contrasted with the postmodern absurdity of disbelief in metanarrative or the 'dissolution of conviction' both Durkheim and Cennini 'believe' or 'see', whilst the (post)modern sounds remarkably like Socrates, remarkably ironic. Of course, irony is postmodernity's most cherished quality; we are *constantly* told as much. But postmodernity is as unconscious of its repetitions as it is of its cultural and political rigidities.

How does Cennini differ from Platonism? In this respect: his form of representing is positively elected; he cannot trade off the paradoxes of already being a speaker who later discovers the treachery of words; painting is not an existential condition in quite the same sense. Nor is writing, especially drama, though Plato routinely ignores the issue by dissolving it in the special status of Socrates. Cennini has no such saviour to command his output, except himself, his vision, his imagination and above all the trust in the relationship between himself and his calling. He is radically more positive (though not unqualifiedly so as we shall see). We are certainly not going to be asked to accept some visual parallel to Socrates' inversion (or identity) of wisdom and ignorance.

In this context, Plato is at times more acute than a sociology or the many forms of postmodern criticism that tend to see discourse or 'text' in painting. He condemns painting because its goal is *essentially* images. Augustine, with greater tolerance, but still armed with the massive scale of generalisation that the distinction between heaven and earth permits, takes this as the tragic two-edgedness of finitude. Cennini, whose essential locus is his *profession*, grasps it as opportunity. In this sense, the difficulty Cennini (and art generally) presents is not that of a formal theory of imagination, nor of artists as a formal category. We are not about to be beset by the enigma of an analytically free domain, which proceeds to structure and limit itself. Instead, we are confronted with an imagination that is directed toward the entirely human, arguably conventional, inescapably pre-structured domain of pictorial possibility. Listen to the difference of resonance between 'possibility' in the philosopher's sense that knows no bounds and the absolute concreteness of 'pictorial possibility'. Durkheim's positions, whilst equivocal, and despite their traditional ties with philosophy and his cited regard for the foundational role of religion, actually lie closer to Cennini and thus also to Giorgias.

Cennini displaces irony with the breathtaking openness of a theory of imagination that is also an explicit obligation to represent: 'it is the *task* of painting....' However, there are certain major points of contact with Platonism especially in the conception of nature, or as Cennini has it, 'the shadows of the natural'. The effect is to place the products of the artist's imagination, or fantasy, in the same relation of constant ironic inversion and re-inversion that energises and destabilises the Platonic conception of the real. This metaphor attains its most extreme development in the work of Michelangelo.

> The artist, it is now claimed, is related to God, and his art is based in the principles of God's wisdom. [Or],..a similar understanding of the artist's activity deeply rooted in discussions of invention.....was raised to the highest power and is compared to divine creation *ex nihilo.* [19]

This sort of claim does not *accidentally* engender the notion that artists are individuals standing outside society; it is instead central to its coherence. Of course it will send many earnest sociologists in search of proofs and demonstrations that artists do not. But that, we suggest, is to begin inquiry in prejudice, to fail to take account of the *different* relation between (another) society and its systems of belief and language. The semantic upshot of the curious admixture of Christian dogma and neo-Platonism is that the totality of social life bears an intrinsically disfigured relationship to reality in *their* sense of the term. Plato's direct analogy is the image of the cave. Unless, then, members generally are going to emulate Socrates' willingness to drink hemlock or be content to live in the shadows of deception, the conception of *grace* visited upon certain individuals takes on an enormous *social* importance. In those terms, grace *cannot* operate asocially but rather functions as the interplay between an ostensible reality and making its imagery. Grace operates in that semantic horizon as the origin of all other *authentic* social action. The fact that (ostensibly) we no longer pay homage to 'grace' is quite beside the point, though perhaps we implicitly still do.

> 'Grace' seems also to have a vertical dimension in Michelangelo's mind that distinguished his thought on the subject from the thought of writers such as Alberti or Leonardo, who, like many others, understood the idea and gave it a central place in their discussion of painting. All agree that grace is a desirable characteristic in a work of art. But only if the term is taken literally, seen at its full height as a divine gift, and thus as a means of transcendence and spiritual return, does it cease to be a mere catchword or formula and become the basis for a religion of the beautiful that Michelangelo so clearly and so deeply felt through most of his life. [20]

Certainly the idea of grace is anti-sociological in the specific sense that it derives from a horizon of meaning that would have directly excluded sociological analyses in the modern sense, but that is precisely its salience; if we fail to accord 'grace' its explicit social claim, we reduce it to nonsensical misuse. To put the matter in extreme terms, neither 'grace' nor its consequent capability, namely, 'genius' can be sensitively addressed as systematic linguistic failures within an otherwise comprehensively egalitarian usage grounded in contemporary forms of empiricism.

At this point, we are sure that the reader steeped in conventional sociology will be 'lost' and in several senses. That reader will be quite unable to share in the solidarity that supports either Michelangelo's grace or his genius. Both ideas will be 'lost' on them. And if we say that we share their misgivings even further confusion will result. Why then do we defend so stratified a visual-semantic order when we have just done our best to undermine its basic doctrines? Our motives will be also 'lost' on this reader. Isn't it the case that the concepts of grace and genius are simply, *unacceptably* wrong? All right, that reader *may* have a point but before we try to resolve the matter may we stay, just for a while, with the extreme, 'unacceptable' otherness of grace?

Nowhere is this difference between Michelangelo and modern sensibility more apparent than in portraiture. They are, deliberately, extremely rare in his oeuvre. The British Museum holds a black chalk drawing of Andrea Quaratesi [21] which is the only finished portrait drawing now known though Vasari refers to a lost half-length, life-size portrait of Tommaso de Cavalieri.

The portrait at first sight might be mistaken for an approximation to the modern tradition of portraiture. After all, this picture is full of willingness to engage pure incident; the treatment of the physiognomy is governed by the uniqueness of the sitter and not by the exemplary qualities of the 'ideal' head or figure that is the more usual locus of his art.

Moreover, to the extent that Michelangelo is prepared to engage incident (the outward surfaces of musculature being the obvious example) it is either because it occurs as a sign of what is intrinsic to the being of the form in question, to its expressive qualities, the dynamism of its movement, to its qualitative differentiation from other forms, or because it stands as an essential element in the visual and semantic composition of his works. If we take a drawing such as *The Risen Christ*,[22] one might take the beautiful lines, full of incident, to betray a delight in purely sensuous qualities, or the deep visual space to show a passion for sensory perception and realisation. However, the significance of the subject matter, together with the

50

flawlessness of a figure that even in scripture bore the *stigmata* argues against this interpretation. If we may put the matter this way: the apparent 'extreme incidentality' of the line finds its root in the *nature* rather than the circumstances of the figure. The uniqueness of the 'incident' of the Resurrection and the need for it to attain an articulate image (recalling Cennini's inversions of the 'shadows of the natural') argue for a conception of Michelangelo's line constituting both a visual edge and a semantic boundary as precise and enduring as those of the Impressionists are fluid and transient.

The portrait, apparently, is quite opposite in conception. Moreover, the subject is clothed, rather than nude or 'robed'; it is dressed according to the principles of fashion rather than decorum or the needs of pictorial composition. Here we see simply this person's clothes. There is also the symbolic resonance between clothing and the 'veil of appearances'.

Much the same applies to the head and the handling of the extremely precise relationships between the neck and the collars. There is no apparent break between appearance, personality and meaning; it is a visual formulation of this man's outward appearance. It may be conjectured that this unusual circumstance is derived from the special regard in which he held the sitters. He was undoubtedly attached to Quaratesi whilst Vasari described Cavalieri as both infinitely beautiful and as loved *infinitamente* by Michelangelo. As Summers places the matter, '.....Vasari's words mean that (Cavalieri) was perfect after his kind, that is, a perfect man.' [23]

That idea grates horribly for us. Even more difficult for us is the idea that his might have been the 'face by which God corrected Nature.' [24] Nevertheless, we urge again that such expressions should not be grasped as failures to accord with our own conventions. Nor is it sufficient to find these 'excesses' simply consonant with the passions of erotic or homo-erotic attachment, for our usage in such an expression as (say) 'the perfect (wo)man' is loaded with an irony that sets highly contextual limitations. And however much we refer to how we 'ought' to look, and however much a certain 'look' becomes a desirable ideal, we do not countenance such a notion as the 'ideal' head or man etc. with anything approaching the sense in which Michelangelo executed such works.

Varchi makes reference to both Cavalieri and another very famous drawing that brings us to the centre of the paradoxes of Michelangelo's art. He is that, 'beautiful person or thing who sometimes awakens us from the dream of human life'.[25] In these terms, the portrait in its uniqueness offers a version of the human person which is equally a denial of its subject. The mediating term is, of course, 'grace'. The uniqueness of the portrait is at once a picture of the rare gift of divine genius and divine beauty. How is this extreme position to be squared with the earlier notion that the term 'artist' refers primarily to a category within the division of labour, or to put the matter in slightly different terms, in what sense does Michelangelo's notion of 'dream' represent a formulation of social membership?

The Dream of Human Life [26] is Platonic irony cast in another idiom. Whether it derives its immediate force from the influence of Christianity - the central figure is surrounded by figures representing six of the seven deadly sins - or whether the flying figure representing fame or emulation belongs more appropriately to Sophism, are minor considerations. The most important issue is the negativity of irony directed toward human life.[27]

Consequently, we see that Michelangelo understood his own abilities to be derived from his relationship to God rather than his social relations with other men. We have seen that Platonic-Christian irony both in order to sustain itself and on account of its disregard of the worth of everyday social intercourse has an endemic need for 'graced individuals' in order that the dream of social life takes place at all. Socrates, with greater consistency, but arguably less intelligence, preferred martyrdom.

Michelangelo's conception of his membership is thus on one hand thoroughly negative but it is no less membership because of that: he is still bound by its conventions, its limits and its learning. Does his special ability allow for any more positive conception? Does the figure of fame that awakens the young man in the drawing point to a qualitative distinction between good and bad forms of membership? Is the true distinction to be made between the paradoxes of a waking and sleeping life? Might Augustine's paradox, the truth of art is illusion, be taken as a genuine truth?

We hope we can find a way to do so but there is little point in pretending that Augustine does anything other than present the paradox simply to find it and art uninteresting. And a man as visually alive as Michelangelo (if the rhetorics are to be believed) could only find two faces worthy of portraiture. The rhetorics may exaggerate the individual facts but certainly point to a socially-organised sentiment. Nor can the idea of grace be easily reconciled with the love of something called illusion. It is then fair to conclude that the socially organised conception of the 'waking' life consisted in a critical withdrawal of consent to the major substance of social life.

Nevertheless, there is a subtle and important distinction between the critical withdrawal of Augustine and of Michelangelo, whose roots lie in their chosen means of expression. No doubt a man of the exquisite sensibility of Augustine could be reflexive upon the possible vanity of writing; but then to do so is to atone, in the sense that the criticalness of language is being allowed to speak. There is here a vestige of the redemption of original sin in terms of the means, and so the fate, that sin engendered.

For Michelangelo, the situation is remarkably different; he is neither content with Socratic silence, nor is he a Churchman. Where he chooses to receive or practice his 'grace' the trumpet of fame that the figure carries in *The Dream* is much more apt. Concretely, this makes his products irredeemably more profane and brought him into relations of both patronage and opposition with factions of both Church and State. Moreover, as those who tend to see the matter in political terms quickly point out, his work is an affirmative feature of the justification and celebration of their power.

But that is only a concrete issue. Of far more importance is the fact that unlike Augustine who could claim to be critical, Michelangelo exemplifies a claim to be both critical and to set limits to criticism. Differently put, where Augustine has faith animated by intelligence, Michelangelo claims to *see*. And that sight has its own intellectual, critical and practical faculties. But *to see*, is infinitely more positive than the mere faculty of criticism. In the terms used earlier, where irony structurally needs a conception of revelation to stabilise or protect itself from its own corrosive power, that need is met by formally articulated negativity. Michelangelo's irony is accompanied by the revelation of substantial form. He does not say 'I am the most ignorant of men' but rather that he is (or tries to be) the most perfect of artists.

Let us try to restate this point in another way: Michelangelo manifestly shares in a negative conception of both mundane social order and sense perception. Yet through his own special position and that of his tradition he is able to positively value certain kinds of social production, gathered around the criticism and making of art. It is problematic, however, whether he is able to conceptualise and so sustain this production as in itself genuine (in which case he is offering a version, albeit critical, of membership) - or whether his works operate as no more than splendid signs (rather like Cavalieri) of the futility of social life. In that case he has virtually nothing to offer; he becomes the irritant that disturbs the sleep of life.

In our view, there is no equivocation here; he was bound to a destiny that entirely crushed the positivity of his art. That is not to say that his late work is of little value; on the contrary, it is arguably his greatest but much of it then remained (and we suggest, still remains) to be better understood. That is perhaps too drastic or perhaps too personal a position, so let us try to make a more balanced account of the more positive components. For our purposes, there are two: the first of these is the valuation of 'sensate judgement' and the second is 'fantasy'.

Michelangelo's continual association with the notion of the judgement of the eye relates him - more than to Neoplatonism - to ....an attitude towards images based on sensate judgement, rather than normative proportion, an attitude that was part of his heritage as a Florentine artist.......Still, precisely because it because it represented a nonrational principle higher than number, the grace revealed by the eye could be understood Neoplatonically, as Michelangelo came to understand it. [28]

The first section of this passage seems to be the most constructive of ideas: it is intrinsically social, underscores the notion of judgement in the activity of the senses, where later and, we think, inferior formulations, tend toward the mechanical and correspondential. Above all it suggests a certain intimacy or aptness between sensory faculty and its objects or Being. Stated at its highest positivity, this 'heritage' seems to allow that there is an intrinsic rightness and intelligence in the activities of the eye. Surely not to be confused with simple instinct, this 'well grounded faculty' is subject to 'meaning' in the sense of both connotation and intention, the demands of decorum and of reason; it can successfully regulate itself without recourse to normative mathematical canons of proportion. Like 'instinct', however, it is already there. Heidegger uses the same formulation for 'language'. The utterly crucial point, that the Platonists, Christians and their derivatives overlook, is that this quality of being 'already there' allows the beginning, only the beginning, of an argument that there is an existential dimension to the activities of speaking, seeing and the activities of the body generally that is not simply the contingent product of convention.

Yet the negativity is implicit in the phrase, '...the grace revealed by the eye could be understood Neoplatonically.' Once the origin of the products of visual work is not the interplay of a no less marvellous intelligence, socially organised and developed in a well-grounded interaction with its physical environment. Once that intimacy is abolished by the corrosive power of Christian neoPlatonism and reduced, as it were, to a tiny crack in the impenetrable armour of Heaven so that now and again a tiny speck of real light falls upon some arbitrarily chosen, absolute 'individual', like Socrates, like Michelangelo, like Cavalieri. Once the lived community of members in Being is severed by this pervasive estrangement, human communal order is reduced to a pointless convention that simply revolves within itself.

Precisely the same problem invades the notion of fantasy. We shall repeat the analysis simply because it allows the richest and most tragic of irony.

One way or another the activity of the fantasy was inevitable. It might hold to the truths of nature or it might wander into things unseen and unimagined. Renaissance writers understood just such an alternative....they described the fantasy as chaos - the state existing before divine order was imposed - or in Christian terms, as sin, departure from divine order. [29]

To put the matter in terms that show the starkness of the irony that is at work: fantasy - the imagination - is denied the regulative power of human order, since (contrary to illusion) that order is estranged from being. However, God still remains absent from the cities of men. Consequently, fantasy is no more than a mark of fallenness: fantasy is the original and the final condemnation to sin.

Fantasy and order are thus irreconcilable principles.. Broadly understood, allegory provided a justification for the activity of fantasy as the servant of higher truth... The artist was finally alienated because his imagination was by definition outside the God-given nature of the world and its exercise led inevitably to the sin of pride. [30]

This interpretation directly contradicts the notion of the graced individual or the 'grace' seen in or by his eye. The positivity images of the drawing, *The Dream of Human Life,* the distinction between the waking and sleeping life have been reduced to the choice between the sin of pride and the sin of sloth.

The reduction of the possibility of portraiture, whether actually or rhetorically, to two individuals may be something we find distasteful, though intelligible. What perhaps we do not see is that the same semantic causes are destined to narrow the possibility of Michelangelo's art still further:

His last works are deeply devotional. They repeat with an obsessiveness that is a kind of husk of his early inventiveness. They are purges of the fantasy. As the religious writers prescribed, he wrote, he drew, then coloured, then carved the saving body of Christ in his imagination. [31]

It cannot be surprising that in a semantic structure that especially severs the senses from Being, that there finally can be only one subject for a visual artist finally coerced by both his age and his society's religion and philosophy into accepting its truth. That subject must be the one instant that Being was genuinely visible in the world. To some readers, this conclusion will simply add weight to the position we first sought to deny - that art is a reflection of, or determined by its society, that it produces the imagery of an ideology. In truth, if Michelangelo were the only artist we could examine here, that case would be exceptionally strong, especially since he is perhaps uniquely strongly related to and shaped by the religious, philosophical and critical language of his day. The relation is perhaps untypically close but that serves, we think, to focus rather than mislead; and it would have been singularly inappropriate to contest the conceptions of reflection and determination by simply citing an artist strongly at variance with his culture. You will recall, however, that we did not deny the relationships between art and society. Indeed we argued that the name 'artist' was essentially tied to an aspect of the division of labour within society and was not, so to speak, the absolute or inalienable property of some 'individual'.

We contested the idea that the relation was one of correspondential reflection and still do, even for someone like Michelangelo whose art is so tightly aligned to Christian neo-Platonism. What, then, do we think is the relation in this case? For even an aspect of the division of labour can 'reflect'. The relation can be simply stated: Michelangelo's practice as a visual artist was partly shaped by but comprehensively failed by his own religious and philosophical language.

Michelangelo's art, whilst related to, is not identical nor should be confused with the religious and philosophical language that accompanied it. It may be that his art is directly impossible without it, but that is still not a matter of identity for in many senses it is also impossible *with* it. The central feature that confounds the interplay of each set of representations is the lack of a principle of immanence that could bring mundane facticity (broadly the world of social history) into a relationship with Being or God that would 'save' human order from the fate of absolute contingency. But there is also a question of degree: the estrangement of the human from the divine order, thus from order at all, is more radical in neoPlatonism than in Michelangelo's sense of 'grace'. This is approximately the same proposition as the difference between Augustine's criticalness and Michelangelo's claim to see.

Without wishing to invoke the entire panoply of Hegelian logic, the problem of the 'flawed infinity' can be seen in radical form if we return to the Socratic discourses, cited earlier concerning the 'real' bed and the 'real' circle. Reality for (Plato's) Socrates apparently consists in the noetic intuition that precedes the possibility of its various, degenerated representations. Notice how ironic are the choices of object: on the one hand, the bed - which simply has to have a derivative, if generic, status: on the other, the circle - which has not unreasonably been understood as one of the fundamental, schematic, organising principles of both perception and production. In either case the unqualifiedly 'real' seems to be precisely qualified by *not* being the sum total of its representations. At the risk of simplification, the Hegelian conception of the real is inclusive of both the idea and its history of representations. One may argue here about the quality of various representations, but that is to confirm his point: representation has an inherent criticalness governed by the nature of the object. Equally importantly, the possibility of representation belongs to both the nature and the revealedness of the object.

Where the Hegelian notion of the real is radically dialectical and historical, the Platonic concept is almost perversely monadic. There is no reasonable account of the presence of any ontic dimension whatever. Hence in several senses we have already seen, Platonism is doctrinally bound to disown the very language in which it is couched. The effect is to force its entire intelligibility to rest upon noetic intuition in the specific sense of an 'intellectual intuition' of determinate form, since the sense of both words and sensory perception is both derivative and degenerate. Stated in slightly different terms, the characterisation of genesis as the corruption of form, forces Platonism into a conception of social order as disorder, or contingency. A republic based on such premises seems doomed but it is as well to remember that Plato ends that work with a section not on the stability of social order but on the immortality of the soul.[32] He is thus consistent with his own usage, if not, arguably, with ours. Of course, *our* usage - especially if we are philosophers - may still turn out be through and through neo-Platonic.

Michelangelo lived in a society dominated by just such a semantic structure and yet practised as both an artist and poet. This in itself is an implicit denial of the radicalness of Socrates' positions, given his analyses of those occupations in *The Republic*. Moreover, through the interventions of a Sophistic tradition of performance and the Christian notion of grace, there follows a further commitment to the rightness of certain works such that the demands of their realisation can no longer be dismissed as merely contingent. If we leave aside for a moment the more exalted claims to grasp the divine order the mundane means of realisation are no less remarkable. When we consider how marvellous an understanding of anatomy is involved in Michelangelo's work and that this is virtually the birth period of that discipline, his ordinary, 'practical' imagination and energy is at least as remarkable as the 'remarkable' realisations of the images of God and the Ideal.

We counsel the reader not to reduce this matter either to a distinction between theory and practice or to a matter of representation if that in any way connotes making a copy. It cannot be 'practice' because we are not speaking of a repetitive relation to a dimension of the real long understood and

57

familiar; we are speaking of well-grounded but fundamentally innovative and hence autonomous intelligence. Crucially however, this is not an autonomy threatened by estrangement. On the contrary, it exemplifies an inquestive and formulating ability highly attuned, responsive and in many ways shaped by an intimacy with Being. We are not speaking of 'copies' nor of correspondence since the entire concept of the animation of the human figure is here being reinvented. It is almost as though the concept of grace also operated in the ontic dimension.

Grace as a doctrinal claim within a Christian worldview, if not acceptable, is at least intelligible for (post)modernity. Yet it acceptability-intelligibility rests upon a deliberate suspension of credence: grace understood fundamentally is - for the (post)modern - an instance of social pathology (which earnestly ethnocentric sociology tries to cure). Grace as a claim within the field of a critical pragmatics, however, whilst tolerable in footballers, musicians (so far as it remains confined to the mysteries of individual physical capacity) is threatening: toward both the concept of universally-equivalent subjecticity and toward the consequent view that 'grace' in the form of practical power can only occur on the rational basis of an aggregation, an organised institution of similarly-concerted subjects. The drawing *The Dream of Human Life* sits precariously between 'grace' in the doctrinal and the pragmatic sense.

Of course, it may be quickly established that Michelangelo's drawing rests upon a more or less definable neo-Platonic horizon without which it would virtually impossible for the work to exist. So also, we may draw attention to the interplay between neo-Platonic rationalism and the surreptitious privileging of the eye in Cartesian models of observation. All manner of correspondences may be drawn between phallocentrism, ocularcentrism, technological control and western visual art. [33] All manner of visual critique may be placed against the project to represent in terms of a monocular convention. We may safely establish, then, that Michelangelo's work is provisional and so depends on a fairly tightly-agreed schedule, a sort of social policy; it is conventional; it could have been otherwise. These are the characteristics an epistemology might consider important; and 'epistemology' here means a certain way of looking that defuses the explicit and fundamental claim of 'grace' by locating it within another worldview, one we need not enter, nor countenance, one we can isolate.

It is not important to our purposes to indicate that an epistemology is also convention-specific and could have been otherwise; that simply perpetuates the convention. It is important to distinguish what else

Michelangelo's drawings do, what else they do that activates 'grace' in a pragmatic sense that bursts through the insulating, encapsulated 'worldview'.

Our reading of *The Dream of Human Life* suggests not simply an accidental relation but a specific, concerted site of dissimilarity between 'practical' grace (that insists on our attention) and 'divine' grace (which we dismiss as fiction). In the first case it stands as a bearer of certain doctrinal and practical idioms. In the second, as (post)moderns hold dear it is also a subversion in several other idiomatic senses we have discussed and do not propose to reactivate. So far it holds itself within the reflexive interplay of representation upon representation, a subterfuge within an economy of signs. But there are several sites, we suggest, where this economy is broken: where the reality is not supplanted by the simulacrum; where the question is no longer the serial, forms of inter-substitution, the 'precession of simulacra' - but where the sign, or better, the discipline, effaces its distinctness in the reconstruction of the real, in the unity of compelling *revelation*.

The first site (also an ironically glossed but distinctly present feature of Platonic drama) - is its eroticism; or more precisely, its homoeroticism. This, no doubt mediated by ideologies of 'perfection' (mercifully misunderstood as bodily perfection) nevertheless renews the aesthetic requirements of the depiction of the nude male figure. Here, the 'giving shape' that occurs in the corporeal mass and power, the repose, the youth, the ambition of the figure, its place as the current object of attention of the fates, a possible corporeal space in which the spirit of grace may unfold - cannot function as sign, image, text for which there is, or is not, a proposed, distinct exteriority. Instead, the distinction, the 'is' or the 'is not' of an exteriority presents itself as unnecessary scar tissue on the face of a continuum, a 'bringing to appearance' not discordant with Cennini's vocational pragmatics. Here, through their erotic charge, the 'outside-textual' items are unlike the generality of 'grace', or the event of Socrates' calling, or the corpus of Plato as disciple, constituting so radical a unity of image-eroticism as to displace any relationship of assumed co-respondence. They surpass the dividing line of a biologically-defined sexuality contingently operating in a social setting; they are wholly *socio*-erotic phenomena. Yet, on the other hand, even from this distance they do not easily square with the economies of preference and choice. They do not present as *substitutable* so much as *compelling*. If from this realised, *sui-generic* visual phenomenon, a visual mythology of origin is reconstructed, a coming-to-appearance, in *this* form of *this* drawing - then whatever else is said, whatever the sexuality, whatever the visual preference, attention to the drawing commands belief rather than disbelief, respect rather than disrespect. There is a persistent visual credibility here that drives through the very heart of the distinction between the original and the social. This social phenomenon is (or at least claims to be) *authentic*; as *sui-generic*, phenomenal, image, simulacrum, or whatever metaphors of distance and interiority we invoke, a powerful resonance of dis-closure remains. It is uninhibited by notions of conventionality; still seemingly uninhibited by the claim of grace; still sufficiently uninhibited to mark out in its chalks, its paper and its 'Cartesian' methodology a relationship of revelation between an archly sophisticated social form - the homoerotic image as 'high' art - and the most corporeal of drives and visual attentions. If, then, the methodic stance of (our) sociology formally insists on irreducible ontological status of a specific 'further' domain of social phenomena as the condition of its existence, then we find to our dismay and joy, doubt and conviction that social phenomena and so also sociology 'spill out' of these formally allotted epistemological boundaries and start to make very compelling claims about authentic realities whose revelation they mediate.

Put more cynically (or ironically) where once signified and signifier conspired in locating a meaning within a convention, here an infinitely more extensive interplay of subject matter and discipline collude in the establishment of a re-presentation. A representation in which the 're' - the renewal - of presence compellingly surpasses its former appearance. Not in any simply 'progressive' sense, - but in a sense which insists that this renewed presence cannot be denied without true human cost. The status of the 'subject-ed' matter now becomes altogether equivocal. It will no longer lie as a disposable component in an economy of preferred signs, but insists on its non-exchangeable, inalienable value.

To exercise the option of ignoring Michelangelo's claim to grace in the practical sense on grounds of epistemological objections to grace in ostensibly more exalted sense seems profoundly inattentive. Better, perhaps to say that they stand in contradiction; for if the higher sense of grace explicitly 'grants' (in contradistinction to the rest of humankind) a kind of knowledge or capability that borders of the perfectable or the divine, then Michelangelo's resourceful rooting in studio anatomy, not to mention the corpse-room, is a particularly graceless manner of receipt. One might say that the ideology of the Elect allows Michelangelo to act like an especially innovative, but ordinary human, with some particularly unpleasant dirt on his hands. But then again we are met with a contradiction.

Consider any of the studies of musculature or even the specific points of realisation within the body of the youth in *The Dream*, recalling again that this did not depend upon firmly-established practice in either art or science, contrasted with the ideological totality of the drawing itself. Is this relentless visual analysis in any sense a consequence of neoPlatonism? Marginally yes. Terms are set; this knowledge of the body becomes ideologically desirable; its demonstration a mark of virtuosity. But beyond that it so spills over the limits of neoPlatonism to become a free-standing means of visual synthesis. Not on account of its givenness; not an account of its desirability to neoPlatonist doctrine; but because it understands the body so well. And whatever epistemological noises we make, this revelation persists. So as a means of visual synthesis, it is not substitutable with any other because it is rightly compelling; it *has* an authenticity. Criticisable? Yes. Ignorable? No. Or in other words the distinction in this case between the innovative and the ordinary is not a deconstructable ideological figure in either verbal or visual terms. Once again, then, despite our post-Durkheimian, post-Derridean emphases it appears that the mythologies of origin, the rationally-warrantable 'nothing' outside text, outside method, outside image, outside convention, refuses to rest as myth or as substitutable alternatives *in this case*. Crucially, we are not speaking of *any* case but of a specific intelligible authenticity that refuses to let our attention wander but on the contrary claims it firmly in any serious consideration of the discipline of drawing. Certainly other kinds of drawing are possible, but their possibility and impossibility, not unlike our earlier invocation of pictorial possibility, rests on the activities of the discipline itself. Crucially, this possible substitution, this proposed series of exchanges is not predicated upon some zero point of formal possibility nor the guaranteed exchangeability of commodities. It is not a 'universal' of that kind.

To return, then, to our reasoning: Our reading of Durkheim suggests an alternative to the predominant contemporary view that being is *falsely* appropriated by re-presentation. [34] This is not intended as a kind of positivist generality but as a matter of judgement on Michelangelo's drawing: that appropriation should be understood in this case in the sense of *appropriateness*. No sense of exhaustive totalising is implied, no exclusive model or system but rather this reversal: in Michelangelo the idea that representation implies a destiny of loss *vis à vis* an original, represents a point of departure in which a sort of neo-Platonic drawing is made possible. Michelangelo's realisation of that drawing, however, increasingly comes to contradict its beginning and instead formulates itself unmistakably as an illumination of a more genuine origin, an innovative, critical intimacy with the physical articulation of the body, that the first, neo-Platonic point of departure never remotely considered and never remotely considered interesting. Michelangelo's drawing then, represents an authentic, critical-practical revision of the relationship, expressed verbally and visually, between origin and representation. That revision, we suggest is therefore central to both visuality and critical theory.

It offers, in particular a remarkable commentary on *'difference'* cited above as 'the disappearance of every originary presence is *at once* the condition of possibility and the condition of impossibility of truth.'[35] For however ironic our reading or Derrida's intention, the semantic and arguably the doctrinal structure remains, of an origin that 'first was present' but has now disappeared in, for the sake of, re-presentation. And despite Derrida's insistence on the contrary, that sense of origin incorrigibly persists as external to the work of representing, the work if not as loss, then as deferral. Then despite the most sophisticated, ironic, inverted readings of these persistent metaphors of distance as intimate enclosure within the work of representation, Michelangelo's visual metaphors come as the most extreme shock: they claim to *inaugurate*. This, arguably, is also Derrida's intention, but the metaphors (the 'language') articulate at variance. Michelangelo's 'language' does not: it insists both that the 'originary' appears through his work of representation and that it appears to originate the work. 'Appears' should here be taken in the sense of disclosure or revelation and not in the Kantian sense of 'mere' appearances set against a formal concept of 'things in themselves' - a formality that haunts Derrida's wordings.

Or again, the sense of 'grace' as critical-practical, compelling realisation, not compulsory appropriation in the narrow sense but appropriateness in the strongest possible sense of appropriate 'discipline', entirely breaks its 'fictive' containment within the confines of a *possible* worldview. Its claims are rather *actual* and addressed to us. Beside that sense of grace operating, as it were, as the interface between the horizon of re-presentative method and 'presence' - (post)modern (Derridean) notions of origin/method, despite themselves, appear to resemble if not neo-Platonism itself, then at least its conversion into the institutional idioms of a philosophy that ostensibly allows us to construe the limits of neo-Platonic and the achievements of Michelangelo's drawing as the same kind of fictive phenomena. This is both theoretically careless and politically inept. It rests upon the same implicit formalism that inhibits contemporary thought in distinguishing great art from the mundane and good politics from evil. But for us, Michelangelo is greater, is more truly graced, than neo-Platonism.

The late *Crucifixions* form the visual site for the development of this contradiction. To reiterate: we consider that what is at stake here is the difference between formalist epistemology and our sense of sociology. We cannot imagine a sociology, a study of social phenomena, that denies the distinct intelligibility of its subject matter by treating them as *formal* possibilities and so implicitly casts their structures as constraints, as disciplines, their very significance, as only active upon another *formal* member. Despite the formality, it's just too much like the cultural dope argument.[36] It is essential to consider here, then, that compared with the *Dream*, the *Crucifixions* do not simply mark another choice but rather another counterpart in a cycle of existence and death mediated by human action. Or again: not a contingently drawn preference within a universally extendable economy of signs but a representation of a life irrecoverably squandered.

Unlike the earlier *Resurrections*, the *Crucifixions* invoke a deeply tragic theme. Of course, the subject is, in itself more harrowing and the sympathy of the artist in the struggle to realise his subject is especially poignant. In a different though related sense, these are deeply human, deeply finite works; they are made by someone to whom transcendence, the ideal, is manifestly denied. Where the earlier drawings present an immaculate figure, held at a distance, highly articulated and intelligible, the later works are close, intimate, at times barely coherent, concealed to the eye but deeply sensible. They are in a sense made by the hand that caresses the suffering form, realising that the intelligence represented by the concept of formality, ideality, is infinitely more distant and less sensitive than the 'physical' body it despises. The essential tragic element is that this admission of the truth of the body occurs precisely at the moment when its dissolution is at hand: close enough to be feared, understood, even desired: far enough away to invoke a lifetime's memory and to be still consciously suffering its final, painful decline.

The several versions of *Christ on the Cross between the Virgin and St. John* [37] are especially moving, largely through the treatment of the sheer weight of the body of Christ. This is achieved through the simple device of tilting the upright of the cross away from the vertical, as though it had been displaced by the hanging figure.

One shocks both because it disturbs normative orientation and throws into focus the points at which the weight is attached, namely the separated hands and the fixed-together feet. This is agonisingly specific work. By comparison, the earlier *Resurrections*, no less exalted in subject matter are formal figures. True, they are articulate; they are vibrant. But they are not 'real' in this latter sense.

What can one mean by so presumptuous a term? Simply that they stem from the doctrine of resurrection, a fairly bizarre denial of reality as the intelligent body understands and fears it. If one were to formulate them dismissively (but not inattentively), one might say that they 'illustrate' doctrine; by that we mean that the entire meaning of resurrection is contained in the doctrine and adequately too; so that its visualisation adds nothing and is, in a sense, inappropriate. The 'perfect' body that is thus awakened is a contradiction (one might say, an illusion) - in religious terms, but is also a contradiction in visual terms. The almost flying figures of the *Resurrections* [38] are beset by a musculature of superfluous weight. Despite the fact that they are beautifully realised works, and will always excite the connoisseur, there are perhaps occasions on which to be more critical: there are many other instances of superb realisation that also achieve a more profound accord with subject matter. By contrast, the *Crucifixions,* conceptually a barbarism of the most sickening degree, are massively ennobled by visual 'representation'. Here again that word has fundamentally inappropriate connotations. We are speaking of an understanding first achieved and realised in the activity of making visual art, of an involvement made possible by art-work. There is no question of a historical 'model' here, to which the work will correspond; it is rather a question of two events within being - the Crucifixion and its depiction - the latter being in the deepest, most resonant sense a realisation of the former.

Why speak of ennobling so brutal an act as Crucifixion, for surely that is open to the charge of unreality? Because it is not the act itself that is redeemed; instead it is the act of understanding, the sympathy of understanding, that is itself noble -in contrast to that barbaric context. There is thus brought to the event, not simply a representation that corresponds to the physiological facts of agony and death, but a question of intention and interpretation. How shall we feel when confronted with this fact of crucifixion? There is little doubt in Michelangelo's portrayal that both its cruelty and its injustice should engage our attention absolutely, but that is as loose as the politician who 'deplores injustice' without defining where or when or why. There is also a sense of inevitability, but that, as such, is indistinguishable from philosophers' formality. In what, then, does this understanding, this censure, this resignation rest? Above all in the coherence of the sense of touch, whether formed in the distraught caress of the Virgin or St. John or in the lines of force that play along the crucified body of Christ.

Whilst there are clearly many versions, for us the most compelling remains the drawing *Christ on the Cross between the Virgin and St. John.* [39] and in particular the relationship between the left-hand figure and the body of Christ. Here, the doctrinal meaning of the figures is abandoned, or better, is refocused in the connection between head, thigh and hand. The plane of speech is severed both by differential height and the enormity of the event. The locus of speech and reason in one, the head, is abolished by virtue of its connection simply to the thigh of the other. The participation of the hand

64

simply adds to the muteness. And yet it understands by drawing upon the warmth of the just-still-living body.

The image is constantly that of the inexorable estrangement of human being from another by the tides of fate or the agency of will. Platonism in a sense, but a radical inversion: it is not the mind that here judges the limits of the body, but on the contrary an understanding that belongs to the body itself. It is touch that caresses, wills and desires to maintain the being that is passing away. It is the mute memory, reduced, constrained and focused in this single enduring contact that understands all that was, all that is left, of this person. It is the mute knowing and understanding of the universality and finality of death.

If we can detach ourselves from the harrowing beauty of the drawing, it may in more general terms be contrasted to the *Resurrection* series by its resignation to the limits of mortality. This drawing sees and understands the fact of death as the catastrophic destruction of the body, its sense and intelligence; there is no suggestion or any hope whatever that any such thing as the resurrection can even be envisioned. Indeed it may be taken as the visual repudiation of the doctrine.

There is one final drawing we shall briefly consider in this context, the Seilern's *Christ on the Cross*. [40] It is almost perfectly symmetrical and drawn with a probing, multiple line that scores the muscular form from the paper. In contrast to the lucidity of the *Risen Christ*, it is again dense and difficult, and invites tactile rather than visual participation. Above all, though, it strikes us as a concerted attempt to re-imagine the agony of Christ through the medium of the body and by the act of drawing. The musculature, once the means to express the lucidity of absolutely embodied grace, now occurs as the tangible features of the topology of pain and despair.

Now in a sense, any artist has to re-imagine every thing, every *body* he draws. But this drawing carries that through to an astonishing degree. It may be fairly argued, then, that the act of realisation, the manner and work of drawing in the Crucifixion series, operates in such a way as to place the substance of the event, as it is understood from the locus of the physically sensate and intelligent imagination, somewhat higher than its doctrinal significance. Its universality rests, if you will, rather more in its being a representation of an act of execution. Perhaps this can be regarded as an accident of the medium and of the kind of imagination that is required to draw. After all, it is the image and not the doctrinal significance one draws; the latter belongs to verbal representing, however much each realm impinges upon the other.

If we can maintain an attempted separation for a moment, this accidentality cuts both ways: perhaps the 'significance' might be grasped as an accident of the medium of verbal language and of the imagination its articulation requires.

Plato's doctrinal position and the general semantic consequences of neoPlatonism might *also* be described as such an 'accident'. If we review the associated concepts of the 'real' bed or circle they are manifestly consequent of verbal representing and, in particular, consequences of the process of col-*lection*. That is, the activity of 'speaking' beds, circles (and so on) *as if* there is an unproblematic continuity between *every* single instance and the plurality of the category. Col-lection - 'bringing together with speech' - *has* to be questionable. Whilst Michelangelo's project is, in one sense, an attempt to subdue his own medium to the demands of 'collecting' (the perfect figure) it is doomed, if not to failure, then to a lack of radicalism in terms of the possibilities offered to Platonism as a verbal tradition. That, of course, accounts for the lowly place, possibly the lowest place, given to the artist's representation of the real. For us this is, then, no question of accident (as it might be for moderns) nor of hierarchy (as it might be for Platonism) but of a contested identity. It is the categorial form of words lending itself to the sort of representation that suggests that the category describes a generic type of which there are instances. The image-forms of visual representing, conversely, are always bound to represent in instances, views, occasions - the category being precisely the denied possibility.

Hence the absolute formalism of Platonic drama: Socrates, 'the wisest of men' able to generate, on the basis of that predicate, the conceptual and representational expectation that there should be no essential difference between men, their wisdom, or the occasions of its exercise. So that *all* men, *all* kinds of wisdom, *every* occasions of its exercise will unproblematically fit within those categories, will make no essential contradiction, no *difference*, and will allow that question of rank to be sense rather than nonsense. So that even Socrates, the chosen One, will not primarily 'be himself' in all of his possible variations but will *first* represent that doctrine of absolute collectability. So that despite the manifest scale and absurdity of the claim - 'for all time, for all men' - (and it *has* stood the test of time) we still have to strain to *hear* the nonsense: it still passes as a possible proposition.

Then the 'flawed infinity' of Socrates may be said to invade his (our) every category, the absence of any principle of immanence being precisely the guarantee of re-collection. (The difference between categorial original and its particular, being merely contingent, reversible, inessential.) Michelangelo's drawing, as explicitly images, as an argument for the salience of images, despite its neoPlatonic shell, despite its col-lective pretensions must break these limits to function at all. Consequently the sense of contradiction that inhabits these works is not contingent nor categorial but on the contrary invokes precisely that embodied human immanence of youth and decay and death and the interventions of ambition and repression and regret. This is a genuine form of contradiction: coming to be and ceasing; burgeoning: fecund; confident; failing; dying; being destroyed. Not a general economy of signs but an excess of vivacity and desire, of lives given, spent, squandered.

If we want to disentangle ourselves from the fate Danto feels is *his,* and by implication *ours,* we need to be little more resourceful in undoing the Platonic testament. Let us try turning the tables. In the first place there is one very large difference between human 'wisdom' being worth *little* or *nothing.* It must be worth at least *consideration* on account of its enormous political and ecological impact. We are after all, if not the most 'successful' then arguably the most powerful species on the planet. This is not a matter of praise or complacency. In similar terms, a certain A. Hitler might once have been 'nothing' but certainly *became* worthy of consideration. That kind of consideration is lost in paradigms of the 'nothing outside text' persuasion and so this section is particularly directed against them.

We can turn the tables by proposing the 'outside text' first. In other words, the conventional form of inquiry assumes that Plato/Socrates has the right to demand that art justify itself before reason and that reason will decide whether the justification is satisfactory. Dissatisfaction will result in expulsion from the republic. Our proposal is the reverse. For us the republic is factually diverse: it includes the making of visual images, the use of spoken and written language and whatever else one cares to name. Just to make sure we are not sentimentalising here - 'whatever else' includes various art forms *but also* political oppression, institutionalised forms of discrimination, psychopathology, stupidity, lack of information. Suppose the pathology takes the form of a serial killer or rapist. We do not act 'wisely' nor with infallible knowledge, - as the shortcomings of justice make all too clear, - but with urgency and pragmatism. And that urgency is not primarily to 'know' but to prevent.

In the case of visual representation, the urgency *to prevent* is not at all clear. But this has not stopped many control freaks ranging from Socrates to Greenberg (and many nastier cases) from trying it on. Socrates' fallible point (he will readily admit this, that is why he needs the Oracle) is that Socrates' failure to justify art (or art's failure to justify itself to Socrates) might be Socrates' own failing or that of the *particular* art form or artist or epoch. In short, it is embedded within the paradigm of Platonism that you *cannot trust a particular* argument even if Socrates himself makes it. This will of course degenerate into a stalemate in which no argument ever takes preference over another (remember Lyotard's unintended liberalism) - *but only so long as we remain within the Platonic testament*. Or, so long as we remain 'inside text'. In other words the problem is not that all arguments are 'relative', nor even is it a matter of *arguments* at all. It is instead that visual art exists alongside verbal representations, - especially those which intend to analyse it, - and has secured its own viability in the sense of continuing to exist though *some* of its forms are undoubtedly threatened - figurative painting being currently the most vulnerable. Platonism must grudgingly accept that it has not and indeed *cannot in principle* 'articulate' visual art's final extinction/expulsion. Our counter-proposal is that the *universality* of visual iconography in human societies is compelling evidence of its *social authenticity*. Against that the categorial ploys of Socrates and signs of the Oracle, Plato's endless bearing witness, Augustine's belief in God and Danto's codicils look, simply, trivial and 'academic' in the most ossified sense. Differently put, Danto (by his own admission) and philosophy (by that charge) have become the province of the Plato *scholar* and Plato *expert* and not that of the critic.

Where there is no 'outside-text' there *should* appear an ungovernable pluralism. This is Plato's/Lyotard's 'unmeant' position. But Danto's 'codicils' and Plato's attack on poets and painters (and not bubble blowers or novelty dancers or even cooks) suggest quite specific targets, or better, *opponents*. In other words - and in the terms of our opening chapter - a structured and co-active complexity with certain characteristic (homeodynamic) co-phenomena. We want to argue that they have a *necessary*, not a fixed, interplay that also generates positive and negative dynamics. Both of those terms are intended in the evaluative sense. We shall describe these structures assuming an analytic 'first' cause.

We may describe the period *before* the first cause as 'chaotic'. This is the kind of plurality that Socrates, Plato, Jesus, Augustine and Lyotard despise, because it is neither Christian nor *liberal* but instead consists of *Babel* (for the Christians) and of *tradition* or *consensus* for liberal philosophy. Then arrives the two-edged 'first cause': on the one hand the pronouncement of the Oracle: 'Human Wisdom is worth little or nothing... he amongst you is the wisest who, like Socrates, knows that this wisdom is worth nothing at all.' 'His wisdom is the knowledge of the negativity of all finite content.'(op. cit.). And on the other the 'doctrines' or speech-customs, or idioms that identify him as 'wise'/ignorant. We shall turn to the substantive idioms shortly but it is crucial to see that this 'first cause' is not a chronological 'first ever' nor even is it a *discrete* event but the postulation of a structure in which Socrates now has first place and 'his' followers (they would say, 'followers of truth') *must* become, literally, *disciples*: they can only operate under the disciplines of that structure. And the counterpart, the active 'life' of the structure is the narrative of its justification and re-justification. The result *is* the social structure of the Socratic republic. Even if (post)moderns think this takes place 'in text' there is no doubt that for Socrates and Plato the matter is one of political reality, complete with 'soldiers' trained by philosophers. It is important to grasp the range of this discipline: the negativity of *all* finite content. Add this to claims of the Christian and indeed the Socratic 'afterlife' and far from Durkhiem's belief that religion is the root of language and thought we have political-religious doctrine that is directed *against* social life as a whole. The only differentiation it permits is the distinction between the disciple and the heretic. The only solidarity it offers is that of withdrawal. And consequently, those who *are* artists (or poets or feminists or any finite determination) *have* to be subversives. This is not 'text' but political reality.

And yet Durkheim is in one sense right. Socrates' doctrines constantly contrast the particular against the general or categorial. The particular is described as something that 'resembles' reality without being it. The 'categorial' on the other hand is taken as the real or as the essential. Of course Socrates does not call it categorial or general (this is a more modern usage) but as the forms or 'ideas' that allow particular *instances* to be generated. In this sense they are taken as the *sources:* the 'essences' that underlie and make possible 'appearances'. This relationship, which we tend to call category and particular, persists in modern usage: not perhaps as the Socratic doctrine of anamnesis nor in its Judeo-Christian form of Creator and creature but as the idea that one form, or structure or one explanation is *right* and every alternative is at best partial or an approximation or simply untrue. Perhaps we relax a *little* more in these postmodern times. We concede a *degree,* a very limited degree, of pluralism but generally in a weak and polarised sense. We concede science the right and the duty to seek 'correct' explanations and we also concede that those phenomena that science *cannot* explain (especially cultural phenomena) - are plural in the sense of conventional and 'could have been otherwise'. We do not generally concede, however that the 'correctness' of an explanation is more to do with the dynamics of ecological viability (that is, temporal pragmatics) than any notion of 'essence'. More problematically, neither do we concede the reverse: that the presence of certain phenomena within any ecology will certainly structure the relations between itself and others *possibly to the point of exclusion.* In this sense, Plato's testament is not so much a theory of art but a proposal of exclusion precisely because no essence of art is conceivable. And Danto's/philosophers' coalescence means simply that they (and we) share the same paradigm. This is why Plato is still important, despite the fact that no one would go along with his proposals. First: because his usage is still embedded within our contemporary phrasings; and second: it persists because contemporary usage has no evidently available critique of Platonism 'at hand'. Simply put, we add codicils to the platonic testament literally because we have no alternative. We are his disciples; we share his discipline and limits; we *are* Platonists for all practical purposes. And in no practical sense *can* we be 'pluralists'. In the language of the opening arguments our usage cannot yet support a theory that recognises complexity *at all*, let alone a developed theory of complexity

Derrida comments on the 'sterility of the socratic seed, left to its own devices' (op.cit.); an interesting metaphor when set against 'there is no outside-text'. Apparently, to the dismay of radical Derrideans, the absence of an 'outside-text' does not imply that phenomena (in this case socratic seed) cannot have determinate characteristics or a 'destiny'. But we cannot go along with 'sterility'. *Aggression* towards non-socratic practices would be a more precise description. In non-socratic practice we may include his traditional enemies (art, poetry, rhetorics) but also every mundane commitment to human value. This why it is so absurd to see Socrates as the ethical or critical counterpart to the 'self-indulgences' of value or belief whether in the forms of art or not. Socrates does not supply an ethics (sterile or not) but primarily an aggressive, fundamentalist ontology whose central commitment is the worthlessness of human thought, action and custom. Its ground and methodology consists in the absurd distinction between (the 'real' form of) bed, circle, or whatever and its 'less-real' *instances*: *a* bed, *this* bed, a circle of a certain size or colour or material. Notice that images (like Michelangelo's) can only deal in determinations like *a* bed, *this* circle, a human or a certain gender or age or physique, whilst Socrates' *narrative* can generate 'bed', 'circle', 'human', without determinations. Armed with an ostensibly higher degree of abstraction, this fundamental ontology can enlist disciples to enforce it: Plato, Danto? Now, the usual, stereotypical, fundamental wide-screen 'monster' will usually only go after its prey. Bigger deal monsters may have genocidal ambitions. But this monster goes further above and further below. Genocide is by comparison unambitious; the aim here is directed at both the species and the self. Or, suicide once the species is convinced of its own worthlessness in every instance of thought or action. Neither does the monster take on any of the usual forms. It is not so massive a creature that you are powerless, nor so insidious a conspiracy that you are constantly under

70

threat. Nor is it minute, a plague-like or parasitic invasion of the body. No! - this monster is only and entirely conceivable within spoken or written language. Born of the narrative possibility of saying 'bed', 'circle', 'human' and of the confusion of essence with singularity, it charges every other form of human representing with the impossible task of aping its own indeterminacy. But beds, circles, paintings, humans, dogs, cats, cities are *essentially plural complexes.* Singularity 'itself' is precisely as irrelevant to essence as any other single instance.

We cannot be so 'unsophisticated' as to make Socrates' mistake, surely? We are far too advanced and plural a society to ask: what is the single, essential form of bed or circle or gender or morality? Surely we know that these phenomena are *essentially* complex? Possibly, or are we still haunted by belief in such expressions as 'the thing in itself'? More of that shortly. First let us see what the (sterile) Socratic seed does to Socrates. As you might expect, its militancy (sterile, remember) brings Socrates into conflict and finally to trial. Let us reconsider Plato's most compelling categorial form, namely the 'real' circle.

Why is it compelling? Because the circle can be persuasively represented as one of the a priori structures of consciousness and as such its controlling power manifestly outstrips its derivatives. In the language of the earlier sections, it is, arguably, 'immediate'. We are not concerned to contest that position. It is finally uninteresting in this context whether or not there are such fundamental structures, since our topic here - Art - is infinitely elaborated, as irredeemably mediate as 'circularity' is not. Then why, beyond reason, do we persist in allowing art in all of its distinct and contradictory varieties, in all of its peculiar commitments, cycles of evolution, points of stasis and revolution, art as the purely visual, art as the fundamentally semantic trace, to be described in one word, one category, as though it were as immediate as the circle and its specific manifestations as derivative? Do we really mean that the funerary practices of ancient Egypt, the irreverence of Duchamp, the 'driven' action painting of Jackson Pollock, the tautologies of Joseph Kosuth, [41] the irony of David Salle, have something *essential* in common? Not simply a kind of important common feature, but one that decisively articulates their common identity, in the face of, despite, and *by effacing* their differences?

The answer is that the category makes a kind of crude sense; or in other words that these phenomena do have certain passing resemblances in common. But this more plausibly depends on our current usage of 'art' then any notion of deep kinship. Which is of course why, when the Egyptians so *ridiculously* buried their 'art' treasures, we saw fit to dig them up and display

71

them *properly* alongside our own. 'Art' as ordinary usage is complicit in concealing this kind of effacement by placing the *expectation* of conformity rather than *difference* in the relationship of particular to category.

We do not comment upon whether some deep connection may be found. We do not condemn a priori the (post)modern artist for his eclecticism (the matter turns of the results), nor propose some preposterous standard of proper attention. We rather intend that common usage does not care about any of this. In general use, 'Art', is a very rough notion indeed. It is thus arguable that precise, highly wrought works do not in any sense 'belong' to the category, 'Art'; in many senses such works are its antithesis.

There would therefore seem to be an identifiable series of contradictions between social phenomena. On one hand: those that can be described as having the general characteristic of being genuinely a priori and categorial, as that to which all subsequent meaning corresponds (such as definition of the circle). On the other hand, there are a series of phenomena that are especially mediate and seem to be a consequence of concerted *will*. It is radically problematic to decide, then, which of these shall claim sociology since the first group seem to take so little account of actors whilst the second take so much account that it becomes a point of honour to say that the truth of sociological analysis is absolutely a matter of members', including sociologists', *will*. Intersubjective will certainly, but nevertheless radically 'located' and with no sense of the range nor limit of such ethnocentred validity.

There is, however, a third and greater problem that sets the terms for the first two. It is this. The term 'art' in its most crude and banal sense may be likened to the 'presocial' or 'preorganic'(in Durkheim's sense) character of common sense or common usage. To put the matter another way, it is relatively easy to erect a stable if crude definition of art so long as this remains merely a matter of ordinary verbal currency: images wrought with pencil, paint, in stone etc... But when one is asked to produce more than passing reference, (that tackles one's social competence hardly at all), when one is asked to *produce*, to *realise* art, either through the so-called 'practical' traditions or through the media of critical analysis, that crude notion quickly turns out to be an aural illusion, (if one has any specific social competence at all). In this sense, the category, be it art or not, turns out to be a primordium that social structure requires to be surpassed. Again, we counsel the reader not to reduce this question to the banalities of a distinction between the 'abstractions' of theory and the 'substance' of practice (for the production may be entirely theoretic). The sharper point is that the demands of semantic order and of the social order, or the division of labour, are radically different.

72

However, since the primary organising principle of both (and we deliberately do not use the term, 'medium') is verbal language, this must mark a radical and decisive inflection within verbal language itself. To energise this inflection in the context of the dynamics of organic solidarity implies, then, a differentiation taking place *in language* at least as significant as that of role or occupation.

The analytic problem for contemporary sociology is the tendency for the formally ordered semantics upon which it depends to erase the salience of this distinction and thus also the difference that Durkheim proposes between philosophy and sociology. In other words if sociology's habitual usage is dependent upon a categorial form, it articulates a solidarity with the expectations of both common sense and neo-Platonism. That expectation, we stress is one of resemblance between category and particular, between origin and instance. To slightly shift the terms of our opening chapter, then, the result is not the ostensible neutralities of formal speech but a surreptitious dependence on both a doctrinal and a structural position allied to common sense. Both, so far as the first depends on a relation of resemblance and the second on a relationship that precedes the production of difference, appear not simply formal but mechanistic, in Durkheim's sense and actively antagonistic to organic solidarity, and hence to sociology.

Where one's topic is an aspect of the division of labour (such as art) and because our focus is precisely the absence in the origins of critical theory of an adequate cognisance of the division of labour, that issue, whilst uncomfortable, is also analytically inevitable.

The notion of grace is surely an impossible recourse for a post-modern sociology; it is the absolute metanarrative claim. Yet here we are being asked to play along with this particular subterfuge in order to evade the ostensibly valid but actually suffocating philosophico-religious roots of our self-reflection - which is equally unthinkable post-Durkheim. That irony is concretely interesting: grace 'saves' the artist (taking his turn somewhat absurdly as the representative of the mundane member) and so, arguably, also saves the sociologist by preserving the object of his study from dissolution in the two acids of Platonic formalism and the Christian doctrine of finitude that audibly persist in his usage. Arguably, that concept of the divine preserves some room for Cennini and Michelangelo to develop their practices. It provides virtually none for their critical appraisal on the part of Augustine. Then the analytic issue for sociology becomes bitingly clear: for us, unlike Michelangelo or indeed Augustine, it is not the divine at whose hand we are damned and from whom we seek grace, but *language*. What is the limitation that language places that severs sociology from its objects? What grace must language bestow so that unlike Augustine we shall be able to critically appraise the activity of representation as a genuine part of nature?

As we said, Michelangelo's art is not identical with the critical body of religious and philosophic doctrine that surrounds it, but is in many senses both impossible without it and yet also impossible with it. Might we then reformulate the interplay somewhat less severely, as a kind of language game, in Wittgenstein's sense, and displace terms such as negativity, illogic, error, condemnation with the more relaxed notion of possibilities within a certain socially-organised limit? In other words, does the inescapable collision between visual artist, verbal 'critical' col-lection and being, show something essential about the processes of representation? Of course, we are not inviting a formal recognition, a religious observance, of 'inevitable conventionality'. We are more interested in a critical appraisal of the different courses of action made possible by the positions of Michelangelo set against those of Socrates.

It is interesting how rapidly the social scene becomes differentiated by the manifold forms of representation. Despite the massive col-lective powers of platonic-Christian thought and despite their foundational importance for Michelangelo's art, his first re-presentative act is to *differ*. The social realisation of his grace consists in representing the perfection of an anatomy: the most differentiated and specialised task imaginable, despite its virtually total compliance with doctrine. Or again, it consists in the mastery of the sciences of perspective, the handling of black chalk, the carving of stone. The analytic consequences of this realised and sustained difference are considerable. If we allow that the 'game' has made possible a sort of transgression of its overt rules, so that a concern with the means of representing the muscular systems and action of the body has become possible. And if further we attend to the positivity of this representing, in the terms we used earlier, as a kind of calling that springs from authentic human relationships with being, then we can already see that to fulfil that calling, there follows a differentiation no less authentic than the originary calling. For it is manifestly impossible to pursue the depth and force of that re-presentative project in either formal or general terms. It demands occupational dedication, expertise, tradition. The concerted act of representation here demonstrates (even if we take it in formal terms with the minimum designation as 'socially organised') the structural necessity of surpassing common sense in the form of specific traditions or kinds of representing.

It is now that the collision with the theoretic foundation occurs, for the col-lective principle is shattered against a burgeoning oganicism which is the direct consequence, not of contingency and fragmentation, but of the authenticity of the relation between being and organically-differentiated representations. *Formalist* col-lection, whether neo-Polatonic or postmodern can never grasp this idea. Its theoretic desire can only be fulfilled in ignorance as a concerted practice, now seen its greatest extent; not merely discounting this or that tradition, convention and so on, but systematic ignor-ance of the authentic relationships between being and representation as a whole. Conversely, it now appears that the structural 'disclosedness' of being now occurs as, in - and *to - organically differentiated* kinds of representing.

May we then succeed in providing the germ of a positive reading of grace, fantasy, the judgement of the eye, in re-thinking ornament and difference as authentic responses to the mani-fold of being and the many possibilities of human's representations? A celebration certainly, but not a sentimentalisation. Think how strikingly the Crucifixions transcend their doctrinal limits but are also free to construct representations of the mortal body ruined by fate and barbarism. Neither can we accept the kind of sentimentalism that says this genuine relationship is a matter of course, for it is directly opposed by neo-Platonism. We cannot play the conventional postmodern here. If Michelangelo's transgressions, by way of Cennini, by way of sophistic performance traditions that were available to him through his praxis, - are authentic, then the limits they transgress (the doctrinal structures of neoPlatonism) - are *inauthentic*. Differently put, Being cannot be held to disclose its manifold self in and through the many kinds of representation and at the same time to withhold itself absolutely by their partiality.

We are aware that something close to that position is put forward by Heidegger (to whom we shall later refer). At the risk of simplification, Being is 'revealed as it is concealed' by beings, represented in ontic speech. Then a kind of grace is claimed for a certain kind of language: for Plato, philosophy; for Heidegger the destruction of Western metaphysics, identified with the 'shattering' of ontic speech.[42] It is easy to see that in either case a limited notion of grace is matched by an infinitely extended 'dis-grace' heaped upon all other forms of representing. Our organic, sociological interest cannot lie in this philosopher's minimal inclusion of certain fragments of the possibilities of verbal representing (only) in the sphere of authenticity. Our sense is quite different and grounded in Durkheim's notion of the foundational or 'natural' centrality of representing within a social order. In simple terms it is the concerted solidarity of diverse representative projects, or better, 'policies' (such as Florentine painting) that is the locus of *possible* authenticity for us, not the utterance of some deliberately self-marginalised policy of ignor-ance.

Socrates' self-defeating conduct at his trial provides the maximum contrast with Michelangelo's resilience. For the history of philosophy (according to Hegel and Kierkegaard) he takes the standpoint of irony, whose primary functions exhibit an amazingly simple uniformity, whether set in train by the ancients or by (post)modern professional academics: absolute negativity directed toward established forms of order (in our terms, policies, solidarities etc.); and absolute because such systems of belief, desire, intention - whatever their concrete value - are determined, a priori, as contingent. Socrates and Mr. Postmodern will share a special solidarity of their own of 'challenging established assumptions'. We note the dismissive description; we note the absence of reflexion. They are *someone else's* assumptions. We note that even when (rarely) the reflexive turn is made the inclusion of one's own position in the firing line still makes for a repetition; irony still calls the shots. But naively, even confusion, seem more plausible descriptions. For us, this consists in the elision of two distinct orders of meaning; an elision which in many senses is a consistent doctrinal requirement but its consequences will not fit; or else, are so misunderstood by the doctrine as to shatter its consistency. In the first place, Socrates recognises the intelligibility of the charges against him:

> Now someone may take me up and ask: 'But what is the matter with you Socrates? Why this prejudice against you?...Tell us what the trouble is then, and save us coming to a rash decision in this case.' Well that seems to me a fair question. [43]

But instead of defending himself at this mundane level of intelligibility, he typically evades the substance, by citing his renowned wisdom-in-ignorance, in such a way as to call into question the grounds of that intelligibility. Hegel calls it the calling into question of natural or traditional law. So far, the position is both predictable and consistent and indeed provides the basis for his subsequent importance in theoretic tradition. But the problem is, Socrates is not actually being asked to theorise *grounds*; he is being asked to defend himself on a specific charge. To the response that such a thing is 'beneath theory', we note the implication of hierarchy; to the related response that the grounds of traditional law *ought* to be questioned we point to the as yet still-confused distinction between the substance of law and the grounds of its authority. For it is immediately clear from any familiarity with Socratic dialogue that the question of grounds for any kind of mundane law, traditional or not, for any kind of mundane practice, will only result in the decisive indication of an absence. So we might sharpen, or better, invert the point: Socrates calls into question rule-guidedness in *every* sense; he certainly cannot be grasped as an ally in valuing modern versions of liberality. As Hegel might have it, the standpoint of Socrates must be surpassed and in this precise sense: it is only after the postulation of an ostensibly more

76

desirable *mundane* order that the questioning of the traditional looks even remotely positive, or indeed possible; for it is immediately clear that Socrates, with immense consistency, has precisely nothing at all to say, even about himself. That *is* his standpoint, his message. And it *must be* his message, since to question mundane justice, traditional or not, presumes that the question has a right to be heard; it is an authentic question within the disclosure of being. Socrates therefore, cannot allow nor engage the question without renouncing the existential priority of his own ignorance, - which is the co-postulate of the refusal to grant credence to the genuine reality of the Being and its delimitations: appearance, becoming, representation, morality. [44] The task of irony - no, that is far too generous - the *ritual* of irony, is to make noises about the appearance of order and its essential contingency. Whilst concretely believed (they are the most common academic stock in trade) they are analytically dismissed by such simple behaviours as visiting the doctor or using a condom and depend heavily on the (mis)use of the metaphors of empirically sensitised individuals in the quite different context of concerted social action. The ritual of irony, then, is literally ignorance, the shutting of eyes, ears and mind to the authentic claim of difference.

If Socrates has nothing to say about the grounds of mundane authority or convention (except that the grounds are unsecurable), he cannot enter, then, into any debate about the justice of its substance. For that is to renounce theory for mundane speech in the precise form of an admission that the insecurity of grounds might be put aside (i.e. be irrelevant to) a specific issue of 'traditional' justice - which may be taken as the exemplar of any such specific or mundane concern. That would, manifestly limit the scope of the theoretic as it is exemplified in Socrates. He would then be faced, both analytically and concretely, with a choice between theorising (in his terms) and addressing the specific charge, in all of its intelligibility. He would have, as it were, to say something rather than nothing, which would destroy his position. He could no longer be exalted through ignorance and so would have to 'trade' with others. Such 'trading', then, would carry the implicit admission that the delimitation of being has a 'reasonable' call upon the theoretic, precisely in the form of remodelling itself in anti-ironic mode.

But intelligibility persists whether traditional or not. Whatever Socrates' speech preferences, this means he is already implicated in a political process. For us, of course, to theorise is to be immediately implicated in a political process, not by default but because a 'policy' of re-presenting is always at stake. The point about politics, 'policies', is that they constitute the existential condition of representing-in-general, the surrounding, the environment, the 'ecology' of the specific act. It is of course a point of honour for Socrates to ignore this, to persist within the limits of his own notion of theory, but ignorance cannot nullify effects. The collision occurs after Socrates is found guilty and is again asked to provide some reason why he should not be condemned to death.

> Since I myself am convinced that I have wronged no one, I am certainly not going to wrong myself by admitting that I deserve to suffer harm and proposing for myself any such penalty. Why should I? To escape the [death] penalty proposed by Meletus? No; as I say, I don't know whether it is a good or an evil.[45]

It is charitable but in our terms misleading for Socrates' subsequent interpreters to speak of his death at the hands of others, (the state, objective political conditions) a kind of martyrdom for the sake of emerging subjecticity as Hegel might argue. *He killed himself.* Partly this was because he could not find reason *to do otherwise*; nor find sufficient reason not to ignore his own life. Or, to put it another way, he could not pursue an apparent (self) interest because the grounds were unclear: 'as I say, I don't know...' Then already he has (in his terms) declined into mundane policies, a matter of alternatives. He has ceased to theorise, or rather 'his' theory has ceased to be capable of concern with him. If there is any positivity in Socrates, it is not due to questioning traditional authority, nor the emergence of subjecticity but rather the illuminating exemplification of a suicidal tendency - not on the part of Socrates the man, but rather as the most complete development of a certain kind of usage - as a perverse possibility deeply rooted in the characteristics of verbal representing.

Theory has done with Socrates (even most of his admirers concede that his standpoint is superseded). At what point? In the distinction between the grounds of law and the justice of its specific acts, or more broadly between the formal notion of tradition as repetitive constraint and the possibility that its specific acts-within-limits may be either ill or well-founded; above all in the refusal to meet the different kinds of intelligibility that are manifest when his speech is itself tested. The trial is but one mundane instance of that testing; analytically he is found wanting by the manifold disclosedness of being itself as he repeats only the absolute possibility of col-lection.

We then come to a point which our traditions warn we must tread warily (indeed they usually say we should not come to the point at all). So perhaps we may be forgiven a preliminary formulation: Michelangelo's claim to see, his grace, (for which he appeared ridiculously culpable) now looks rather more authentically rooted in being than Socrates' ignorance (for which modesty he is so often praised). If we began with the notion of a game and its transgressions, it still appears that Michelangelo's *Crucifixions* maintained a community, an attention, a traditional *and* authentic care for the visible, manifest and intelligible, whereas Socrates *practised* ignorance. Theory and practice? If so, then at the price of recognising the most complete inversion. The point then, that tradition says we really should avoid: Michelangelo, by way of Cennini, by way of a sophistic tradition of performance, even in the conceded spaces of a game, entirely surpasses neo-Platonism. We have ourselves been brought to the point of trial and verdict: in the face of the theorist's traditional distance we are forced to choose on grounds of quality. Raised to its maximum salience: traditions, constraint, policy are words for solidarity. We have chosen solidarity as more ontologically defensible, more authentic in its care for being and in its own resilience, than the so-called 'critical' theoretics of Socrates. Differently put, for us, sociology does not, or better, *cannot*, share the history of immanent subjectivity to which philosophy, for example in the work of Hegel and Kierkegaard, refers.

That, to recall our opening passage from Danto, is our response to what philosophy would be without art, or better, when Michelangelo's art has broken its destructive embrace.

Notes

1. Danto, A. (1985).
2. See Rosen, S, (1974) pp.37-8.
3. Seilern Collection. See *Drawings by Michelangelo* (exhibition catalogue) British Museum Publications 1975 pl. 128 & pp.109-110.
4. Kierkegaard, S. (1965) p.197.
5. ibid. p.199.
6. These are components of Derrida's reading of Plato, see Derrida, J.   'Plato's Pharmacy' in Johnson, B. trans. (1981) and below.
7. from *The Sophist* 234b/c and cited in Summers, D. 1981 p.42.
8. Plato 1974 p.424.
9. Plato (1973) pp.137-8.
10. ibid.
11. Derrida, J. (1981) p.136.
12. ibid. pp.153-4.
13. ibid. p.168.
14. Summers, D. (1981) p.18.
15. ibid. p.43.
16. ibid. p.48.
17. ibid. p.51.
18. Durkheim, E. (1976) p.18.
19. Summers, D. (1981) p.448.
20. ibid.
21. *Andrea Quaratesi* British Museum (Wilde 59) *Drawings by Michelangelo* pl.119.

22. *The Risen Christ* ibid. pl.47.

23. Summers, D. (1981) p.217.

24. ibid.

25. ibid. p.215.

26. *The Dream of Human Life* Seilern collection Drawings By Michelangelo pl.128.

27. A comprehensive analysis that reworks Hegel's criticisms of Socrates is available in Kierkegaard's *Concept of Irony*. An extremely interesting review of Hegel's position also occurs in Rosen's *G.W.F. Hegel*. We have not the space to analyse their positions extensively but cite them as support for the infinite negativity of irony and for the important co-phenomenon that is often glossed: the comprehensive negativity of irony cannot be a derivative concept without being threatened by itself. One might put the matter another way by saying that irony carries with it a strong conception of the revelation of its own truth. Hence the 'daimon' of Socrates.

28. Summers, D.(1981) p.449.

29. ibid. p. 458.

30. ibid. p.458.

31. ibid. p.459.

32. '...since [the soul] is not destroyed by a single evil – either its own or an alien – it's plainly necessary that it be always and, if it is always, that it be immortal...And if it is, you recognise that there would always be the same souls' (*The Republic* 611a) Socrates is as ever consistent. The problem is that the constant priority of the immortal over the mortal means that his 'political' philosophy is irrelevant, or better, dysfunctional.

33. These are noticed or perhaps invented by disciples of Hiedegger. Their common ancestry is the concept of 'enframing' (subsequently reworked by Derrida) and their common prejudice is against technology..For a more detailed discussion see Jay (1993); for the anti-technology and pro-Heidegger stance see Levin (1988); for criticism of that position see Smith, J. in Heywood & Sandywell (eds.) (1998).

34. Durkheim's alternative - that society is a part of nature – could be taken as sentimental. That for us misses the point: that human society is an autopoietic possibility. For us the followers of Heidegger are the sentimentalists: they sentimentalise Being through a series of metaphors suggesting everything from balance to divinity which human representation 'distorts'or conceals. This both overstates the role of humanity (a sort of negative humanism) whilst at the same time denying the need for human animals to protect themselves 'from' Being. It is in the context of this sentimentalisation of fate that Heidegger can see fit to acquiesce, if not praise, Hitler. See final chapter.

35. Derrida, J. (1981) p.168.

36. Cultural dopes are dear (and dangerous) to sociology in the sense that they justify the sociologist's 'corrections'. We do not want to avoid the politics of that problem, but to pretend that formalism is an adequate analytic or political response is beyond credibility. It's just the academic's old trick of hiding a refusal to judge in a list of the possibilities that lie open: the more formally put, the 'better' the obscuration. The best current obscuration is pluralist hypocrisy, essayed after Lyotard. See above and later in the context of Duchamp's apparent playfulness.

37. *Christ on the Cross between the Virgin and St. John*; Windsor, Popham Wilde 436 & 437 *Drawings by Michelangelo* pl.178 &181.

38. *The Resurrection* and *The Risen Christ* both British Museum, Wilde 52 & 54.

39. *Christ on the Cross between the Virgin and St. John*. British Museum, Wilde 82 *Drawings by Michelangelo* pl.183.

40. *Christ on the Cross* Seilern Collection *Drawings by Michelangelo* pl.179.
41. See Kosuth, J (1991) or Harrison & Wood (1992) pp.840-9.
42. The most straightforward account of Heidegger's position is in Rosen (1969) Ch.2.
43. Plato (1980) p.33n.
44. These delimitations are from Heidegger, M. (1961) *Introduction to Metaphysics*.
45. Plato (1980) p.57.

5   Impossible Representatives

Heidegger: 'in Kant's definition:.. Being is *merely* the positing of the copula between the subject and the predicate.' [1]

This is probably the most complex section of the book since it questions and in many senses destabilises one of the foundations of Enlightenment thought, namely the human 'subject'. Some of the arguments, then, will seem counter-intuitive; others will treat habitually-used and familiar concepts as unreasonable. It would be as well, then, to sketch something of our intentions; to indicate some points of reference in a preliminary way.

We *choose* three 'impossible representatives' - this is not an inventoristic history of subjecticity but an argument for paradigm-change: David's paintings, *Oath of the Horatii* and *Death of Marat* and Kant's 'transcendental subject' from *The Critique of Pure Reason*.

For the paintings, we shall argue, despite the specification indicated by the titles and the ideology that surrounds their production by one especially politicised artist, that the representations exhibit an extraordinary degree of what post-structuralism might call 'instability'. We prefer the term 'autopoesis' in the sense that the representations constantly restructure themselves *despite or because of the* chronology of 'original' and 'subsequent' meanings, components, contexts. This temporal frame of reference in which '*re*-presentation' is active and mediate is crucial to what follows.

For Kant's 'transcendental subject' we shall seek to displace his emphasis on a subject that creates or 'synthesises' itself according to specific laws (the structures of 'pure reason') *and,* or despite, its similarity to Maturana and Varela's 'bringing forth worlds' instead treat the human subject as contexted and co-dependent. First, as an instance of consciousness that is not unique but shares common development and ancestry with other carbon-based life forms; second, if 'carbon-based' connotes an inter-dependence between living and non-living structures, we also want to emphasise *social* contexts of inter-dependence. Differently put, 'our' subject is not an abstraction that *becomes* a member of a social unit on this planet but is always, even before the event of its self- awareness, a concrete *member* of a community that rests on the complex, inter-dependent homeodynamics of the non-living, living and social environments. Crucially, this should be understood as *systemic at every level* and not simply at the macro-level of large-scale social 'artifice' built 'upon' or 'added to' a natural or physical environment. That additive, macro-only approach seems to us the characteristic fallacy of much 19th Century sociology, especially Marx's, and is in many cases responsible for an anti-materialist regression in 20th Century thought.

> Two main currents appear in French painting after the sixteenth century: the rational and the irrational. The first is apt to be moralising and didactic; the second is free of such ethical tendencies. The rational trend stems from France's classical epoch, the seventeenth century, and continues with more or less strength throughout the eighteenth; the irrational current is less constant but appears most splendidly in the first half of the eighteenth century. Both, though in a variety of transformations and mixtures, can be recognised in the complicated structure of French painting of the nineteenth century and continue even to our own day. [2]

Whatever the contemporaneous professional evaluation of Michelangelo's achievement and its contextual influence upon the history of art, it remains analytically true that the broader critical tradition of his day regarded 'professionalism' with a mixture of indifference or dismay and best disguised under the rubrics of grace or genius. Fundamentalist tendencies within Christian and Platonic discursive horizons could easily reduce the division of labour to a matter related primarily to original sin or essentially contingent limitation, with no response at hand other than interesting but philosophically unsystematic derivatives of Sophism allied to some vague notion of pragmatics. For both religious and platonic critics, the decisive matter in the division of labour is that of the 'Elect', the chosen, graced individual whose production is in some way consonant with the structures of Being; the remaining social organisation and perception of labour remains merely mundane and uninteresting. Unhappily, Michelangelo and his supporters, potentially the most positive and cogent opponents of this dramatically limited idea, are seduced by the ostensible strength 'grace' offers to them as individuals, at the expense of both their profession and the reinvigoration of the theory of Art.

For David and the revolution he supported, this virtual identity of social order and the state of sin is repugnant. The genuineness of the social structure proposed by the Revolution is founded in morality as an order revealed to and in the activities of Reason and the reasonable, virtuous citizen.

Interestingly, this position allied to concomitant attempts to identify the subject matter of painting with revealed moral virtue is not a consequence of revolutionary fervour (though perhaps it is re-animated and re-directed). Rather, it is a persistent characteristic of the French *Academie* from LeBrun to Ingres.[3] From our point of view the essential consideration is the explicit formation of a relation between painting and the State through the imperative of morality. Contrasted with Michelangelo, the practice of painting may thus potentially appear as an act of civic responsibility rather than religious devotion. Contrasted with the notion of freedom as it is represented in contemporary thought, Republicanism may be seen as the attempt to achieve a union of rationality with desire such that the merely mundane or practical are re-forged in a form of secular *devotion* or social solidarity. David displays a commitment both to painting and to Republicanism that marks out a social space for a determined series of specific actions that begin by repudiating such glosses as 'the dream of human life' or, indeed 'disbelief in metanarratives'. Differently put, the commitment here is one that Platonists, or, more pressingly, Mr. Postmodern can easily recognise but not easily concede: where they point to locatedness as a general condition and so, implicitly or explicitly, formulate the mundane as a whole from which they differ as the extra-ordinary, Republicanism distinguishes between various kinds of instances of the ordinary, (practical, mundane etc.) and argues that this one is *better*.

Honour offers an account of David's *Oath of the Horatii*, which largely corresponds with the didactic and moralising currents within Classicism:

> David suddenly reached full maturity. Completely emancipated and completely in command of a new and rigorously purified style, he achieved a perfect fusion of form and content in an image of extraordinary lucidity and visual punch.... a clarion call to civic virtue and patriotism. [4]

Perhaps our difficulties with this formulation stem from the various limits of (post)modernist critical convention; we should, very likely, be more impressed by its spatial coherence, especially when compared with its Rococo predecessors. We are likely to find that the terms, 'completely emancipated' and 'perfect fusion of form and content' derive more from the rhetorics of eulogy than the analytics of criticism and to find the both the form and the content of the 'clarion call' staggeringly absurd. Nevertheless, it is arguable that such responses repeat current prejudices and undeniable that repetition differs fundamentally from analysis. Consider this reasoning, then, which may well have been available in some form to David's contemporaries:

> he seems to have turned to Livy for a "true" account, both historically and morally, of how the three Horatii brothers agreed to settle a war between Rome and Alba by personal combat with the three Curiatii brothers and how the only survivor, returning to Rome in triumph, found his sister mourning one of the Curiatii to whom she was betrothed. The survivor thereupon killed his sister, was condemned to death and only reprieved after his father pleaded publicly for clemency. [5]

Can it be argued that this picture, then, answers to the variously formulated demands, from Rousseau, from Winckelmann, from Diderot [6] and so on, for an art that portrays or brings to mind exemplary virtue and provides maxims for personal conduct, rather than indulging the taste of the *amateur* for the sensuous qualities and hedonistic subject matter upon which Rococo was (ostensibly) based? Does it, or can it, satisfy Diderot's appeal: 'First move me, astonish me, break my heart, let me tremble, weep, stare, be enraged - only then regale my eyes.' [7]

Does it act upon Winckelmann's advice that painters should 'dip their brush in intellect'? [8] Or is this the customary prejudicial inversion that places visual art primarily in illustrative service to verbal reasoning, whilst at the same time implicitly denying that visual creativity (dipping one's brush in colour) has anything but a marginal connection with the intellect?

Before we try to respond to these questions, let us try to sharpen the focus, In the first place we shall not seek in any way to deny the justice of Diderot's or Winckelmann's requirements as a reaction to the greater excesses of Rococo, though it would clearly be barbaric to dismiss the achievements of the likes of Watteau in the spirit of such programmatic reforms. Nor can one deny the worth of the essentially creative impulse that elects critical parameters, earnestly felt. The question is rather this: whether painting has acted, or indeed, can act viably within the limits of the sentiments expressed; whether the sentiments themselves, whatever their innate worth, can in any sense appropriately shape the practice of painting. [9]

Now if any artist has the potential to operate successfully within these conditions, it *has* to be David because of the depth of his involvement in French intellectual and political life; the conditions are the very opposite of external constraint but an expression of his deepest ambitions and commitments. (As a matter of accuracy, it was not until 1790 and after David had become actively engaged in politics that a directly Republican meaning was read into this work. Nevertheless, it remains in its inception, an undeniably moral work.) Moreover, the 'quality' of the picture is not generally doubted and so we are in the best possible position to determine, given the visual strength of the picture, given David's commitments, whether it actually does, whether it actually can, answer to the demands of Winckelmann and Diderot.

He apparently began the *Horatii* project with a sketch representing a different moment of the story, the father's plea for clemency at the surviving son's trial, only to reject it since, ' Horatius was acquitted more in admiration for his valour than the justice of his cause. He had displayed an admirable patriotism but a deplorable lack of the main stoic virtue, self control.' [10] He chose instead:

> the one moment in which the highest Roman virtues were crystallised in their finest and purest form.....when the three youths selflessly resolved to sacrifice their lives for their country.
>
> By selecting this scene David was able to extract and isolate the essence and reveal its inner meaning, the nobility of Roman stoicism, with a correspondingly stoic directness and economy of visual means. Moreover, the solemnity of the oath-taking, heightened the effect by adding an extra dimension to the moral, universalising it and generalising its human relevance. Thus whilst the message is conveyed in personal terms which were immediately understood by David's contemporaries, it was clearly understood as a lesson applicable to all men and for all time.
>
> David extols an heroic world of simple, uncomplicated passions and blunt uncompromising truths. Masculine courage and resolve is contrasted with feminine tenderness and acquiescence....' [11]

For Honour, then, David appears to fulfil Diderot's requirement, since the only mention of anything that might 'regale the eyes' is minimal: 'Masculine... is contrasted with feminine.' Why, then, in the context of manifestly discursive purposes should he seek to produce an 'image' of an incident?

What is to be gained, or lost, by such an illustration? The basest level of answer, one that allows the least independent value to be attached to the act of painting *per se*, would run roughly as follows: Art stands in the service of the discursive intellect and therefore its highest function is to stimulate and aid the discursive imagination by means of evocation and illustration. [12]

But it is equally arguable that the image does nothing to advance the course of discursive reason since it proposes the circumstantial limitations of a visible instant as a representative of a discourse that is both moral and extensive. In this sense, for example, the finalised form of the *Horatii*, 'crystallised' as it were, fails to contain the cautionary force of the later murder or the questionable justice of Horatius' acquittal. The Socrates of *The Republic* could undoubtedly argue that whilst the picture may be moving or forceful it shares in the intrinsic 'falsehood' of the arts when they are contrasted with reason: only the latter could claim to grasp or contain *The Oath of the Horatii* in all of its ramifications whilst pictorial representation can only produce various, concrete and dispersed images or moments from the 'real' subject. Nor does David attempt to produce contrasting portrayals of, for example, the abandoned moment of the murder nor the brutality of combat.

If, then, we put aside at this moment of analysis our taste for pictures and any possible admiration we may have for this painting, we might justifiably argue that David exhibits similar failings to those of Horatius and his father; he is willing to abandon the stoic commitment to reason for the sake of the emotive force of a picture; sentiment takes precedence over morality and justice. Bluntly, it becomes difficult to square the moral commitments of either David or Diderot with their taste for visual art. But it remains in question whether their fault lies in the character of their tastes or the character of their reasoning.

Let us remain for a moment with this question of the relation between the 'entire' discourse, and the necessary limitation of visual representation to, at best, a series of moments. Remember also that this image is supposed to stand as a 'lesson for all men and for all time'. The argument that David's critical audience would have known the 'total' context is spurious - or else justifies the most limited and partial reasoning on precisely the same grounds. Yet equally absurdly (or laudably, according to your view) the Horatii stand for the entirety of Rome and the Curiatii for the entirety of Alba. Perhaps that is perverse; perhaps the point is not that certain other citizens of Alba might feel they could have done a better job, for example, by outnumbering the Horatii - if Classicism hadn't set the rules in advance. Perhaps we 'ought' to see that the Horatii, perfectly in David's single image, more equivocally in Livy's subtler account, personify the essence of civic virtue in the extreme form of self - sacrifice. Perhaps we can be accused of confusing neo-Classicists' conceptions of the real with our own.

Then we must respond with an objection on two counts: the first being a reiteration of the inappropriateness of form between the single image and the manifold series of events and the second being the extension of this principle to the corresponding problem at the discursive level between the specific acts of the Horatii and 'self-sacrifice' as such, (as an issue for 'all men at all times' etc.). We may now generalise this as a rebuttal of the most salient and objectionable characteristics of neo-Classicism whether verbally or pictorially manifested, namely the tendency to allow one event to stand as the exemplar and archetype of many events whose relationship to the original has no other apparent source than this theoretic habit. Hence the chapter title 'impossible representatives'.

That, we concede, is far-reaching: it is to refute not simply this use of exemplary *image* but also to place in radical doubt any immediate recourse to the *categorial*. It also places in question (not without hostility) the presumed, traditional ability of verbal language to re-present the manifold of arguably similar phenomena through *categories* (such as 'art', 'painting' or even 'the work of David'). Where the fundamental etymology of 'col-lection' means 'bringing together with speech'; and if this is lost in our customary and careless use of categories so lax as to be meaningless or contradictory, then we aim to emphasise that 'bringing together with speech' is more a forceful than an innocent *act* of re-presentation. Such re-presentations may also be 'impossible' for reason to tolerate.

In this sense, the *Horatii* provides for us a double image: (1) on the one hand the concrete exemplar in the brothers' substitution for and subsumption of Rome, in which the latter is both represented but deprived of its sovereignty (the corresponding Curiatii/Alba substitution illustrates this rather better); (2) on the other hand, quite unlike the situation in Michelangelo, the *imagery* of col-lection (the mis-use is deliberate) is here more radically illustrated in *pictorial* rather than verbal form.

Livy, after all, is more diffuse in his story-telling; he has other fish to fry than relations between form and instance. David, in contrast, is propelled by his moral-pictorial project precisely, hopelessly into the representation of a form (applicable to all men at all times...) in a single, aserial image. This is a project of compression at least as ambitious as Socrates' yet which, ludicrously, is *consciously* a fragment of its referent. The double image is then, the concrete form of the exemplary and the practised ignore-ance that surrounds its construction. The *Horatii* is like Socratic irony, wrenched form its habitual, lithe transparency and concealment in words and represented in a visual form that shows its cumbersome construction, omissions and evasions. It would seem that painting has exacted a kind of revenge for an attempted subjugation.

If, then, we stand accused of confusing neo-Classic with our own notions of reality, the truth we signal in advance is that a subsumption is eventually at stake, one that points to a continuity and a supercession, which may well in turn ruin our own coherence. Suffice to say at this stage that an opposition is indicated that may well backfire upon us but which cannot be equated with the spurious (il)liberalism of 'posterities' that never affect one another adversely.

How can it occur as a credible event in Classical discourse that three brothers stand for Rome? How is it that in neo-Classical French painting a moment of Roman history ostensibly offers a maxim for moral conduct not simply for eighteenth-century France but for all humanity? If the actions of the Horatii are not to be reformulated as foundational myth (in which case the unique force of their personal sacrifice would be lost since there would be no supportable concrete distinction between the Horatii and Rome and the entire tragic tale becomes a dramatic or Sophistic appendage to a moral position, arguably very like David's picture) - they take place in a social context that has virtually nothing to do with Davidian Classicism; except by the assumption that self-sacrifice has a single, uninflected character. This may perhaps be true, but only at an extremely banal and shallow level, in the worst and most misleading sense of 'image' and will invariably be confounded by specific actuality. One is here speaking of an image of the basest, oldest and commonest kind, that Wilfred Owen characterises perfectly: '...the old lie: dulce et decorum est pro patria mori.' Now that old lie trades off systematically concealing the inevitable collision between the generality for which the sacrifice takes place and the individual who both bears the cost and is in many cases and senses severed from community by death, injury or simply his experience. Whilst this question takes weight and shape in Owen's poem, there is virtually none of it in David's image. Consequently, the poem, intrinsically a suspect medium for Platonically inspired neo-Classicism can justly be described as more 'reasonable' than the picture or its moral supporters; in a sense, their positions are neither reasonable nor unreasonable but at best unbalanced and analytically inadequate; at worst, in Owen's sense, blatantly false.

On the other hand, there is no overt visual nor critical reference to the inevitable contextual differences between these heroes of Rome and the possible heroes (or victims) of the French Revolution. It is arguable, then, that David does not address either the Roman or the French context, despite the apparent appeal of the former for the latter. Nor does he address the difference between social structure and individual member, despite the fact that the picture is addressed to the 'responsible citizen', supposedly the incarnation and support of that very relationship.

One is perhaps open to the charge of confusing morality with circumstance, or to put it slightly differently, of making a moral objection on the grounds that the facts lack credibility. Precisely so. This is Classicism's continual recourse: whether or not the individual circumstances are convincing, is analytically irrelevant to the principled character of the moral act. A rejection is cogent on several grounds: firstly, since it severs morality from its social context: secondly, because it removes the moral act from its immediate results and costs: thirdly, because the charge simply reflects the characteristic negativity of Classicism toward the circumstantial. To that theoretic habit and hence to the charge above one must reply that a moral act divorced from its circumstances is simply not an act at all. Unfortunately, the virtuous citizen is irredeemably an actor on the social scene and so is apt to bear the consequences.

Socrates' *Republic* is crucially flawed by the complete absence of a principle of transcendence that genuinely relates the realms of eternity and temporality. Hence drinking hemlock provides an 'adequate' answer to the injustice of his condemnation. David's Republic, whilst locating the possibility of transcendence in the moral dignity of citizenship is finally betrayed because the civic spirit of humanity is infected by the concrete form of a (pictorial) language that is incorrigibly 'socratic' and so cannot fulfil that potential. It is thus hugely ironic that David should choose to portray the sacrifice of individuality for the sake of the justice and security of the state since it is precisely this relationship that cannot be realised in neo-Classical language; nor can his picture assert anything but a highly questionable role in the matter, even in his own critical terms, and culminates in the most forceful self-refutation, an image of its own culpability and impossibility.

Given these considerations the status of David *qua* 'painter' and (say) Livy's verbal account takes on a new theoretic dimension. Let us prepare this matter carefully: the difference between a 'complete' (let us say reasonably just and balanced) account of the story of the Horatii and a picture of the Oath as such couldn't be more marked. It is not at issue that all such accounts are fundamentally incompletable and constantly re-opened, (as we do now), since the picture has no more nor less of a complete 'physical body' than any series of text and its significance is also fundamentally open to re-negotiation, (as we do now). It is rather a different kind of incompleteness that is at stake in each case; for the picture is, above all, momentous in all the ambiguous senses of that word. It is the representation of a moment in such a manner that it is constantly, preciously recalled; so that one can sustain, dwell in and re-animate the sight and emotive resonances of the sentiments expressed, isolated at their height and kept from the taint of the passage of time and the play of circumstance or contradiction. No words, however often repeated, however minimised their serial quality, can match that almost hallucinatory quality of absolutely constant presence.

David is marvellous at sustaining this quality, principally because of the entire lack of contradiction in his principal works between the 'contingencies' of mundane surface and essential significance. His *Death of Marat* is a most compelling picture of this type. On the one hand there is practically nothing within the 'realist' traditions that can surpass its sheer corporeality; the body of Marat is immensely, sympathetically tangible. On the other, there is nothing of the later demands to portray transience or the dissipation of portrayal within the 'reality' of surface. The picture brings together the grief-ridden moment of death, sympathy at its peak, the salience of bodily presence and the sentiments attached to this man in an instant that constantly re-presents itself. Though the picture fails to treat adequately the force and agony of death, the visible absence of animation and the sickening evidence of its loss that is so catastrophically present in Gericault or Goya, that absence is consistent with the warmth of sentiment that is felt for the man. In Goya or Gericault, the victims are made absolutely anonymous by the force, scale and precedence of violence as such as subject matter. In this picture above all, David entirely surpasses the Modern's charge that he, that Classicism, is blind to *particularity* ('modern life' in Baudelaire's, Zola's or Manet's sense), but at a price that destroys the theoretic cohesion of his critical support and undermines the visual claims and values of the *Horatii*.

Think how wrong Diderot must be! There is virtually nothing discursive in either *Marat* or the *Horatii*, for the entire experience of the absolutely constant moment lies totally within the representational possibilities of visual art. Nothing else achieves this transcendence. How ironic is the phrase, 'only then regale my eyes'! The entire force of David's image originates in the very faculties that Diderot, as a representative of the verbal traditions of neoclassicism would prefer to place in the last position. Whilst the visual commitment in the *Horatii* may be understood negatively, what David achieves in *Marat* produces is a potent, self-contained and absolutely visual image that is designed to and manifestly succeeds in moving its audience. It has all the character of persuasive presentation, its sentiments spilling out and frustrating all criticism or caution. In the context of a quasi-Platonic affirmation of art that is itself a contradiction in terms, it is a nice example of Sophistry. [13]

How maddeningly frustrating for the moral defenders of David's painting; how irritating for David himself: faced with the challenge of being voluntarily associated with a political commitment, painting has apparently betrayed the trust and found the specific forms of its own autonomy rather more compelling, in both senses of that word. For Platonism, apparently also for neo-Classicism, the visual arts demonstrate their capricious limits. For an organic conception of re-presentation modelled after Durkheim we confront instead the assertion and development of a sovereign difference namely *painting* - that, crucially, belongs primarily to a public, socially-organised, autonomous, discrete but *dynamic* tradition; not to the moral intentions of writers; not even to the specific intentions of a certain M. David.

One is thus again forced to the conclusion that neo-Classicism, despite its concrete pretensions, analytically has no means to articulate its affirmation of painting. As the language of a republican society, it is incoherent or demonstrably silent upon an aspect of that structure, that it desires or appears to value. In a very real sense, then, despite its surface appropriateness, it is arguably not the language of that society; or, conversely, and more radically: this society has no language of its own. Might this be the irony that supported 'history' painting into the late nineteenth century? Might this be the irony that continues to frustrate our realisation that the division of labour implies a differentiation in language at least as significant as that in role or occupation?

The visual critical tradition from which David springs is couched in a semantic idiom dependent upon the re-animation of a specific and very ancient conception of the relation between nature and the 'Ideal' - or, in more familiar terms, nature and judgement.

> By the ideal (wrote Mengs) I mean that which one sees only with the imagination, and not with the eyes; thus an ideal in painting depends upon the selection of the most beautiful things in nature purified of all imperfection.[14]

On the same matter, Reynolds is characteristically practical:

> It is from a reiterated experience and a close comparison of the objects of nature that the artist becomes possessed of that central form .....from which every deviation is deformity. But the investigation of this form...is painful and I know of but one method of shortening the road: that is, by a careful study of the ancient sculptors.[15]

It is tempting to dismiss the 'Ideal' as an elaborate inflation of a taste for the antique. However, the relationship is anything but a question of taste; the sentiments expressed reject the very idea: 'By nature, I understand the general and permanent principles of visible objects, not disfigured by accident, or distempered by disease, not modified by fashion or local habits. Nature is a collective idea, and, though its essence exists in each individual of the species, can never in its perfection inhabit a single object.'[16]

On the face of it, these ideas provide the perfect space and justification for neo-Classical artists' practices. In a manner highly reminiscent of Cennini's 'shadows of the natural' but now recharged with a strong sense of social duty. They are in a deep sense 'required' by Nature to reveal itself adequately, 'reasonably', essentially, to society; not just in terms of simple appearances, but in seeking, portraying those special moments when the confluence between the physical order and the moral order is, so to speak, 'absolute' or at least 'authentic'. The *Oath of the Horatii* represents, ostensibly, one such moment in which the truth of Nature in this special sense is revealed. Thus the artist was wedded to the notion of essence and to some version of the practice of decontexting. And that duty uniquely intervenes in the relation between presence and re-presentation so as to transform the latter from superfluity into necessity. But as we have seen, the image (say, of the *Oath*) is, per se, innately contextual and this produces radical tensions between the limits of painting and the limits of criticism.

Without wishing to repeat the arguments, the *Death of Marat*, is an infinitely more convincing picture precisely because it accepts an absolutely specific context. Of course, one can simply argue that *Marat* as a subject is 'possible' because it is temporally a unity, where the *Horatii* is impossibly ramified. But that view conceals three important considerations: Marat's death produces ramifications at least as complex as the *Oath* and so is equally 'impossible'. It cannot be justified in terms of the practice of elucidating Nature described above. As an image that remains potent to this day (and certainly to its own epoch), it has successfully escaped the trammels and imperfections of finite contextuality in the narrow sense but in a manner that has absolutely nothing to do with neo-Classical conceptions of that possibility, since the image is most certainly 'disfigured'. It may be, then, in an echo of the status we argued for Michelangelo's *Crucifixions*, that this picture has the potential, as it were, to indicate or teach a better speech. Similarly, by 'better' we intend a speech directed toward an active, ontic solidarity whose differences relate to the authentic, disclosed manifestness of beings. Differently put, *Marat* as visual representation potentially outlines the possible utterances of a republic whose actual critical discourse is determined instead by the stifling silence of irony.

The Death of Marat as an image indicates a series of sentiments, certain talents and education on David's part, in short, a sensibility that is both socially constructed and yet uniquely his own; no one else realised this image, though an entire tradition is involved in its possibility. Moreover, if there is any justice in the reasoning above it erupts upon a language that is in many senses critically hostile. If an alternative view existed within his profession, it would be highly specific to its idioms. The effect is to throw the focus of possibility upon painter and painting, the *profession* rather than upon the social whole and indeed, to circumvent its ideological structure. Sensibility, its perceptions and its traditions thus become crucial. You will recall that it was the professional idiom and members' individual sentiments and sense perceptions that Platonic Classicism most despised, especially when the profession was the painting of images.

Before we turn to the substance of Kant's 'transcendental subject', it may be useful to summarise our analysis of the *Horatii* in more formal terms. We have not yet done with *Marat*.

Our opening sections argued the need for a theoretic model of complexity that did not rest on a kind of surreptitious 'pruning' (or emasculation) that allowed fundamentally opposite or actively opposing worldviews to be subsumed *under* the 'posterities' of liberal, secular postmodernism. As any attention to current affairs or to the more informed radio debates on 'new' books, ideas and initiatives will show, 'postmodernity' is actively vilified by paradigms as diverse as religious fundamentalism, nationalism neuroscience and *realpolitiks*. Our next task involved the examination of Platonic-Christian notions of the real and derivative, essence and (mere) appearance, sacred and mundane (or whatever you wish) - dedicated to the proposition that ordinary complexity - the mundane world - is literally ignorable. It doesn't 'count'. We examined how neoclassicism in the visual arts both made use of and subverted this idea and was made to pay a price set in terms of the social limits it then *had* to concede. Art became a matter of 'genius', directed quite deliberately away from the broad social order in which it took place, shared an uneasy alliance with privileged patronage. But this, we argued was the consequent social substance and structure of Platonic-Christian *ideology* - and not necessarily a description of the social limits of visual art. We cited Michelangelo's *Crucifixions,* as opposed to his *Resurrections,* as formulating a crucially different subject matter (or at least a crucially different way of representing it) and as potential originators of a quite different view of what kinds of art and social action might be possible. Our emphasis was placed on these points of social differentiation, - and their autopoietic possibilities, set against the suffocating closure of neo-Platonism.

For Socrates, and for Augustine, the world of social-political 'representation' has no consequence: it shares no real community with what is essential, be it the foundational 'Ideas' or the creating-condemning 'God'. For David and his critics, an attempt to represent positively the 'ordinary' political processes of republicanism as good or better or necessary (set against what went before) is crippled by an image of community that still lacks authentic notions of complexity, we argue, because its speech and visual idioms are still neo-Classical. In other words, Davidian painting still feels the absurd need to 'compress' the manifold of visual possibility into impossible representatives - *of all men* - such as Socrates, or the Horatii. This is doubly ironic in that both Socrates and the Horatii rest precisely on a concrete and explicit principle of exclusion. And it is precisely the many possibilities of social action - whether artistic, military or philosophical that are excluded. Put differently, Davidian painting and politics *wants* to articulate an authentic image of (republican) community but lacks both the visual and the verbal language which could *include* that complexity. We have implied above and shall argue below that David's *Marat* shatters this limitation, but at considerable cost.

Kant's *Critique of Pure Reason*, first published in 1781 before *The Death of Marat* was painted in 1793 had placed sense-perception in the forefront of the possibility of Reason, thus reversing Platonic formalism:

> How should our faculty of knowledge be awakened into action did not objects affecting our senses partly of themselves produce representations, partly arouse the activity of our understanding to compare these representations, and, by combining or separating them, work up the raw material of the sensible impressions into that knowledge of objects that is entitled experience [17]

Notice that in addition to the conventional empiricist's position, stress is placed upon the interpretative and synthetic elements of experience. For Kant this must be so because: 'Experience teaches us that a thing is so and so but not that it cannot be otherwise.' And from this it ostensibly follows that: '....if we have a proposition which.....is thought as necessary, it is an *a priori* judgement.' [18] There follows a series of amplifications of this idea that need not concern us here. The essential point is the *a priori* disposition of sensate intuition to structure phenomena according to the laws of its own conceptual structure. Consequently,

> in the relation of the given object to the subject, (the object's) properties depend upon the mode of intuition of the subject, this object as 'appearance' is to be distinguished from itself as object 'in itself'. [19]

So begins the modern tradition of phenomenology, essentially as a bifurcated and hence critical empiricism. From our point of view, it confers advantages and disadvantages of considerable importance: on the one hand it potentially liberates experience from the suffocating limits of the Platonic theory of forms and the Christian concept of finite 'falsehood': on the other, it places at least as strict limits upon the validity of experience, and on grounds arguably more rational and hence more binding. Our emphases in a moment will be collected around the consequences for the relationship of representation and time. First let us try to formulate our preliminary reading of Kant in a more accessible way and *begin* to distinguish it from others' readings.

There has been, unfortunately, a tradition of interpretative 'correction' of Kant allied to a grossly misunderstood selection of those aspects of Kant which can be more easily assimilated to common sense notions of reality or the empiricism of science and technology. Both tendencies tend to transform Kant's radicalism to the purring of a paper tiger or to the often-voiced assertion that he was a good thinker who, nevertheless, could not express himself clearly. [20] Our reading, like Heidegger's, places Kant at the foundation of modern thought: 'The modern form of ontology is [Kant's] transcendental philosophy which becomes epistemology.' [21] Though our criticism of Kant will differ from Heidegger's we insist that his, and our, conclusion is unmistakable and correct: the knowing *subject* becomes the foundation (the *only* foundation) through which Being can be addressed. As Heidegger puts it: 'In that truth becomes certainty and thus the beingness (*ousia)* of beings changes to the objectivity of the *perceptio* and the *cogitatio* of consciousness....knowing and knowledge move to the foreground.' [22] This then, is the Kant that begets Hegel's radical idealism and all of its feeble derivatives, ranging from 'there is no outside-text' to the supposition that everything that lies outside the *subject*, and its conceptual, linguistic and social structures, is random and orderless.

For Heidegger and for us, Kant is the burden modern thought has to bear[23] simply because Kant is still deemed to be credible. For Heidegger: 'Epistemology is the tile for the increasing, essential powerlessness of modern metaphysics to know its own essence and the grounds of that essence.' [24] For us: the insistence that every form of necessity and certainty is derived from the *subject* and not from experience (in other words Kant's criterion itself) isolates both the modern subject and thought about that subject from every other viable, terrestrial manifestation of 'consciousness' and from every other viable terrestrial '*discipline*'. In other words neither the modern subject or, consequently, the disciplines that attempt its formulation can enter into an ecological relationship with other beings or other disciplines. That is the burden we seek to re-place.

We shall turn to more specific clarifications (where possible) and more specific refutations in due course. We return to questions of representation and time.

'Genesis' in either the Christian or the Platonic sense, allied to the determination of mundane life by the concept of sin, reduces sense perception and ultimately experience to the status of arbitrary semblance. Kant's transcendental 'aesthetic' (the analysis of intuition) injects an order, albeit a 'phenomenal' order, that bears striking formal parallels with David's depiction of Marat. Kant speaks of three 'syntheses',[25] those of apprehension, reproduction in imagination and recognition in a concept; each of these is in turn rooted in the 'transcendental unity of apperception'. (In more familiar terms, the unity or identity of the subject or of consciousness.) Without entering into the technical details, these syntheses structure the possibility of perception through stabilising the unity of the individual *vis à vis* the manifold of time and space. Where the Platonic-Christian 'subject' is radically dependent upon circumstance, the Kantian subject is both a mediating principle and a shaping agency.

Consider David's image in this light. Certainly, it is circumstantial in respect both of the event and of David's relation to that event. But as a response to those circumstances it is anything but passive and avowedly synthetic. As synthetic reproduction in imagination and in the concrete image, it constantly, literally 're-presents' and so transcends its immediate circumstances; it intervenes in and mediates radically that which in Platonic-Christian thought is the immediate, absolute determinant, namely temporality itself. The enormity of that intervention, for us, renders the argument advanced by Mengs, Reynolds *et al.* concerning the relationship between the contingencies of individuality and the perfection of Nature quite superfluous. We are simply not speaking about an 'individual', if that term implies anything connoting instance or occasion because that temporal limit is precisely what the image has surpassed. Instead, we are speaking of nothing less than the social mediation of temporality. Nevertheless, we are not speaking of absolute stability, of truth in the sense implied in the neo-Classical conception of nature, but rather of the mediate social 'phenomenon'. And that would appear to reinvest temporality with all of its original corrosive power.

A matter of contrast is then generally held to be important, indeed unavoidable. Kant's proposition – experience teaches us that a thing is so and so but not that it cannot be otherwise - trades off the empirical limits of the belief that such and such 'is the case' contrasted with the infinite variety of undefined possibilities that we may imagine. It is thus always possible to suggest that the firmest belief is actually contingent upon a meagre set of circumstances, set against infinite variability. Nevertheless, whilst this professed logical necessity follows from the contrast between finite and infinite, the grounds for the necessary application of the contrast itself remain inadequately thought. Of course, the contrast (or in Kant's usage, more properly, the 'criterion') is intended to distinguish *a priori* propositions (that display the characteristic of being necessarily true) from all other *contingent* judgements. That is supposed to firmly determine the general ontological status of the latter, but experience rather takes its revenge for this cut-and-dried schema. Instead, we shall shortly argue, the contrast itself, and so the ascription of necessity or contingency, tends to be used as and when experience demands. It is then, in a sense, not necessity that governs the application of Kant's position but the absolutely concrete movements of perceived circumstance. So far the strict Kantian may maintain his case by arguing that this *ad hoc* application is a characteristic of ordinary usage, set against the intellectual rigour of philosophy. More modern social theorists, for identical reasons, are apt to distinguish between the 'natural attitude' and their own formulations.[26]

Pursuing, however, the ironic idea of a necessity that is contingently invoked, we may construct a complex series of propositions about Michelangelo or David and it would take a maddeningly dotty version of Kantianism to insist that the 'totality' of possible experience is in any way relevant. We are rather implicitly addressing a certain horizon. Moreover, within that series of propositions only a certain group could be reasonably held to be potentially contingent. Then the application of Kant's axiom is in some sense itself dependent upon judgement. And that sense begins by structuring the ostensible, immediate necessity of the contrast between a circumscribed finite and an absolute infinity, into a series of finite horizons of relevance. It is therefore Kantian phenomenology, and not ordinary usage that lacks rigour in its very attention to the infinitely extended. In a precise echo of Michelangelo's openness set against the 'rigorous' closure of Socratic irony, ordinary judgement appears to see what Kant, for all his intelligence does not: infinity is nevertheless *manifold*. We appear to be again beset by a critical tradition whose first impulse is formalistic, radically categorial or col-lective: the modernisation of irony not on account of the Oracle at Delphi but on account of the oracles of customary verbal impulse. In other words Kant's 'necessity' is not *a priori* except in the strict sense of a recognisable *idiom*.

Or again: the image of community essayed in this idiom is that of a formal and undifferentiated infinity set against the sole structure of subjecticity. Subjecticity thereby 'gives' this void its distinct character but only as appearance *for* the human 'subject'. Kant calls this 'contingent apperception'. This is not 'bringing forth worlds' but the determination of the void 'according to concepts' of the subject. Since there is no other order (no outside-text) - only (or despite) the randomness of sense-perceptions the transcendental subject determines 'his' own appearance to himself [27] and (in principle though this remains unstated) that of every other phenomenon including every other human. The 'thing in itself', - for Kant the 'pure beyond of thought' [28] put more radically, includes *everything*.

Stated in slightly different terms, if the *thing*-in-itself remains a 'pure' beyond of thought *and no more than that* - despite the superficial resemblance to 'bringing forth worlds' - there can be no *ecological* relationship between the manifold we call 'things' and the various orders of representation. This remains true even if Kant's analysis of the human subject may be taken as a representative of the possibility of consciousness-in-general. Another impossible representative, then: by implication every impulse of awareness has its own 'pure beyond' *and nothing else*. It is easy to see that in this total void in which the synthesis of any awareness takes place (for no good reason) that *necessity has no place*. Of course Kant needs to find a way to 'explain' necessity, but entirely because his paradigm-idiom excludes it in the first place.

If we want to underline the contrary - the mutual autopoiesis of 'things' and their representations, then 'necessity' becomes associated with an alternative series of cognates: vitality, viability, vigour. In short the primary resonance of 'necessary' (whether we speak of external things or the orders of representation) is not the 'fixed' but the *vital*. And the vital *can* perish. In this sense, the supposed rigour of Kant's icy formalism is displaced by the mundane (but *vital*) pragmatics of contexts, possibilities, probabilities. Do not mistake this for Lyotard's softer pragmatics. Stress instead mortality, structure, pattern; the possible is framed by the impossible; the probable by the improbable. Vitality has its allotted span.

Before we leave this preliminary on the issue let us consider its application to *Marat*. If we think of the burgeoning series of issues that lead to and from his death and indeed from the existence of the image itself (such as this text), the axiom may be apt. But remember that in saying so we have as yet touched none of the issues themselves, whether verbally or visually formulated. We have maintained a polite, possibly prudent, disinterest in exactly the same manner that formal relations between acquaintances are managed. We have not, as it were, even attempted to enter 'their' society. David's *Marat* invites quite the opposite response: the maximum sympathetic response of mourning. It matters that David 'knew' Marat; it doesn't matter what we know about 'him', so far as the image is concerned. Both cases, however, image making and response depend totally on 'experience'. Shall we now judge it seemly to deploy Kant's axiom? Of course it would be an act of philistinism, and this itself points up a contrast. In David's making the picture and in our responding we trust our (socially organised) sensibilities and experience without the formal caveat Kant advises. Supporters of critical phenomenology may see this as a consequence of the difference between common sense, or 'ordinary' and analytic reason. To be sure, there is a difference, but their formulations tend to grasp that reductively: one as social action and the other as its potential analysis.

We have already encountered Lyotard's contradictory legislative-pluralism and its emphasis on overlapping clusters of language games and performance criteria - without metanarratives. But Lyotard thereby offers something also approaching a metanarrative, which his opponents clearly *resent*. Our point can now be put somewhat differently: it is not the propensity to construct worldviews that is objectionable in either Kant or Lyotard; indeed they are inevitable. The problem is rather subsumption: Kant, Lyotard, Derrida gloss the higher rank they place on their writing-idioms over and above their subject matter. Diderot and Winckelmann are at least more explicit, if unfashionable. Notice that we said *their writing-idioms* and not *writing*. This differentiation is deliberate and crucial: it is fundamentally unreasonable that 'writing' and the unique authorship of *any* of these names can substitutable. Nor is this a question of 'blame'. It is simply to note that in the curious absence of metanarratives in Lyotard's illiberal universe he chooses to place a certain tradition and discipline *above others*. These form his subject(ed) matter. From this it follows, that David also made a choice, a decision about rank and worth. And despite, alongside, perhaps *because of* the critical tradition that generates Diderot and Winckelmann - *David chose to put painting in the first rank.* That is, of course, strongly akin to Michelangelo's paradoxical choice of visual art in, despite, because of, neo-Platonism. That difference of discipline will turn out to be crucial.

If Kant's transcendental subject cannot 'bring forth worlds' in any way that is a convincing or reasonable alternative to creation *ex nihilo*, then neither can any 'social' collection of such subjects do so. In principle, the 'collection', the society, is no more than the multiple appearance of subject(s) to subject(s): the one(s) the formal synthesis of the other(s). This abstract being will not then strive to constitute its (and others) membership by the act of some will to concretion - a sort of destiny of deformalisation that paradoxically ends in a conventional 'member' rather than a formal subject. In short, the Kantian subject is an impossible representative of

101

human subjecticity because it can have no history other than its own peculiar synthesis.

If instead, human history is a dynamic of *members* then Durkheim's notion that Kantian 'categories' (the rules of the perception, representation and language) 'really' belong to the collectivity [29] is at best an improvement but not a solution. It preserves one of the most objectionable features of humanism: that *human* language, perception, representation are discrete phenomena and not the systemic outcome of interactions with other phenomena in the planetary eco-systems. The proposal is, then, for human consciousness to have a history *at all,* it has to have an extra-human history *as well.* It has *evolved.* We accept this in relation to our bodies, but it is a stubborn prejudice of the most critically-advanced 'postmodernity' that human consciousness is *too special* for similar considerations to apply. (God's image and all that?) Put differently, the antecedent of human consciousness is not 'subjecticity' in either the strict Kantian sense or the more ordinary but *formal* sense but a 'vital' antecedent located in a previous society and ultimately in a different species and a different ecology. This is the 'outside-text' of subjecticity, or better, of membership. In this sense, Durkheim's revisions of Kant indicate something of the *difference* that marks out the sphere of the human-social but little of its *relationship* to phenomena on the periphery or external to that proposed closure. Its edge, so to speak, is too hard and impenetrable; neither nourishment nor danger pass from one side to the other (just as in Kant) and that is deeply unreasonable.

We may grasp something of what is at stake here by analysing possible definitions of the system of social phenomena - or more generally: what defines *any* system? Durkheim's pragmatic definition treats social facts as *sui generic* phenomena. On that basis we might construct a provisional working definition of a system for our immediate purposes: any group of phenomena that is capable of structuring and sustaining itself for a certain time. One extreme reading of Durkheim would insist than *qua sui generic* the system of social phenomena is 'closed'. Readings of this kind would be helpful to arguments that see power relationships - between genders, the old and the young, accreditations of achievement and non-achievement - as 'traditional' or entirely self-founding and therefore potentially self-transforming. The opposite reading - that the system we call social phenomena is radically open to its asocial environment - that certain structures are *consequent* upon this relationship and therefore necessary. The classic uses of this argument of course concern gender and forms of unequal status. We deliberately choose a radical/conservative polarisation here simply for the satisfaction of showing that it is completely irrelevant.

We are not dealing with a moral or a political issue here. The question is *first* ontological: that of theorising viably the *existence* of the class of social phenomena. The question of particular desirability for interested parties is as yet a long way down the line. 'Vitality' belongs to the system itself, along with the loss of vitality, and any other question posing as necessity presents a false trail. An unpleasant truth, certainly, but it is only a naïve and sentimental humanist that reserves extinction for other-than-humans.

If that rather abstract formulation still does not satisfy the moralists that theirs is a second-order concern, let us form a reversal of the conservative/radical schema above. The drug-related culture described in Irvine Welsh's *Trainspotting* is hardly conservative Also, however closely the characters draw on a 'reality' outside the narrative, we are still presented with a story, a film, a fiction is which we can rehearse our identifications and responses *as if* the situation were our own. A more radical and arbitrary declaration that humans 'invent themselves' would be hard to imagine. Yet it depends on the openness of the ostensibly invented social phenomena to the biochemical systems of drug *effects*. At a possibly slighter level, the questions of clothing and lifestyle rest upon the acceptance of a set of available resources ranging from benefits, a drugs market, cheap housing, a shared set of intentions and the rejection of others: for example a rejection of certain styles of clothing, body styles and so on, coupled with an acceptance of others no less ready-made. Jeans, first available as workwear are used as markers of rejection. But, availability of ready-made 'alternatives' is limited and sometimes ludicrous. Think of the number of violently-opposed alternative cultures that *have* to use very short hair because medium is 'straight' and long hair is the registered trade mark of the sixties and hippydom.

Similarly the 'closed' system which in the earlier example aided the cause of those attempting to *change* power relations (for example between genders) - may just as easily be an ally in the preservation of *any* status quo. Hence the obsession of totalitarian regimes with secrecy and (literally) closed borders.

Our interest lies not in closures or in openness but relationships between stabilities and instabilities. Crucially, this instability does not lead to chaos but to *patterned complexity*. Physicists have recently shown interest in Fisher information - usually shortened to I. The central idea of Roy Frieden's [30] new book is its application to unifying the laws of physics.

The key relationship is that between two statistical distributions *I* and *J*. *I is* a measure of the information you can squeeze out of a system given the errors in the system (random disorder, temperature anomalies, error caused by the very act of measuring) given that such errors are governed by statistical distributions such as the bell-shaped curve. *J* is the amount of information bound up in phenomenon you are trying to measure. This information-processing model does not quite square with our earlier approach but because we are less interested in the laws of physics than a general ontology that begins with complexity - rather than trying to exclude it - you will see that it does not matter (and that we make quite radical alterations). Sticking with the information-processing model for the moment, *if I - J* (literally the difference between the information 'as it is' and what we know about it) - the 'information difference' - is as small as possible, the result will be law-like. Or, (for those who spot ghosts of things-in themselves), more precisely, the representation will be viable *as* law.

The assertion is in a sense tautological: laws are effective descriptions of phenomena. That is not in itself objectionable, if slight at this stage. In the hands of mathematicians and physicists, however, a number of spectacular pay-offs occur. We are not competent to understand let alone assess the mathematics or the experimental results. We can, however, derive a number of extremely interesting results, precisely because both our competence and our interests lie elsewhere. First we can apply the *I-J* 'test' (our deteriorated version) to Kant's formulation of the laws of reason. Second, but closely related, we can point out that the desired outcome of *I-J* for the generality of humans and other species is not the viability of the *laws of physics* but *viability* as such. This is the point at which he information-processing analogy becomes congruent with our earlier formulations of 'bringing forth worlds'.

Recalling Kant, we repeat his fundamental criterion for *a priori* knowledge: 'experience teaches us that a thing is so and so but not that it cannot be otherwise' (op. cit.) The chosen candidate: Every effect must have a cause. This might either be represented as a tautologićal 'law': that which engenders effects is named 'cause' - or, as an instance where I *minus* J=0, for all practical purposes. The problem arises when we start to ask about the *context* in which cause and effect take place. We find the answer in the transcendental aesthetic - which modern readers and users of Kantian 'phenomenology' tend to ignore - with good reason. The context, of course, is a time-space continuum (not a problem in itself) except that it too is *necessary* and is also, therefore, *a priori*. Now there are at least two ways to handle this. Kant's is quite explicit and equally explicitly ignored by his modern supporters:

> Time and space, taken together, are the pure forms of all sensible intuition... But these are a priori sources of knowledge, being merely the conditions of our sensibility, just by this fact determine their own limits, namely that they apply to objects only so far as objects are viewed as apperances and do *not* present things as they are in themselves. This is the sole field of their validity....This ideality of space and time leaves, however, the certainty of empirical knowledge unaffected. [31]

In other words, space and time are *merely* the form in which we construct *appearances*. A second way (our way) is to say that some form of a space-time continuum is essential to viable existence in the biosphere. This does not imply that the notion of relativity is questioned or that the fly or the seasonal flower inhabit a Newtonian universe. It simply says that *some* relationship, represented or not, to a space-time continuum is a common characteristic of species and a primary condition of such 'higher' phenomena as locomotion. Kant is able to concede *something* similar [32] but characteristically adds that this can be none of our concern. It *is* our concern and it *does* affect knowledge. This, then, does not point to a simple absence in Kant but rather to a fundamental difference in the *location* of what he calls the *a priori*. For Kant its location is unequivocally *mind* and its character is formal and uniform. For us (and this is essential to the notion of complexity and our whole project) its location(s) is the various systems and subsystems of the biosphere and that consequently its character is not a priori but autopoietic, not formal and unified but manifold, concrete and differentiated. It may exist in one form in the type of colony we call a beehive and in quite another in the colony we call a human society. Both will be subject to the law of viability as it presents itself in that location and at that time, that is *ecologically*.

To illustrate: All the hunter (human or other) needs to 'know' (*I*) about its foodstuff/prey (*J*) is its location, that it *is* edible, the means to secure or kill, some measure of the risk involved, some way, perhaps, of warding-off competitors. The 'system' (in this case the dependence of predator on prey) is structured around a 'vital' requirement but its boundaries are highly elastic. Similarly the relationship *I-J* is determined in *each* of its components by need, process, environment. In other words, the hunter (human or not) may understand the 'law' of the need to eat but that law in itself specifies the relevant components of both *I* and *J*.

Nor is I/J simply a question of ecological niche of particular species. Whether we take the example of the domesticated hunting dog or indeed of the industrial worker who does not produce food, human organisation intervenes in the I/J relationship by forming other viable feeding arrangements. The information needs and 'competence' of the shopper or the domestic dog are not the same as their hunting counterparts. In this sense, neither I nor J are *species* properties but *system* properties. And 'laws' in their widest sense, belong to the interrelation of phenomena and *not* to the formulator (human or not). Differently put, the law the physicists or sociologist or hunter formulates gains its viability or non-viability not from the *a priori* of mind but from the evolved viability of embodied *thinking* within the biosphere. Therefore, to describe social systems as 'open' or 'closed' is simply ridiculous since it presumes for no good reason that all social phenomena have the same relation to their environment. The question: open or closed? - may indeed be an idiomatic habit but outside of something like the Kantian paradigm, this *categorial* form of address is less an imperative and more of an obstacle. To the categorial imperative that authors the question 'What are social phenomena?' our response must be that the question is unreasonable. That speech-law has been superseded in exactly the same way that is no longer necessary and no longer reasonable to ask: 'On what support does the Earth rest? This does not mean, of course, that we cannot address 'social phenomena' but instead of expecting a category of uniform type, we should expect an array of phenomena exhibiting complex patterns of differentiation, some remarkably stable, others highly provisional.

We can now return to and develop a previous position. We objected to the traditional rank of theory and its objects by pointing out that even if we the absence of metanarratives it is still the case that to write or to paint implies a choice and a preference for the adequacy of one over the other. There will, moreover, be complex nuances: Shall we write within the discipline of philosophy or in the form of the novel? Shall we paint in figurative or abstract modes? Of course, this has *nothing* to do with rank in any absolute sense. It has everything to do with context and the appropriateness of kinds of representation to members' interests, habits, proposes, talents. Stated in the terms above, we should not expect different disciplines to tend toward a uniform 'core' identity. Expect instead, differentiation, incompatibilities, different kinds of I, but different kinds of J - *as well*. Heard in its fundamental key this does not simply mean different kinds of representation but different ways of founding information - in short vastly different social possibilities.

It is relatively easy to see that Socrates' position cannot provide for pictorial possibilities, except for the ingenious spin that Florentine neo-Classicism puts on his doctrine. It is also easy to see that Diderot and Wincklemann have serious problems squaring their critical position with any genuine regard for art. In other words, they could not *be* painters - however close the ostensible relationship - without, in their terms, demeaning themselves. Put more cryptically (the sense will emerge) their positions are not *pictorial* possibilities; in themselves they do not generate pictorial possibilities; they generate other, possibly subsequent, 'higher' verbal possibilities.

Our position suggests also that the *Horatii* never was a genuine pictorial possibility at all: it generated nothing new, indeed it demeaned the story [33] On the other hand, we are determined that *Marat* is incorrigibly pictorial and that the proximity of neo-Classic and phenomenological usage refuses to enter the question of what that might mean.

> ....there are no subsidiary figures to set the scene or point the moral. The bare fact of death dominates the work. It is not like earlier death scenes, an exhortation to face death bravely but an image to provoke meditations - a secular Pieta. ..... But, of course, no allusion to Christ was intended - another Jacobin said that to compare Marat with Christ was to slander Marat! [34]

An interesting sentiment that we shall explore in another manner; we shall compare the image of Marat's death with the crucifixions discussed earlier. It follows from that analysis, to put the matter very briefly, that the enduring power of the image of the crucifixion consists firstly in the darkest of understanding and second in the palpable formulative and evocative power of (Michelangelo's) drawing. Both belong together and stem from the agency of the eloquent and inquestive body; both would find Kant's axiomising trite, sterile and irrelevant.

The salience of the image consists, then, precisely in its re-presentative power; it re-calls, recognises and reproduces for enduring contemplation, an event that is not only ancient but on account of its sheer violence, can only genuinely have existed for a very short time. But it is not the real or imagined correspondence between event and image that evokes; the image is rather the mediating term of an understanding that is formed in both the physical and social body. To draw or paint the crucifixion, or the sheer, unredeemed fact of death, as in *Marat,* is in a deep sense drawing's and painting's maximum point of introspection, where the act of representation faces the prospect of brute extinction and thus also the extinction of the representation for its maker. It can, as representation, only have real and transcendent power where it is given up to another, in fact, to a social order that is able to sustain its potency.

For Platonic-Christian doctrine, this potency is equivocal, apparent, illusion, Augustine's two-edged truth: at first compelling but finally false. Perhaps we have the vision but as yet not the voice to understand that whilst image and image-maker face and formulate the catastrophe of annihilation, to bequeath the image is actually to challenge this sense of mere illusion. We might resolve the contradiction by suggesting that Platonic-Christian perspectives confuse the limits of the individual and the social body by theorising only the extent of the former. To put the matter in slightly different terms, the image of the limits of the individual body is already an absolutely social representation that surpasses that limit. One may restate this kindly. One would surely not suggest (in this case) that the significance of Michelangelo was limited to his own life and exhausted at his death. Or ruthlessly: his actual death is a minor event in the significance of his work. Finally, whilst the individual may keenly feel how empty is the potency of imagery for himself, in respect of his mortality, social structure, whilst not immortal, is not limited in quite the same blunt way. Thus 'Michelangelo' is a deeply contradictory concept from a sociological point of view: both an individual and an 'institution'. Whatever may apply for the former may well not apply for the latter. [35]

Consequently, with the deepest irony and with the most unfortunate consequences, both Socrates and Christ, who perceived primarily the limits of individual mortality are amongst the most important social actors in European history. Unhappily, we persist in attending to the concrete, doctrinal sense of their pronouncements and not the ironic, analytic significance of their continued social existence in representation. Both perceived that their lives were deeply contradictory with their representations, their understandings and doctrines, but then set limits on understanding. In truth, this is the freer of the two. It was their life that was far more limited. And in a sense, each of their deaths was far more false than their own genuine attempts to theorise, for each was barbarism masquerading as justice. Similar notions may have been familiar to David:

> Under the impact of the Enlightenment the concept of eternal life in another world was giving way to one of immortality on earth: the Christian day of doom was beginning to seem less real than what Macaulay was later to call judgement at the bar of History. [36]

Marat's death was also false in the sense of unreasonable or unjust, (so we are led to understand). The image, moreover, is familiar to thousands who know little of the circumstances of either his life or his death. In a very real sense, for a significant proportion of European society, *Marat* is *simply* this enormously beautiful and potent picture. Perhaps this does not really fulfil David's aim of immortalising a man he admired and mourned as a political martyr; perhaps such connotations like so many memorials are bound to lose force as memory fades and the representation takes on a new series of interpretations. But it vastly increases both the power and the complexity of the survival of the representation beyond the life, immediate significance and intentions of (in this case) both Marat and David. Hence whilst the work is grounded in 'experience' of a highly complex and ramified, though 'located' kind, it is not bound by the formal limits of experience and certainly not by the limits of individual experience. The use of post-Kantian phenomenology could here be accused of transforming the Platonic-Christian elision of individual and social body into the confusion 'private' with 'public' life.

It is this difference (between a phenomenology of the subject and the phenomenology of intersubjectivity, which is never quite made explicit in Durkheim) which he certainly requires to justify the status he gives to the structures of intersubjective representation. Crucially, for us, this is not a matter of perspective or election but of a necessity which the intersubjective phenomenon relentlessly underscores; in the case of *Marat*, visciously.

Contrasted with the *Horatii*, it is instructive to consider what image of the masculine body is presented in *Marat*. Where the former are archetypically masculine in physiognomy, bearing and resolution, the latter is almost harrowingly gentle. There is a beautiful and touching reversal of the 'ideal' here: a loved and admired friend, a good man possessed of a tangibly soft, (no longer) warm body; the head, diminutively angled, fallen forward through the space of the picture such that it is almost pressed toward the viewer; the face so unbearably tender. It invites touch.

Where the *Horatii* are impossibly distant by virtue of the sheer scale of what they stand for and its consequent demands - Rome itself - *Marat* is fundamentally human, fundamentally close; and ironically so, for it is despite the non-humanity and distance of death. Indeed, the fact of death functions to carry him, in imagination and sentiment, into the care of the viewer.

There are several other uniquely personal emblems that have to an extent lost their force, on account their 'memorial' quality: Charlotte Corday's self-condemnatory letter and the quills and inkwells that are so much the instruments of his life. But the iconography consists of several other, far more enduring elements that relate to the intimacy of personality. These are the fact of nudity and the simple apparatus attached to the interrupted bathing of his body. It is speculative, but not idly so, that such items as the sheets, the towel around the head and the enclosure of the figure within the bathtub play an important role in the later developments, usually associated with the female figure, that one sees especially in Ingres and Degas; not forgetting that both stand in a direct line of tutelage.

Diderot argued: 'To make virtue attractive, vice odious, ridicule forceful: that is the aim of every honest man who takes up the pen, brush or chisel.' [37] We need not dispute that this idea may have been close to David's stated or conscious intentions. But a man who makes pictures like *Marat*, anyone who stages and sustains that quality of intimate physical presence, does not primarily spend his professional life on questions of morality; he is instead passionately, questioningly and formulatively involved with the life of the senses and the world of 'appearances'. David may also have held Marat in high esteem; that may also author the picture, but the realisation of the picture itself authors that, for example, that gorgeous balance between the slightness of the chest, the soft weight and disposition of the shoulders and head are far more important. Tacitly or not, David simply could not be a painter unless he accepted this authority that is intrinsic to the act of painting itself. In slightly different terms, if David claims authority as a painter, it is not vested in him as an individual, but is held jointly with the traditions, demands and critical significance of his profession. Diderot has a weak position in that he perceives his taste to be inferior to his reason and thus in many senses a distraction; David, by contrast, trusts painting and could never be a painter without that trust.

Painting as it is exemplified here, asks you to believe that representing the towel around Marat's head is more important than representing the ideas generated therein. That is perhaps an extreme formulation of a simple truth: the theoretic substance of Marat's ideas can only be engaged by writing; we are here concerned with his appearance in the context of a specific event. That event is most significant, but that too is best engaged in writing; or rather, we are here concerned with its visual significance and that finally has very little to do with his political martyrdom. It is thus no accident that this picture is received into *pictorial* tradition virtually at the expense of Marat's political standing and thus Macaulay's remarks on the 'bar of history', whilst promising, are also wide of the mark. He again implies that it is the actions of the personality, preserved in some way like the disembodied soul that are judged but we can reasonably say that Marat's example shows that it is instead the character of the representation and its continuing tradition that is at issue. And that is why Kant's reasonings, though ingenious, are completely superfluous: no *individual* act of empirical apperception is in any way involved. Similarly, (though more subtly) the life of the *image* has virtually nothing to do with, indeed in many sense directly contradicts, the supposition that it was produced or in any way sustained by David *qua individual*, except in the most residual way. David *as member* is a different story - so long as we realise that his, individual, death eventually bequeaths the substantive remains of his membership to others who will decide to deal with it according to their own will.

Of course, similar considerations apply in principle to written representations, except that we should not gloss their difference. For the moment let us say that the above remarks are in no way intended to devalue painting but rather to indicate that it desires, performs and bequeaths a wholly different function from that of writing. Had *The Death of Marat* instead been a discursive text, the qualities of the chest and the towel would have minimal significance for that tradition of representation. There are other possibilities: poetry, for example, that might coalesce visual and verbal images. But our intention is neither inventory nor formalism; we want to stress, however that to enter the web of re-presentational traditions, associations and purposes (whether as maker, viewer, critic, re-maker) with which this specific picture interacts is indeed to place towels above politics. Of course, one may then leave the gallery and go on the hustings; neither was David apolitical. For the moment, we want to stay in the gallery; neither are we apolitical.

Perhaps it would help to dispel any remaining suspicion of *moral* asymmetry (David *qua* painter being less moral than Diderot *qua* writer) if we rework that sketch as an *I-J* interaction. Consider the statement, 'Marat was a political leader.' For a writer this is entirely unproblematic. The *J* (so to speak) of his politics is everyday material to the *I* of writing in the most general and banal sense. The *J* might get a bit tougher for the *I* of political critique but finally comes down to the (relative) pragmatics of research and opinion and criticism. For painting, 'Marat was a political leader' is a complete pain on the canvas. The image is stuck with the fact that he was murdered *in the bath*. Ouch! What a requirement! O.K. What *J* do we need for the *I* of painting? What shape was his bath? Was he wearing that towel round his head? Did he fall forward or back? Can we find a model to substitute? Does a reasonable likeness exist? [38]

The *J* (of painting) couldn't be more different from the *J* (of writing), The same applies to the *I* (of painting) and the *I* (of writing) - let alone the Hollywood version or the Republicans or the monarchist supporters or more modern art students. But then David cannot - as a painter - leave out the bath; it would be inauthentic. And if the bath, then the bathroom, then the towel and the likeness and the physique (even if that so-ordinary, lovable body breaks every neo-Classical rule). [39] Even a novel would have to spend far more time

111

on *why* he was in the bath, the circumstances of the murder. How she got *in*. Whereas political critique really couldn't give a damn; it would be inauthentic to worry too much about that. The paradox is, of course: any old speaker can 'make' a painting: David's *Marat* shows the political leader murdered in the bath. It is a very moving image. You are advised you to see it. Subtext: don't bother with/ don't bother *me* (political critic) with the description. But only painters can make paintings.

This is not an argument about genius; only about differential distribution, according to circumstance, according to interest, according to purpose. Another way to say this is: painting sets up a social space that *inaugurates* the possibility of examining, combining, formulating, or better, *grounding* new kinds of information (*J*); a painter is someone who, for whatever reason, comes up with a viable *I*, or painting. It is crucial to see that the patterned complexity understood by 'painting' includes in fact and in principle the possibility of rejection essayed by artists such as Duchamp. These are the raw materials of autopoiesis, the drives and energies that engender patterned complexity. It is truly strange that we still persist in this context with formulations such as 'contingent' or 'conventional'. It is the rich determination of social phenomena, like natural phenomena, to structure themselves into different *kinds* that should really interest us. Or are thinkers too bloodless, too androgenic, too categorial to risk confronting this voluptuous unfolding?

Notes

1. See 'Sketch for a History of Being as Metaphysics' in Heidegger, M.1973 p. 65.
2. Friedlander, W. (1952) p.1.
3. ibid. See also Bryson, N. 1981. For example p.31: 'The atmosphere of the *Academie* after 1668 became fiercely linguistic.'
4. Honour, H. (1968) p.35.
5. ibid.
6. See Friedlander, W. (1952) pp. 1-12, Bryson, N. (1981) Chs. 6 & 7 and Brookner, A. (1980) pp.13-38.
7. Friedlander, W. (1952) p.7.
8. Honour 1968 p.19.
9. Fried, M. (1980). Distinguishes between 'absorption' and 'theatricality'. The latter being the condition of theatre is seemed inappropriate for painting which should not invite or appear to invite your participation, or so his argument runs. Our comments should not be read as an implicit reference to that distinction, nor as tacit support. We are not about to make reference to the distinction between absorption & theatricality on the grounds that the difference can only rest upon some version of what painting *is*. If we are not to understand that *is* as a matter of Fried's taste or desire qua

112

member, (we take it that is also not his intention) then we are again in the midst of implicit Platonism, not Sociology. The issue will be developed later and below.

10. Friedlander, W. (1952) p.35.

11. ibid.

12. This is approximately Diderot's position at least at certain points in his writing. For a fuller discussion see Bryson 1981, Chapters 6&7.

13. To re-work note 9 above: notice how the sophistic connotes ornament & destabilisation whilst absorption instead connotes criticalness, self-reflexivity, 'essential' functions or principles. For Fried, *Marat* is more absorbed (than *Horatii*) but not absorbed enough; he will find 'better' more 'essential' - not *different* - work later in the Tradition. In other words, if David's implicit commitment is sophistic, Fried's is platonic.

14. Honour, H. (1968) p.105 A series of examples of critical writing by Mengs, Reynolds and Diderot can be found in Eitner 1971, Rosemblum 1976 and Bryson 1981.

15. ibid p.106.

16. ibid p.105.

17. Kant E. (1973) p.4.

18. ibid. p.43.

19. ibid. p.88.

20. We have Cassirer in mind: 'when...I began to read Kant .my instantaneous reaction was what it has remained ever since. While perfectly ready to admire his surpassing greatness as a thinker, I felt at the same time intensely irritated partly because of the clumsiness and obscurity of his manner of writing and partly because certain of his tenets seemed to me thoroughly wrong-headed and even perverse.' Cassirer (1968) Preface p.10. Or again: '...he [should have] left alone the question of what was to be held responsible for our sensations and the state of passive responsiveness which is an essential ingredient in perceptual awareness. The issue should not have been raised at all, if only because Kant ought to have realised that he could say nothing useful about it at so early a stage of his argument.' (ibid.p.28). Having received similarly imperious comments, we can say they are invariably made by those who have completely missed the argument and are consequently reading against the grain. In case anyone is in doubt, our objections to Kant are *not at all* to do with style; his *Critique* is, for us, *conceptually* inadequate. Similarly, Kant's radical idealism is absurdly assimilated into such doctrines as Popper's notion that statements can only be falsified, never verified. This is conceptually *identical* to Kant's criterion: experience teaches us that a thing is so and so but not that it cannot be otherwise. It is equally absurd: *some* statements can be verified and those that are falsified depend absolutely on the verification of the criteria by which falsehood is decided. Popper cannot in that sense be deemed an 'advance' on Kantian critique. Kant is at least more consistent since he begins with the formal subject and formal necessity. However questionable this abstraction, it is perfectly clear that Popper as an adherent of experimental method has no grounds whatever for *his* formalism. On the contrary: in the material world of technology, statements are true or false *entirely* in the context of probability and efficacy.

21. 'Overcoming Metaphysics' in Heidegger, M. (1973) p.88.

22. ibid.

23. The credibility of Kant over Hegel and Marx is crucial. It is simply placed by Rosen: 'Hegel is frequently blamed....as one who discredited reason by claiming to much on its behalf.' Rosen (1969). Its more complex history is summed up powerfully and influentially in Lyotard's denial of credence to metanarrative as the mark of

113

postmodernity. An informative account of Kojeve's readings of Hegel and Marx and its influence on the direction of subsequent French thought can be found in Pefanis (1991). The fact remains that if Hegel-Marx are discredited, the major influences on modern critical philosophy are Kant-Nietzsche and therefore the subject's *will* to being, mediated, of course, by Heidegger's criticism of that emphasis, or better, that 'closure'.

24. Heidegger, M. (1973) pp.88-9 Note that 'essence' is not intended in the Platonic sense but as the authentic source of the possibility of thinking.

25. See Kant, E. (1973) pp.111-128.

26. The distinction marks phenomenology as practised by Husserl, Merleau Ponty, or Shutz- from the 'positivist' pragmatics of scientific method. The difference between phenomenological 'reduction' and technology's interests in efficacy is, for us, not a fundamental (or ontological) difference but a matter of strategy. See Smith, J.A. 'Three Images of the Visual: Empirical, Formal and Normative.' in Jenks, C. (1995)

27. Kant p.1967 pp. 165-6 B153.

28. That is at face value a simple tautology: the 'in itself' always contains more than is 'known'. But that is itself a formal trick. We may not, for example know 'fully' the nature of something we use or eat. But a used or surpassed or eaten 'thing' is in no position to insist that a proportion of itself has been somehow missed. The dinosaurs, for example, are extinct 'in themselves'no matter how much of their nutrient or DNA content has been recycled. Similarly Kant 'in himself'is dead and gone no matter how long his texts excite interest. The key insight is that the thing in-itself (or not) is not *specifiable* outside of its ecology and in that context is a range of *possibilities*. Crucially, these are not determined by 'itself' but by its interaction. Ecologically, the thing *in itself* can have no meaning; in the context of an evolutionary ontology the same is true. In-itself, like god-himself (literally and necessarily) belongs to a creationist mytho-ontology.

29. For an author rightly pursuing the strategy of establishing the distinctness of sociological phenomena as a *sui-generic* class perhaps our criticism is misplaced. On the other hand Durkheim offers this foonote:

    'For example that which is at the foundation of the category of time is the rhythm of social life; but if there is a rhythm in collective life, one may rest assured there is another in the life of the individual and more generally in that of the universe.....In the same way the notion of class is founded on the human group....Classes and species are natural groups of things' Durkheim (1982) p.19.

    It should be said, however, that other footnotes on the same page are confused and confusing. Suffice to say there is a case for thinking that 'sui generic' and 'things in themselves' are just too close. This will be discussed more fully in later chapters.

30. Roy Frieden, B. (1999).

31. Kant, E (1967) p. 80/B56.

32. ibid. p.82.

33. To that extent our usage overlaps with Fried's. However our intention was to emphasise difference, not to provide rules for its future course. We cannot then be concerned with 'unavoidables' like paint, canvas and supports precisely because they are utterly avoidable; or again, the weakness we address in the visuality of the Horatii does not in any way preclude the stupendous visual power of Reifenstal gathered similarly, but to vastly more sinister, political ends.

34. Honour, 1968 p.155.

35. This is our reworking of an idea familiar to the Renaissance – that art in some sense 'defeats' mortality. But, as will shortly become apparent it is less the question of persistence than that of qualitative trangression that interests us.

36. Honour, H. (1968) p.153.

37. ibid. p.80.

38. The likeness is much idealised. Brookner (1980) describes Marat as 'hideous in real life as is attested by abundant circumstantial evidence.' (p. 109) But he is not idealised in the manner of the *Horatii*. The body, its clothing (towels) and its circumstances differ from neoClassical strictures. However, we are not saying that *Marat* does away with the totality of Neoclassical conventions; merely that they are so far stretched that a different potential 'prototype' begins to declare itself.

39. Brookner (1980) writes: 'Delecluze notes that David's involvement with the political events of the Revolution caused him to 'forget' everything which he had previously learned about artistic theory and practice. In fact he did not so much forget as discard. His extraordinary subliminal sense of timing moved him out of the worlds of Winckelmann and Diderot into a situation for which there were no aesthetic as well as no political precedents.' If the absence of predicates is a reasonable position then the determinist reading of aesthetic change 'caused' by political change looks decidedly tenuous: there is insufficient time especially since the changed political 'ground' had yet to stabilise and define itself. But if both the aesthetic and the political influence each other we have a spontaneous and simultaneous autopoietic field that also generates the *difference* between the aesthetic and the political. *Nothing* asserts that this temporal relationship should persist in the same form and therefore as we argue elsewhere and below, determinism has a particularly weak notion of temporality and especially of the *future* evolution of significance. Brookner is right, we think, to insist on 'discard', not 'forget' but the clear point is: David did not discard *everything*; he remained primarily within the altered sphere of the aesthetic, rather than the altered sphere of the political, or at least this painting did and *still does*. That is why it is an *aesthetic* prototype and so is politically unstable because it essays a kind of autonomy.

6   Manet's *Olympia*

In the studies of Michelangelo and David we did not concern ourselves so much with 'theorists of art' as that might be understood in the contemporary sense. Our focus was instead the tacit *professional* undermining of neo-Platonic and neo-Classical aesthetics and so the sources for our analyses were Plato and Socrates on the one hand and on the other, what can only be called 'pragmatic aesthetics' - Cennini being arguably the most versatile pragmatist. Our other major source was Kant and in particular *The Critique of Pure Reason* which we provisionally described as a modernisation, or apparent rationalisation of something akin to the Platonic standpoint. We now turn to what must be one of most the dominant contemporary theory of art and certainly the most unified. Unquestionably, its roots are nurtured in Marxism - but long-modified by the 'cultural shift' of Habermas and Adorno and contemporary feminism and critical aesthetics. This theory - or better, school of theorists - seeks to explicate the imagery, content, manner of production of works of art through reference to their social context.[1] As we have already argued this strategy can produce the most crass reasoning summed in the statement: art is a reflection of society. It would be a scant gain to repudiate that kind of crudeness. Our focus and our protagonist will therefore be T.J. Clark and his book *The Painting of Modern Life* - chosen for its scholarship, its influence but above all, its subtlety.

Manet's *Olympia* [2] is anything but a subjectless painting. At the same time, it does not hold its subject easily; there is a tension, perceived at the time as both savage and destructive, between subject matter and the manner of representing. Jean Ravenel (Alfred Sensier, friend and biographer of Millet) described it cogently as, 'Painting of the school of Baudelaire, freely executed by a pupil of Goya.'[3] This double origin appears to describe the limits of contemporaneous criticism: there are a number of references to prostitution, to bodily decay, ugliness and so on - set against generally adverse reactions to the brutality, incompleteness or intrusiveness of Manet's 'handling'. More detail in a moment; the parameters appear as follows:

> If contemporary life was to be represented with its banality, ugliness and mediocrity undistorted, unromanticised, then the aesthetic interest has to be shifted from the objects represented to the means of representation... if the

subject..... is aesthetically indifferent, then the aesthetic significance comes to rest entirely on the style.[4]

One's immediate reaction is perhaps to dismiss this modern (1984) statement as a curious persistence of 19th Century critical prejudice; after all, the 'realist' tradition referred to here, was destined to shortly claim Impressionism as one of its consequences whose very practice (the cult of open-air landscape painting) is, unquestionably, aestheticism. Nor could one nowadays deny the beauty of *Olympia vis à vis*, say, Ingres' *Mme. Moitissier(s)*. However, on closer inspection, it turns out to be a serious argument, if perhaps on slightly different grounds to those proposed by its authors, Rosen and Zerner. But firstly the matter of detail:

References abound to ugliness: 'A sort of female gorilla, a grotesque in india rubber'[5]; to corruption: 'her body has the livid tint of a cadaver displayed in the morgue'; to dirt: 'she is a coal lady....never outraged by water'[6]; to her occupation: 'the little faubourienne, woman of the night from Paul Niquet's'[7] Clark sums up:

> It was as if the work of negation in Olympia - and some such work was surely intended, some kind of dissonant modernisation of the nude, some pitting of Baudelaire against Titian - were finally done but done somewhat too well. The new Dona Olympia was too much the opposite of Titian's for the opposition to signify much, and the critics were able to overlook those features the two pictures had in common.
>
> What the writers saw instead was some kind of indeterminacy in the image: a body on a bed, evidently sexed and sexual, but whose appearance was hard to make out in any steady way....sexuality did appear in the critic's writing but mostly in displaced form: they talked of violence...uncleanliness...a general air of death and decomoposition.[8]

In the context of Clark's writing, the terms 'modernisation' and 'indeterminacy' are crucial; they indicate his notion of the connection between the substantial reform of social relations and of painting. His argument is massively detailed - but for our purposes can be reduced, approximately, to the assertion that 'Paris' (one includes its physical and social topography) became one concrete occasion, perhaps the most 'visible', of reform in the name and interest of commodity capitalism:

> The essential separation of public life from private, and the thorough invasion of both by capital, has (had) not yet been effected. The public idiom is not standardised satisfactorily, not yet available to everyone with the price of a newspaper or this season's hat. In this sense, the 1860s are

notably an epoch of transition. The great categories of collective life - for instance, class, city, neighbourhood, sex, nation, place on the 'occupational ladder' have not yet been made into commodity form, though the effort to do so is impressive. And therefore the spectacle is disorganised, almost hybrid: it is too often mixed up with older, more particular forms of sociability and too likely to lapse back into them. It lacks its own machinery; its structures look flimsy alongside the orders and means of representation they are trying to replace.[9]

Thus the corresponding reading of *Olympia* which:

> makes hay with our assumptions as spectators ...but this negation is pictures as something produced in the social order, happening as part of an ordinary exchange of goods and services. The painting insists on its own materiality, but does so in and through a prostitute's stare, a professional and standardised attentiveness.[10]

Yet in a telling footnote we find:

> The value of a work of art cannot ultimately turn on the more or less of its subservience to ideology; for painting can be grandly subservient to the half-truths of the moment, doggedly servile and yet be no less intense. How the last fact affects the general business of criticism is not clear.[11]

But of course it *is* clear: *Olympia* is matched as 'a picture of modern life in Paris 1865' by a thousand justly forgotten paintings, drawings, newspaper illustrations, photographs, jottings, journals, songs and a thousand more antiques; but is quite unmatched as the founding of modern painting. The upshot is this: some of the concrete details of life in Paris in 1865 may be necessary, but never sufficient, conditions of Manet's project. Others are as inessential to *Olympia* qua painting as the items in our little list of curios to the tradition of modern figuration; certainly photography, certainly newspaper illustration, exerted influence: think of Degas, of Van Gogh; but it is not the fact of their dating, nor even their subject matter that is important, but painting's mediation and intervention. Differently put, influence is exerted the other way round. That is the *decisive* analytic character of re-presentation in our reading.

Of course, if one really wants to talk about Haussmann's rebuilding, the commodity form, the centrality of prostitution, then do so. But one cannot then pretend to be genuinely discussing *painting's* re-presentations, except in a secondary way. We shall not repeat the attendant arguments that appear in previous chapters. Suffice to say that if painting is the genuine subject and not simply the occasion for another, then painting is the first order and despite its size and sociologists' prejudices, society, (in this case Paris, 1860s) is necessarily the second-order mediation.

That proposition is deeply counter-intuitive for a discipline ostensibly rooted in nineteenth-century preoccupations with the priority of the material conditions of production, relations of reflection, dependence, correspondence, 'base to superstructure' - and the supposition that that the phenomenology of words can easily and transparently substitute for that of visual images, as though the difference never existed. Clark's footnote continues:

> one thing that does not follow is that viewers should ignore or deny the subservience in the hope of thereby attaining to the 'aesthetic'. It matters what the materials of the pictorial order are, even if the order is something different from the materials and in the end more important than they are.[12]

We can now see this opposition between 'materials' (or subject matter) and 'aesthetic' to be false; that is not to champion the facile formalist resolution of the subject matter in the 'primacy' of the physical attributes of painting. The issue is rather that the subject matter - in this case ostensibly a prostitute, so far as it appears in a painting at all, *always* belonged to the painting, was always subject to its mediation, always an aspect of the unity that is the painting's re-presentation.

It is simply not very important to say that the subject is a prostitute, nor to try to re-establish the context of its production as though that were central to its meaning, as though its meaning were in some way tied to a particular period of time. It is inessential because *Olympia* is not a correspondential sign but, above all, a reverberant re-presentational image around which the profession of painting has collected and established its direction(s) ever since its production. It does not matter at all that some of these directions are, or appear, mutually contradictory and the question of their greatness or feebleness rests entirely in our perception of the worth of their products. That one school of thought is persuasive or successful in no way defines *Olympia* itself; or better, such definitions - such as seeing *Olympia* as the first Modernist painting - in no way foreclose other possibilities - such as seeing *Olympia* as a highly traditionalist picture that contests neo-Classicism's claim to that tradition.

To insist that *Olympia* as sign should be in some way restored to its 'original' meaning sorely confuses the status of member and individual. It cannot be restored to Manet, the individual and his unique context, because Manet is only at issue as member, as painter; and painting does not belong to him or Paris, or 1865. Still less does it belong to eminently disputable, however scholarly, reconstructions of the period. But we cannot escape and must face the fact that *Olympia* has forced us to concede its centrality and importance for a century - and that finally has very little to with the fact that there were lots of prostitutes in Paris in 1865.[13]

It is not that we have forgotten; rather, the prostitute is re-presented *qua* 'painting', and in that her prostitution is effaced. It may be that for Paris in 1865 (or even for Manet) that effacement was not complete. Then *Olympia* was, as it were, not 'completely' a painting - or not *allowed* to be a painting; it was all too easy to allow other representations to intervene. Of course, we can (and Clark does) insist that the verbal representation, *prostitute* persists or takes precedence. But then we looking at painting as a way of representing or are we insisting that painting be represented in some other way? If the latter (and we grant the possibility - no inviolable - i.e. asocial - status is being claimed for the painting qua painting) then that is tantamount to presenting a case for displacing and replacing. It is to say that *visual* primacy and centrality of the painting's mute image should be verbally amended - 'she is a prostitute' - on the ground that its function, for example, as an informative sign is more important. That may be the case; it may be that the prostitute in Paris in 1865 is of the utmost sociological importance, far outweighing the relative 'triviality' of whether her life be represented in visual art, literature, or photography. One might turn to a text that expressed such a persuasion and expect to be enlightened on prostitution; one would not, however, expect to be enlightened on visual art, literature or photography.

We can put the matter more briefly by saying that the autopoietic possibilities opened by *Olympia's* visual silence are decisively altered by the *verbal* connotation of prostitution. It is not that the wording is blind to the image; quite the reverse in both Clark and contemporaneous criticism. It is rather that the autopoietic possibilities of *visual* silence allow one to approach the painting and *forget or efface* 'prostitution' in a way that is just not open to the verbal project of Clark's (re)contexting. This is a matter of *difference*, not of rank. Clark cannot *explain* the painting called *Olympia* however well he researches and reinstitutes other non-painting dimensions precisely because he cannot explain how the image is capable of generating entirely new 'contexts' by its interactions with other viewers and other visual work. In short, in denying *Olympia* its distinct, independent but social life, Clark is forced into an implicit proposal of 'essence and appearance': most Platonic and completely non-sociological.

Olympia's continuing centrality to painting has little to do with prostitution, or Paris, or 1865. In our view, it has everything to do with the processes of seeing and representing *through painting*. *Olympia* is important *as a painting* because it reconstructs sight. That implies that to *see*, like any other socially-organised activity has its specific decorum; *Olympia* is an intervention in that crucial set of manners.

Think the matter through in terms of the *I-J* relationship. There are at least two quite distinct sets here *I-J* (for Clark) and *I-J* (for Manet). That's before we begin to take into account *I-J* for a new reader and/or a new painter. Each is interested in quite different things and quite different orders of representation. Each stands upon a different valuation of what is at stake. Clark's interest is in persuading us of a kind of ideological causality; however complex, a kind of closure. Manet's interest is pictorial and for us rather more open. For the former, Manet's interest in Spanish painting is either an aberration or a question of fashion, which begs the same question. For the latter, the stylistic possibilities of Goya and the rejection of modern French Neoclassicism is crucial. For us, the entire object of interest is the autopoiesis of the difference; not because we want to pretend a greater democracy or sensitivity but because of the theoretic imperative of *inclusion*. In other words, Clark *has* to leave out Goya because there's no real place for him in the model of ideological causation. That is, we claim a better model even if, as is certainly the case here, we cannot intensively pursue the patterned complexity that it illuminates.

Olympia may be a prostitute, she may have outraged Parisians on that account, but these finally are words and categories. It is far more important that the picture has bite as a visual image, and in many ways the critics who pointed up the sense of dirt, decay, disease are perceptive, if prone to exaggeration. It is, in contrast with its predecessors, explicit and intrusive, aggressively sexual where its contemporaries often portrayed nudity sweetly and coyly. Of course, such renditions carry codified sexual signals, in the pose, the texture, the events, but Olympia transcends all of this. It is tremendously frank, enormously challenging, not simply in the 'shamelessly flexed hand', nor the directness of her gaze, but in the weight and physical presence of the body and above all in that we (still) perceive all of this 'action' to take place in a recognisable social setting that we ourselves might encounter. This is the essential difference from the peculiar mix of nudity and history-painting that was then current; their ancient or mythic time simply does not claim and disturb our attention so urgently. Doesn't this re-instate Clark's position? No, because what is remarkable is not a series of correspondencies that can be verbally documented, dated, and dispensed with when their time is over, but instead the willingness of a reflexive tradition of visual representation to engage and re-engage the contingencies of its own (and by implication) our - social environment. We are here speaking of the diametric opposite of the 'perfect type of the human figure' or of the suppression of the 'living and accidental' that characterises neo-Classicism. This commitment is far more plausibly seen as the repudiation of neo-Classical decorum.

Is it not reasonable, then, to concede Rosen and Zerner's point: Manet's position reforms 'sight' in such a way that it no longer selects but frankly accepts its environment and the aesthetic interest consists primarily in the *performance* of representation? Can't the image of the prostitute be partly taken as a mark of a 'debasement' of the eye, that once claimed to see beyond the 'shadows of the natural'; the virtuosic but unconcealed handling a resignation to the fact that manual technique is the sole real manipulative agency in a material world that the eye must itself accept and be swept along on the tides of fate?

The answer lies, we think, not as Rosen and Zerner propose in a shift in the concept of the visual from the willed and 'aesthetic' to the correspondential and 'natural', nor as Clark implicitly suggests, from the 'traditional' to the rational, economic or 'commodity' form, again based upon the presumption of a correspondence to social life not unlike Science's 'observer'. It lies instead in an altered conception of the natural but on that account is no less an act of intervention, of will, or of the aesthetic, and is in no way severed from these dimensions. So we must re-phrase our point above: 'repudiated decorum' should read: 'qualitatively different decorum; otherwise we shall only see (Manet's) Modernism as a *lack* of (e.g. Ingres') neo-Classicism. The question is, then, what sense of nature is at work? What sense of decorum or ornament?

It must be conceded that Manet's figuration seeks to correspond with its world in a manner that is both affirmative of that aim and contemptuous of neo-Classicism's repudiation of the contingent, ephemeral, imperfect, fashionable: top hats, elegant dresses, steam trains, balloons, night clubs, bars, waitresses, prostitutes and dandies replace the characters and moral claim of history-painting; in the place of highly wrought portraiture stands a paint surface sometimes frankly incomplete, sometimes disgustingly oily, sometimes wonderfully virtuosic, usually ambiguous, always evident.

What has happened to the Classical rhetorician's desire to convince or delight through ornament, to the grace of the artist? What has become of his ability to assess and criticise the imperfections of appearance? Hasn't an ideology curiously balanced between Platonism and Sophistry simply collapsed into an equally ideological, manifestly unstable collision of artist and scientist such that the greatest artist will be a camera and photography will be standard by which painting will be judged? (Aided and abetted of course by careful inventory of the social conditions to which the photo-painting once corresponded).

The answer is perfectly obvious. *Olympia* is not a prostitute, nor a photograph of a prostitute, nor even a 'picture' of a prostitute; that usage is simply too loose. It is a painting (possibly) of a prostitute, certainly of a woman whose sexuality provokes, connotes, issues of that kind. But these are things we *know*, independently of its being a painting and as a painting it shuts out all further inquiry. *It is not relevant* (unless you have other business) who she is, where she lives, what she's like, how much she charges. You are instead brought up abruptly against the fact that this connotative image, framed placed on the gallery wall, gorgeously composed and coloured is itself the ornament; it is indissolubly a painting. At that realisation, all thought of correspondence and inventory, science and cameras, falls away.

As a painting of a prostitute, taken as a single unity it raises (at least) three crucial questions: What version of painting's tradition and project does it exemplify? What relation does it bear, how does it mediate, this specific subject matter? What arguments, if any, does it advance for the worth and purpose of painting? These questions are, of course, the specific outcome of the earlier, general question concerning nature and decorum; the form of decorum is here painting itself; and 'nature' constitutes its subject matter.

As far as Manet's tradition and project are concerned, a number of general perspectives exist. To the extent that they differ, there is still remarkable agreement as to his dislike of the then current Academy and, conversely, his affirmation of Baudelaire. Whilst there is further acknowledgement of his debt to Spanish painting, there is then little cogent discourse on the difference between the two traditions represented here. Ironically, then, his espousal of older Spanish influences is taken as an aspect of his Modernism. The discursive lack is that we do not address why Manet found an older Spanish tradition (amongst other influences) preferable, or more pointedly, superior to the French. To say that Spanish painting was in some way more amenable to the representation of modern life (as our critical reticence implies) is an ironic charge that simply blows apart ordinary conceptions of the relations between art and social order. To say that Manet rejected his immediate tradition on the grounds of its obsessions with history (whilst he preferred the modern) is to leave the matter to differences of taste. How then is our taste so unanimously in favour of Manet?

The whole matter resounds with the characteristic imprecision of the *amateur* whose 'job' consists in imagining and collecting. Manet's job is surely much more decisive and certainly more limited; he *has* to make choices. He can be reasonably taken as saying that the *Academie*, history-painting, is a corruption of painting, where Velasquez is not; that the *Academie* produces non-art, where Goya makes great art. He cannot, like the *amateur*, square the presence of even an Ingres portrait in the same 'set' as his own. He *must* be a visual polemicist. The question that critics, historians and sociologists politely leave out is whether we agree. One can see why (and it runs to the very centre of the distinction between artist and *amateur*) because our agreement or disagreement involves a formulation of what painting ought to be. Moreover, so far as we address 'painting' as an aspect of the division of labour, this moral question at least involves painting's relationship to its social world and, by implication, the status of representation in its generality.

Recall David's *Horatii* and the images of self-sacrifice in war it represents. We shall not repeat earlier arguments except to say that no convincing, specific self and hence no sacrifice appears. Set that against Goya's series of etchings, *The Disasters of War*, and despite their caricature-like quality, it would be an insensitive viewer indeed who did not respond to absolutely specific, tangible horror and cruelty they depict. And yet, in a far more extreme version of the same issue present in *Olympia*, they were made to be exhibited on a gallery wall. For anyone who has actually seen this series presented together in the original, the tension between the graphic means and the significance of the issues represented is awesome. They are magnificent as etchings, tremendously inventive in the use of the medium's tonal possibility, marvellously interesting and vivacious in line - and relentlessly intrusive, tangible, nauseating. To the extent that such representations, whether Goya's etchings or memorials to the Holocaust, are intended to make permanent an issue that is in itself sporadic and finally forgettable, the *Disasters of War* fulfil this function absolutely. They are entirely unforgettable.

Perhaps David's 'restraint' could be called false. Perhaps its omissions are actually both cynical and manipulative. Perhaps, however, it is at times important for a society to systematically forget the destruction and mutilation of its members for some greater good: the war against Nazism would be a fair example. David's restraint might be thought to function in that manner. But that moral dilemma is here less important, or better, less extensive than the moral status of representation, for David's tradition requires that we leave out the imperfect, contingent and specific: there is no 'neo-Classical' way that Goya's subject matter or handling can exist *at all*. The *Disasters of War* are in a deep sense invisible to neo-Classicism in precisely the same sense that painting is uninteresting to Augustine and that the *Republic*, for Plato, is second-order, derivative and illusory. This means that to the extent that neo-Classicism persists in Platonic-Christian beliefs that portray the specific order of the mundane world as disorder, and so far as its implicit Sophism cannot overcome this characteristic, it is radically impossible to represent the mundane in either word or picture. Despite its apparent clamour, the ordinary and finite is, for neo-Classicism, finally not visible and not audible. One intends this analytically, of course; David, for example, made studies of the victims of the Revolution; but it is no less binding on that account. The invisibility and inaudibility rather consist, concretely, in having to turn away (as Michelangelo did from portraiture); analytically, in grasping the appearance and the sound of finitude as incoherent reflections and shadows of *another* form. Goya's position and Manet's affirmation allows mundane social order to represent itself through painting, to look at and see itself, to formulate its own visual and social coherence. This is, for us, the decisive moral superiority inherent in Manet's invocation of the Spanish tradition over the French. The *Academie*, on the other hand, invited the practice of an Art that is close to worthless because it had ruled in advance that it was, in principle, unable to represent its own society. Now this is a perhaps over-radical proposition and carries with it the danger of providing a simple rule whereby the whole of neo-Classicist representation can be critically ignored. The proposition points to a central difficulty in neo-Classicism; *however* it cannot *define* neo-Classical painting - which owes so much of its possibility to Sophistic rhetoric. Nor can any such axiom substitute for detailed critique. Michelangelo will remain great, though perhaps for reasons other than divine grace.

It is important to concede, however, that Manet was prepared to be radical, was prepared to shift the type and handling of his subject matter, was prepared to argue that his notion of the possibility of representation was superior to that of history painting. His champion, Baudelaire was also unreticent:

> There are many kinds of beauty and since all centuries and all peoples have had their beauty, so inevitably we have ours. The

Academic schools have denied this, for they have a strong interest in ceaselessly depicting the past. But in their love of general beauty they have neglected particular beauty, the beauty of circumstance.[14]

What is beautiful about the disasters of war? Nothing - but then Goya did not exhibit a mutilated corpse - or at least if he had, the subsequent reporting, in words and pictures would be infinitely more important than the stinking flesh. Damien Hirst uses formaldehyde to similar effect. In either case, the issue is never one of actual correspondence but rather of inflections within the social order of representation. Or, the persistence, modification and construction of representation is of infinitely greater importance than some set of data to which they may once have roughly corresponded. To underscore an earlier argument: the limits set about the physical conditions of an event's occurrence and its direct observation are radically different from those set about its socially-organised representation and dissemination.

It may be that, then, Manet invokes a Spanish tradition more sensitive to circumstance, but that is not to say that it is dependent upon events. It is crucial to see that the *Disasters of War* is more important as an active indictment of war's consequences and an attempt to keep them (re)present(ed) in he public mind long after the event or even that form of warfare has disappeared. To say that the etchings match an event is to miss the point; to say they 'record' the events is better; to understand that 'recording' arrests, intervenes, shapes and determines the temporal chain for intersubjective purpose is essential. Consequently, Manet's/ Baudelaire's postulation of the moral superiority of so-called Modernism over the *Academie* was not that it passively matched events, but on the contrary that it could represent modern life and so share in bringing it visibly under the sway of intersubjective purpose. Ironically, it was Classicism that was passive *vis à vis* the mundane and the modern because it was no part of its project to represent it. We may now move to the second question, that of specific subject matter.

Clark approaches *Olympia* sensitively from several directions but with obvious unease:

> The achievement of Olympia..... is that it gives its female subject a particular sexuality, as opposed to a general one. And that particularity derives....not from there being an order to the body on the bed but from there being too many, and none of them established as the dominant one.[15]

> (Hers)....is not a look which is generalised or abstract or evidently 'feminine'. It appears to be blatant and particular, but it is also

unreadable........It is candid but guarded, poised between address and resistance - so precisely that it comes to be read as a production of the depicted person herself......it is her look, her action upon us, her composition of herself.[16]

A few pages further on he inserts a footnote describing Bataille's argument with Valery:

given over to absolute nudity, she makes one think of all the remnants of primitive barbarism and ritual animality which lurk beneath the routine of prostitution in great cities.

This (from Valery) is contested by Bataille:

It is possible (though questionable) that in a sense this was initially the text of Olympia but this text is a separate matter from the woman.... the text is effaced by the picture. And what the picture signifies is not the text, but the effacement......what she is, is the 'sacred horror' of her own presence - of a presence as simple as absence. Her hard realism ....consists in the painter's determination to reduce what he saw ...to the mute simplicity of what he saw.[17]

Clark comments: '...vision for Bataille is always wrapped up in some such complex act against meaning.'[18] This argument is important and deserves more than relegation to a footnote; it manifestly deserves more than Clark's dismissal: 'Whatever else one might want to say of this criticism, it has little to do with the simpler narratives of modernist art history.'[19]

Manet and Baudelaire have proposed a reform that apparently allows a representative project for the modern painter but its commitment to 'particular' beauty also involves a quite savage demonstration of painting's own particularity, especially the fact that it is not discursive. The notion of 'particularity', which first appears to be a relatively simple reform of subject matter, turns out to be dialectic that is potentially reflexive upon both the subject and the means of representation. Perhaps unfortunately, it is also capable of, and in many senses actually calls for, so striking a demonstration of pictorial means that its fictive project is undermined.

It is essential to see that the 'realist' potential (understood in the sense of representative intervention in modern life) is actually coextensive with the formalist potential of demonstrating the reality of the various means of representing. Or to use perhaps more current but to us less useful terms, the confusion between modernity and modernism should be seen as a unity simply because the latter is a topicalisation of representation as an aspect of the former, in the form of then-current (painters', writers') practices.

Moreover, the distinction between verbal and visual forms of representation is here quite fundamental. Because discourse cannot be separated from meaning, the most we can do is disrupt the sense we have established. Painting, on the other hand, is absolutely visible as an object and as such can completely severed from meaning. That is why Bataille's argument is important: because it hits on an issue that is intrinsic to painting. On the other hand, whilst meaning as 'reference to' can be effaced from painting, meaning as *intention* cannot. Consequently, painting as 'object' finally has little to do with its physical components because they are second-order mediations of a socially organised project. That point is lost on the critical descendents of Maurice Denis who begin with the notion that a painting is 'essentially' a plane surface and proceed to claim a greater truth for the 'real' materials over the 'illusions' of (say) pictorial space. The 'essential' is rather the decision that demarcates such a plane as an occasion for the practice of painting; and the materials of that decision are certainly not physical but are social.

Bataille's argument can be understood on a further level: contrasted with Clark, the critics of 1865, and possibly Manet, possibly Baudelaire, who insist on the importance of Olympia's being a prostitute, he says that for him that connotation is far less important than the 'mute simplicity' of what the painter saw. To see this as an act against meaning, given the argument above, is somewhat limited. To see painting, as Bataille implicitly does, as an act against verbal and correspondential meaning is quite another. One may search in vain for any irreducible coding of the category 'prostitute' in the painting but it is not there; Manet's intention is far less explicit than (say)Vermeer's in *The Procuress*; and the tradition that springs from and cites him as origin is arguably far more concerned with surface and process, rather than prostitution. So this path threatens to end with uncertainty as to his specific mediation of this subject: on the one hand 'it is *her* look, her *action* upon us'; on the other, 'she' is primarily an occasion for 'making marks'.

The issue, we suggest, can be resolved, though in no way does that produce simplicity, by realising that the relationship between the handling, the seeing and muteness is an essential one. At the risk of breaking the unity of the painting, we want to treat that question in sections that correspond to the stages of production and the various parts of the picture.

Arguably first stands the question of the pose. The derivation from Titian is reasonable enough, though the model ends up higher in the painting, more central and closer to the viewer. The frankness of the look is arresting; unlike the Titian, it is unmodified by a diminutive curve of the neck. The result is bolder, perhaps less alluring, certainly tinged with an open-eyed sadness where the Titian is insinuating. Beyond that, a body both 'on display' and in repose. Mattresses and pillows serve to emphasise both luxury and the palpability of her body, its weight, its points of contact and to set a cool key that plays up the warmth of the body tones. The whole is surrounded by near-black colours that make up half the picture; other items later.

It is *her* look. Does she look at you as a prostitute? You say yes. So what? What next? Its all finished with and either you do or don't approve of its being on a gallery wall but the next step, if there is a next step, will involve discourses on prostitution, women, class etc. The painting qua painting will be over. But Manet didn't write *Olympia* nor is he exhibiting the sexual process, paid for or not. But he *is* exhibiting the process of seeing, not 'in general', but in and through *painting this* woman. May we suggest that there is rather more to see once you accept the (to us incontestable) fact that this disturbing gaze is literally that exchanged between the painter and model? Of course that carries erotic overtones. At some other time, perhaps? But if critics cannot see that 'what he's doing to her', here, in this picture is painting her, then we cannot see any point in either painting or prostitution (unless painting is one of those 'adult games').

Olympia, in this sense, is disturbingly 'visible'. The harsh, illuminated isolation in a claustrophobic void of near-blacks adds to this; it concentrates the project of looking at her. She is disturbingly 'only' visible: there is no trace of conversation, only a gaze that responds to the matter-of-fact business of measuring, drawing, brushing on colours. One looks at a woman who has been posed and arranged for that purpose; she, the painter, and by implication you the viewer, have agreed to limit your relation to this. It is a crushing limit. One suspects that the speed with which critics reach for an alternative discursive dimension indicates how little they value it. It is also an intense limit: it draws the processes of seeing and representing to enormous heights of consciousness.

It is mute. Manet 'says' nothing (about prostitution) when he chooses the white, blue-grey range for the linen. But he thus allows himself that delicate range of grey-violet and yellow-white for the skin; contrasted with the blues it still appears warm without recourse to those overblown pinks one finds in (say) Ingres. Nor have we any doubt that the key that determined this scheme was the model's own colouring.

130

Similarly, the choice of so much black may suggest the mood of the brothel. Conveniently, it also allows the suggestion of enormously high illumination of the body and yet another way of contrasting and describing its contours. Thus the hair dissolves ambiguously into darkness, allowing two readings, long or short, whilst the orchid flames in contrast. The contours of the left arm and thigh soften into the deep browns, whilst the legs are brilliantly lit and defined. On the right hand side, body-contour is defined in relation to material, either linen or the coloured shawl, and runs in and out of ambiguity as it is variously covered and exposed.

The greatest passage, however, remains the extraordinary line that demarcates the left breast and the curve of the stomach from the left arm, plunges down to constitute the thumb, moves rhythmically on to establish the flexed fingers, then to define the overlap of the legs. Here Manet revels in the characteristic ways that painting represents: the simple play of dark and light forcing the canvas to recompose its flat self as image, but constantly touching the tension between the two. Above all, the drawing of this line is so right; it produces contour and space and such tellingly correct proportion that it is through and through erotically charged.

Surely this raises the notion of correspondence yet again. Yes and no. Yes - because the attempt to draw the model faithfully, accurately is paramount; none of the geometricising tendencies of Ingres or Goya's caricature are present. No - because these lines and others are first established only in this painting. We do not mean they are merely a new juxtaposition, consequent on the pose. We mean that Manet's painting made this line visible in this way for the first time; it is a consequence of his pictorial concerns. 'Correspondence' is a subsequent possibility. This is crucial generally for 'modernist' figuration: the attempt, variously expressed, to paint 'what one sees' is misunderstood as a simple one-to-one approximation. On the contrary, its very novelty, urgency and moral claim lies in the sense that these things have not yet genuinely been seen; they are there, to be seen but they have not yet been subject to the processes of representation (whether in word or picture); they are thus 'visible' but the act of seeing has not been questioned, developed, educated, by representing; they are not yet socially organised.

Of course this is also why the simple notions of correspondence and the passive observer are generally of no use to us; if representation were not a defining, refining, deepening organising and collectivising process, we would still be primitives, organised by instinct. In truth, that simple idea may be valid to a very rudimentary biology; it cannot have any sociological significance from the moment 'observation' has any social history or tradition. Manet's achievement is to bring certain 'new' phenomena under the sway of that organisation. Does that re-activate the notion of the gifted individual? No - because however brilliant and original a painter Manet was, his 'genius' consists in the invocation and reform of tradition; his genius is that of reflexive member and that surely must be an essentially sociological concept.

One of the interesting modifications he makes concerns the relationship between colour and form. It had been common (neo-Classical) practice to think of a form as having a certain hue, more or less modified by tonal value. Whilst this describes, for example, the way Ingres organised colour, it owes its coherence as a recognisable practice as much to the Impressionists' opposition as it does to predecessors' clear intentions. Nevertheless, the suppression or restriction of local colour (again an instance Impressionist critical hindsight rather than design) tends to produce spatial difficulties along the margins where colours meet.

For us, *Olympia* both draws upon the greater strength of Velasquez in respect of spatial organisation. The essential difference between Velasquez and (for example) Ingres is that the latter is set about by the ideology of the perfect and so is apt to suppress local colour variation, the incidents of handling and 'soft imprecision' as accidental and undesirable. Similarly, his insistence on the precedence of drawing over painting suggests perhaps that he prefers the graphic medium, but certainly regards colourism as in some way also the medium in which the accidental and degenerate thrive. Thus *Moitissier* (seated) is flawlessly enamelled but spatially chaotic.[20] Velasquez seems content to brush on a certain shape and colour, to work wet into wet, with immense plasticity and transparence, rejoicing in both the visibility of his action and the sheer malleability of the form-building process. The result is a willingness to 'through-compose pictorial space, leaving in full view the traces of that process, and in that relation, the ostensible 'guilt' of deep, illusionistic space becomes a non-issue: the display of means is such that there simply is no break between the actual graphic, two-dimensional mark and its spatialised images. Ingres' procedure is, by contrast, clumsy, cumulative and inventoristic.

Manet's achievement lies in using the simple, malleable regions or large shapes (the body, the bed, the darkness) that are characteristic of Velasquez's composition process and in being willing to work into and keep open the relationships. Similarly, the handling process is kept in full view. The result is a space that is somewhat shallower but certainly more consistent than Ingres'. (One would not want to claim that for all Manet's

132

painting.) The sense of the weight of the body on the bed, the volume of mattress and pillows and the spatial cohesion of the parts of Olympia's body is marvellously sustained. And the colour truly sparkles in the shawl and the flowers

The flowers, whether on the shawl, in the bouquet or in the hair, serve to lift the total mood and key. But what of the black woman? No doubt the cream of the dress is a compositional and textural device that is supposed both to continue the colour-range of the body into a new shape that occupies the black void on the right, and to set off the differences in substance and drawing. Why is she black? To avoid two competing heads, such that Olympia's look is the absolute focus.[21] But the black maid *did* exist.

A truly wonderful painting, one of the greatest pictures of the European tradition, and indeed one of the few occasions where the female body is the true subject. (The problem of the cat we leave to you.)

We believe its status to rest on the qualities we have described but it is arguable that many painters found the frankness of its handling more important than its creation of form. Manet himself seems to vacillate between an almost destructive emphasis on surface and the full space we see in his larger pictures. It may be that he regarded his smaller pictures as sketches and it is certain that some of his lesser work (think of the National Gallery's *Man in a Blue Smock*) is utterly unresolved. Of course it is rather hard to call Manet 'unfinished' since that is precisely the position of the critics of 1865 occupied, and subsequent developments (to say the least) question their judgement. It is even harder to admit the weakness of *Man in a Blue Smock when* the 'value' (in both senses) is determined by its historic rather than its aesthetic significance.

Let us compromise and say that 'Manet as represented in the Galleries' - which does not necessarily coincide with his judgement, or even 'good' judgement - is extremely inconsistent. And yet it is the mark, the high colour and not the space that consistently excites many of his descendents. Think of Degas' pastels, and Impressionism generally. The import of 'space' as a preoccupation seems to lapse until Cezanne. But that precedence does not close the issue: it is, in principle, possible for successful painting and criticism to re-assess Manet's significance.

It is in this context that we must raise the next question - of the worth and purpose of the painting exemplified in *Olympia* - for the project of representing that is evident there, seems to be partly closed by his descendents. Manet, in *Olympia*, but not in his lesser paintings, seems to give himself over to both subject and to painting such that there is no break, no guilt, no embarrassment, no question of rank, but a fruitful give and take that also frankly admits the limits of that relation between painter and model. His followers, to be sure, invent new possibilities of subject matter - like the Impressionist landscape - but somehow the suggestion grows that any subject is, in absolute truth, merely the occasion for painting. Thus occurs a matter of analytic rank and with it a moral duty: painting 'itself' is the one true subject and should be shown as such.

To say that this kind of position is first formulated by Zola [22] is perhaps to claim too much: the idea of the 'subjectless' painting was inherent in Romanticism and of especial interest - in our view, destructively so - to Delacroix,[23] and there have always been painters for whom the visible processes of painting deserve the highest possible rank. Nevertheless, Zola seems to have made current this approach to Manet in the face of then-current objections to 'immoral' subject matter. Equally, where Delacroix's solutions seem stale and reductive, Manet offers a development of both the range of subject matter and the character of its handling. In this sense, it is hard to see who would stand as an heir to Delacroix, while those who claim to be Manet's are legion.

It is not, then, the formal proposition of this strange notion of 'painting itself' that excited interest but the way Manet accomplished it. It is thus hugely ironic that the claims of what is correctly seen as formalism lie in Manet's establishing a successful, concrete idiom for its expression. Zola's comments thus help unleash an ironic, at times almost comical series of events, which includes much of the greatest Art of the 19th and 20th Centuries.

Detail of Zola's position will be kept to a minimum, because the principle advanced, in the sense above, is always less than the idiomatic, pictorial solution. We should understand, for example, that the 'shockingly' nude woman between the clothed men in *Dejeuner sur l'Herbe* derives only from the needs of colour, design, composition. Whilst one might accept that as a faintly bizarre reading of the *Dejeuner*, one could not accept it as a reading of 'Olympia'. Nevertheless, a truly important issue arises: to say that Zola's formalism explains *Olympia* inadequately is quite different from saying that one's relation these formal aspects is more important than one's relation to the subject matter.

Degas' pastel, *After the Bath* [24] underscores this difference savagely: it can readily be understood as the visual assertion that not only Manet's critics but Manet himself were mistaken about *Olympia*, that the painterly trace was by far the most important thing. The pastel medium, the size of the marks in relation to the scale, the resolution of the calligraphic trace itself, set against the irresolution of the bather's body, the complete precedence of two dimensions over three, all add to this sense. One might take this as a difference of emphasis and then argue that despite the need to achieve and approve a practice called 'painting' for various social purposes, this definition is traditionally open and permissive: Degas does not so much oppose but rather stands beside Manet as an artist of somewhat different intentions.

We admire the Degas; we have no wish to make a choice; no desire to construct a hierarchy. But faced with the need to construct painting, whether concretely or analytically, we are again bound by the difference between the amateur and the artist, the amateur and authentic criticism. And in the light of this requirement we must argue that the Manet is the greater and for several reasons.

Notice how quickly the attempt to engage the problem of 'seeing modern life' is reduced to a repetition of the bravura mark, the calligraphic trace. This is true both of this Degas and the lesser Manets. We do not say that there is nothing else in the Degas. We do say that it threatens to replace the representative process with one of presentation, so that what is available is not the outcome of having looked, but merely the presence of the physical trace of the hand working the pigment. That seems to us to leave the question of the social organisation of vision completely in abeyance. With horrible irony, the modern thus allies himself with the history painter by saying that the substance of modern life is not the genuine subject, whilst both prefer instead 'what painters do', being the various debased and idiomatic forms of 'painting itself'. On this reading, the moral claims of Manet's-Baudelaire's sense of outward-looking modernism have been reduced to a relatively fixed idiom, a series of ritual moves that, providing 'unique' traces, stand for 'particular beauty' but avoid having to deal with it. They are *codified* recognitions that the concept of 'particular beauty' might be a good idea (at least better than history painting) but formal recognition is as far we will take the project. In this sense, the Degas is the very opposite of *Olympia*, but no more so than the lesser Manets. Both threaten to overwhelm the open visual inquiry called *painting* with a codification closer to words and horribly susceptible to ritual or dogmatic limitation.

The opposition might be presented as a failure to balance subject with means of representation and thus merely an exacerbation of a tension inherent in *Olympia*. At first sight straightforward and plausible, this argument turns out to be an oversimplification that produces false parameters. In the first place it assumes the viability of the view that Manet's synthesis of subject and 'means' is in fact 'tense' when, by implication, some other synthesis is *not* tense. It is rather hard to fill in concrete examples of this analytic 'not tense' relationship: certainly neither David nor Ingres fit the bill. We thus tend to fall back to mediocre academic, the uninspired so-called 'realist' as our example. Not surprisingly, then, criticism post-Manet is full of references to seemingly transparent work in both painting and literature that the eye and the mind 'passes right through' without once noticing the activity of representation. This is, of course, nonsense: the creaking devices of painters' craft is never more apparent than in academicism; indeed, the academic often presents his realism as honest craftsmanship, (against the pretensions of the avant-garde). Nevertheless, one is not supposed to notice 'the business'; oddly, we generally comply.

Consequently, when Manet's handling shouts loudly enough to make everyone notice (and believe they are *supposed* to do so), a little chain of events slips into place without anyone really wanting it, genuinely believing it, or reflecting upon it. The academic's painting is bad; his handling is 'invisible'. Manet's painting is good; his handling is visible. Good painting has visible handling. Dare we argue that the crass proposition - very good painting has very visible handling - has operated as a central critical notion?

Perhaps that goes a little too far. We are not really that bad at looking at art, are we? Then let us simply agree that Impressionists' handling is more visible and frank than ...What? Yes it is horribly difficult to fill in a name; and we know that any half-decent examination of a more traditional landscape will come away bursting with visible devices. And yet we will still agree the Impressionists are more frank, more visible, more inclined to draw attention to painting *qua* painting, and certainly not asking for their marks to be 'transparent'. If that position is not already tenuous enough, let us try to draw it over the edge of its absurdity.

Without wishing to engage in a discourse on Impressionism that is beyond our scope, it is nevertheless generally conceded that they were, amongst other things, specifically concerned with the transitory colour and movements of light. Their very name, first applied as an insult, suggests a willingness to accept the impact of the ephemeral and not to try 'complete' the image in a form that looked somehow permanent and free of circumstance. This might be seen as a refutation of Reynolds' cumulative Classicism, cited earlier. In one sense, then, their method at least implicitly claims greater 'neutrality' than (we shall again leave that open). How does neutrality square with the frank demonstration of painting *qua* painting? Not at all.

But it is *not* neutral; *qua* painting it is a *mediating* process. Then what does it seek to mediate, to see, to reflect upon? The transitory effects of light, etc. So might we not more cogently solve the riddle of the nameless artist who organises his practices perhaps somewhat along Reynolds' lines but whose procedures are invisible, unless we look; and the perplexingly frank Impressionist (who apparently has nothing more than a camera has to be frank about) by saying that the difference rests rather on what is topicalised.

In other words, Impressionism comes out like it does because its subject is somewhat different; its painting is different because it is painting a different range of phenomena. It is far more convincing (more 'transparent', if you like) as a rendition of light than many of its predecessors. By the same token, they are more 'complete' in the various special idiomatic senses that belong to an art that is never completely the same as its subject, whose truth is illusion. (We have seen several different such idioms in Michelangelo, David, etc.) This is not surprising when that is precisely what they aimed to do.

Manet's predecessors' handling is perfectly visible but differs from his. If the processes were truly not visible, neither would be the image they construct. This difference is qualitative and not quantitative: the forebears do not *lack* Manet. More importantly perhaps, neither does Manet lack his descendents. This finally is the failing of the formalist position: that to diminish the importance of subject matter directly falsifies the means of representation by suggesting it is somehow independent, or worse, that it belongs to some *quantitative* continuum.

Then what is the worth and purpose of painting as exemplified in *Olympia*? We suggest again that it presents the relationship of painter to model, that is, to *subject,* as a frank limitation of each to the practices of painting; whose sole use consists in the reflexive and formulative contemplation of what one can see: the social organisation of sight via the mediation of painting. It tries to see, and in so doing accepts the manifest social complexity of that act.

Notes

1.   The contexts of art's production are interesting, not least because they fade more rapidly than specific works. This school of thought once dubbed 'the new art history' is essentially a restorative enterprise. This and later chapters will focus on the ontological complexity involved in enduring, fading, restoring, re-animating.
2.   *Olympia*, Musee d' Orsay, Paris.
3.   Ravenel in Clark, T.J.(1985) p.88.
4.   Rosen and Zerner (1984) pp. 149-150.

5.   Clarke, 1985 p.94.
6.   ibid. p.96.
7.   ibid. p.88.
8.   ibid. p.96.
9.   ibid. p.64.
10.   ibid. p.80.
11.   ibid. p.78.
12.   ibid.
13.   Clark's detailed accounts of the reconstruction of Paris and the renewed cultural place of the prostitute form the major part of his text. This is hardly surprising but it still does not concede that many others have found Manet significant for quite other reasons. (See for example 'Greenberg's Notion of Competence' below.) This obvious lack and a proper treatment of the problem is more often than not hidden behind a political correctness that treats other options as reactionary or badly-informed. However, even Clark can no longer sustain the conceit that neo-Marxism is correct. Hence his latest title: *Farewell to an Idea*.
14.   Cited in Gay, P (1976) pp.88-9.
15.   Clark, 1985 p.132.
16.   ibid. p.133.
17.   ibid. pp.137-8.
18.   ibid. p.138.
19.   ibid. p.139.
20.   See Bryson (1984) pp.171-5.
21.   For those persuaded by the need to reconstruct Paris 1865 as a prerequisite for addressing this painting - yes, there was an identifiable black woman servant that might be taken as candidate for this portrait. Presumably there were also white ones.
22.   See Hamilton, G.H.(1969) pp.81-87.
23.   cf. Rosen and Zerner 1984 p.163.
24.   *After the Bath* National Gallery, London.

7   Duchamp's Intervention

A decisive turning point now occurs in our analysis, so a review of the position so far is appropriate. However, this simple mapping should not substitute for the necessary complexity of the argument to this point. We began with an outline of the several senses in which (for example) Lyotard's concept of pluralism contained unintended and mutually-negating consequences. We argued against what we saw as the prevailing descriptions of social phenomena as either *unified* or *arbitrary*. We were persuaded that a theory of interactive, patterned complexity provided a better model and that this model was fundamentally *autopoietic*. From that formal position we began a more concrete focus on the troubled relations between Platonism and neoClassicism as aesthetic and counter-aesthetic doctrines on the one hand and the disruptions caused by visual images on the other - images, which were ostensibly 'suggested' by and under the auspices of neoClassicism, but set up crucial patterns of interference and at least potentially opened up a new and further layer of complexities within the manifold of social phenomena. These were not, we suggested, simply nuances or variations but specific, new images of community which could not be 'voiced' within neoPlatonic or neoClassical discourse.

The images we chose in particular were Michelangelo's *Crucifixions* and David's *Marat* both taken as visual images formulated because of and despite the visual idioms and doctrines of neoClassicism - or because of and despite those artists' other work and beliefs. That is to say the disjuncture is itself autopoietic. A pre-existing set of idioms is an essential component, confronted by events - such as the crucifixion of Christ, the murder of Marat, their religious and political significance - and the response of artists raised in but eventually not bound by neoPlatonism or neoClassicism.

A further image, the Kantian 'subject', was rejected partly on logical grounds. And that his (or any) *general* definition of subjective experience cannot account for the complexities of discrete instances of experience, shared experience amongst contexted humans or the possibility of shared conceptualisations with other species. We said that the Kantian subject could not have evolved and could not evolve *into* 'membership'. Or, events, people and their significance do not collect seamlessly into a prehistory called 'formal subjecticity', nor do they emerge from it. Instead they appear, act, react in complex patterns of congruence and non-congruence. The presumption of a formal sameness *is not to be expected*. It is just a speech idiom, stretched beyond rational use.

Similarly, events, persons and accounts generate 'modernity' in a number of interacting ways, *one* of which is: modernity-as-a-topic-for-painting; and some foreclose the viability of neoclassical notions of perfection and of didactic constancy in the form of 'history' painting. But the new, specific disjuncture roughly named 'modernity' also generates attention to the specificity of painting *as medium* and therefore reflexivity in the form: What is painting? What is art? All of these we argue are possibilities, not determined outcomes. The evidence for that is quite clear. The determinist model would require the attention to medium to be a *modern* problem but it is obviously a *renewed* concern of the tradition, ranging from Rembrandt to Manet's more direct influences in Goya and Velasquez. How can determinism account for that? - let alone anyone as extreme as Turner.

More precisely, the reflexive question for early modernism is: What is it to paint modernity? Specified in that question are two active principles: to paint and modernity. Relations of causation and correspondence are absurd here. They do not evoke nor represent the differences of presentation – temporal, spatial, class-related, income related, gender related – that either term must have. Far less do they attend to the homeodynamic of their interrelations. Put in graphic terms - think of a Venn diagram. One set consists of 'modernity' – it is new, vast, varied and burgeoning. Another set is termed 'painting' – it has a long, contradictory and influential history and is also developing. It is riven by new opposing factions and reinterpretations. A certain M. Manet of a certain located class has an opinion about painting and his own painting. He succeeds in causing a fraction of the set 'modernity' to overlap fractionally the set called 'painting'. What he succeeds in producing is a specified subset, minute by comparison with its neighbours called 'Manet's painting' and elsewhere 'the first modernist painter'. Its originality should not obscure the modest scale of the action. The modest scale should not obscure its fertility, nor its inter-relation with similar work. The fertility, the scale and the chains of relationship are functions of each set as fluctuating possibilities – not fixed entities, not the shuttle of mechanisms   - but autopoietic complexity, defining and redefining several sets of boundaries against many others.

This chapter will concern itself with a paradox that might be expressed in several ways; amongst them:

How is it that Duchamp who's phrase 'as stupid as a painter' is well-known becomes if not the most influential 'painter' (the term will be justified later) then at least the greatest single influence on 20th Century painting, eclipsing (we can argue) even Picasso?

How can the reflexive question - What is it *to paint* modernity? So quickly degenerate into the morbid quasi-platonic essentialism of: What is *art*? Notice that the entire domain of social action is effaced in the shift from the active verbal form *to paint* to the noun (or name) *art*.

How is it that the freedom essayed by Dadaist significant objects (Duchamp's *Fountain* amongst them) can without contradiction or radical doctrinal alteration make Abstract Expressionism look at first promising, then ridiculous and culminate in the ostensibly *necessary* end of painting? How can radical freedom and suffocating censure be identical consequences of the same programme?

How can Manet's modernist *enterprise* culminate in Greenberg's citing both Manet and the distinctly not modern Kant in the service of 'competence' and anti-enterprising formalism, again without apparent contradiction? How can the self-seeking *Flaneur* formulating and relishing the spectacle of what he can *buy* (Olympia included) metamorphose without apparent contradiction into the painter who pays his dues and does his duty? How does the complicit sparkle of *Olympia* carry within it the destiny of monochrome black rectangles?

How does the pleasure of Manet become Richter's hopeless despair? Can the mediating term be guilt? For what crime?

There are those who argue[1] that it is not so much *crime* but loss of confidence through loss of *market* - to photography indeed! - that seeds the decline. What utter nonsense! Put a 'quality' photograph - let alone a snapshot - next to a Rembrandt portrait, or an Ingres, or Manet, or a Picasso, or a Freud (The originals, that is, not more photos.) The difference isn't just apparent, it's enough to shake the foundations of any 'replacement' theory. Or, to take a parallel case, why didn't the same happen to music? How come music's essayed abolition is so feeble when compared to painting's? Or more narrowly, why hasn't Julian Bream been 'superseded' by Eric Clapton? And of course there is the question of how much painters relished and used photography for their own ends.[2] No it cannot be a question of being nudged out of the marketplace by a more cost-efficient product. Even mundane markets don't work in that way or else there'd be no niche for the upmarket car, or modern forms of equine sport. It is, in our view, a gradual recriminalisation of painting, largely on account of its use of imagery, even in the limited form of abstraction, and for much the same

141

reasons advanced by Plato for his exclusion of artists from the Republic. There are, we think, two sets of reasons: the persistence of a quasi-Platonic paradigm for social action (as we argued above); and, as with Plato, its politicisation.

Again we shall choose one protagonist - this time of an entirely different kind from Clark - precisely to show that despite the ostensible difference, the same paradigm, the same exclusions and the same contradictions appear. This time we choose Thierry de Duve's *Kant after Duchamp* and ask again: What image of community is essayed here? What does it embrace and what does it exclude? The choice is made out of respect for both his scholarship and intellectual agility. It is a difficult argument.

The opening section is titled *Art was a Proper Name* - a counter-intuitive move if ever there was one. How does he account for its necessity? He begins with an imagined extra-terrestrial sent to do observational fieldwork on humans' passion for art but the observer soon becomes 'implicated'. These are the stages: art lover, critic, historian of tradition, aesthetician or theoretician of art, genealogist or theoretician of tradition and finally archeologist. [3]

> The roles.....can only be played one by one and in that order of entrance...And since you yourself played all of these roles in turn, this applies to you. [4]

That, of course is an explicit paradigm claim: you must have and you must do this; *this applies to you*. He continues:

> You are allowed to be a mere art lover.....but it would be absurd to call yourself an art critic without being an art lover. It is perfectly honourable for you to practice art criticism...without claiming to write history in the heat of the moment but it would be unthinkable to write the history of an art tradition without judging as a critic and from within that tradition. You can practice art criticism without theoretical ambitions, but conversely, if you sought to produce an art theory without reflecting on the actual activity of the critic you would be caught in a formal and sterile exercise. Finally, it is entirely legitimate for you to want to add to the jurisprudence by relying on the jurisprudential record, whether immediately or belatedly, but you would fail to grasp the historicity of the tradition if you did not reflect as a theoretician on the jurisprudence in which the critic and the historian are, in other respects, immersed. (And how could you do so if you hadn't had the experience of the critic?) Only then, when you have played these five roles in order and in full awareness will you be able to reinscribe them back into the period that gave them birth. [5]

We haven't quite reached the stage of 'art was a proper name' but an interim interpretation is worthwhile. Notice the central role of criticism: it is the energising term that sets out and sustains the destiny of the subsequent roles. Notice that strange word 'jurisprudence'. It is entirely apt: we are speaking of critics' judgement and of appeal, indeed of a permanent court of appeal (de Duve's term) - hence the need for a jurisprudential record. And you - remember: *this applies to you* - must address that record *as a theorist* to grasp the historicity of the tradition. Now this is a complex, confident and, above all, ambitious position as we shall shortly see - and quite unlike Clark's. Unfortunately de Duve does subscribe to the view that painting and photography were disputing the same market but let's say that painting's *loss* operates as opportunity or catalyst rather than cause. Apart from that, which is not central, the driving force is a theoretical understanding of aesthetic judgement - jurisprudence - and not ideological relationships. In other words de Duve's position is anathema to Clark's school of thought. He continues:

> Only then, looking back to this period called modernity will you gain an overview of this culture that sustained itself on the idea that art was autonomous and on everything that, of necessity, contradicted that idea. Only then will modernity begin to reveal the fruitful mistake on which it fed: whereas it proceeded from a regulative usage of the idea of art as proper name, it believed or wanted to proceed from a conceptual or speculative usage of art as idea. And this - belief or idea - probably authorized that - regulation and production.[6]

Now this is very tough reasoning so let's take a step back to the critic. These are de Duve's words [7] but we've edited and simplified the steps:

1. you a critic will be judged on your judgements;

2. the injunction is a command to produce the referents of the sentence as you pronounce it case by case: 'this is art';

3. and *not* the referents of a supposed general concept of art *nor* of an unlimited set of artistic signs.

Notice the judicial tone of: 'the sentence as you pronounce it case by case'. He continues:

The word "art" is a linguistic sign, no one would deny it. But it is not a logical concept. It is thus not a common noun, even though it is common to all the things you call art. [But] This communality results from the namings you have brought about through your judgements: it is not prior to them in the manner of linguistic denotation or conceptual extension. It is of the same order as that which assembles all the Peters, Pauls or Harrys: they have their name in common.....They owe that to the act of baptism...and not to any.. property or meaning they supposedly share.[8]

This is a really interesting but difficult proposition in that it essays a counter-view to the essentialism that nags away at every set of interests, every innovation and every counter-reaction in the form: Is it (really) art? And de Duve is really quite radical in the extent to which he is prepared to push this, which is refreshing since most academics turn very meek when the name 'art' is mentioned even though they *know* its central to the human sciences.

You must not forget you have arrived at it [this is art] not through deduction nor induction but via the reflection you have made on your feelings as an art lover, in other words, on the conviction or the certitude (and what is certitude, if not the feeling of knowing?) that you are dealing with art when you express your judgement with the phrase, 'this is art'. [9]

Feelings and lovers and certitude are not the stuff of ordinary academe, more's the pity! Clark's account of *Olympia* is as dry and exclusive as the definition 'prostitute'. But just as the complexity of human feeling is at last admitted alongside the complexity of 'accounting-for' the difficulty is the conflation, or oversimplification, of baptism with judgement: Harry can't be un-Harry'd but 'this is art' can and *will* be contested in (de Duve's words) a permanent court of appeal. Moreover, we don't care to un-Harry Harry because that proper name is *arbitrary* whilst 'art' is a question of judgement, a baptism and (literally) a 'sentence'.

Among certitudes of this sort, the particularly fragile and totally unjustifiable feeling that Duchamp's urinal "contained" a theory of art was the one on which you reflected most, for this object is the most exemplary, the most paradigmatic of all works of art, inasmuch as it begs you to call it art and nothing else.[10]

The central difficulty of the urinal - and we all know it - is that it gives you nothing at all with which to make the judgement because 'it' strips away all the forms in which aesthetic feelings might be expressed -

such as being beautiful or even being extraordinary. *It* refuses to 'aestheticise'. It demands simply to be named, or baptised (joke intended), or not, as art. De Duve is a little evasive we think in his generalisation: '[It] reveals more explicitly....the antimony that results when a personal feeling is cast into a predicative proposition with a claim to objectivity.'[11] We were under the impression that its uniqueness rested on the precise *exclusion* of any dimension such as personal feeling or aesthetic judgement.   It's at this point that the tired old geezer at the back of the conference room suggests that perhaps Duchamp *chose* the urinal for its aesthetic qualities. Have you noticed there is always one? He's far too old to be there and he always wears a hat! He *must* be Duchamp's ghost. He is backed up by some young blade who has picked up the iron, 'egalitarian' grammar of post-structuralism and yet sees fit to 'correct' the old geezer by pointing out: No! Duchamp is insisting that both the urinal and the acknowledged masterpiece are aesthetically worth as much or as little as each other. The issue is the *refusal* to judge. An established academic who happened to be dozing in the corner and who also knows his late modernism from a more wakeful past now joins in by citing figures such as Johns, Rauschenberg and Judd and applauding the said refusal (embodied as the pisspot) as a political position and an icon in the quest for pluralism. It does not occur to him, even in his waking moments, that 'this is art', as a sentence about the pisspot, is also a sentence that says art is to be put *in* the pisspot. This is not pluralism - to repeat an earlier point. It is, however, a juridical sentence; and this text is a submission to the court of appeal. But de Duve is not going to side with the dull academic. He has a much sharper point

> The phrase "this is art," as it is uttered by art lovers who use it to judge by dint of their feelings and of the conflict among their feelings, is a baptism. Art lovers....may have many motivations, some cultural and learned, others emotional and sensual, still others intellectual and even moral; *but it is with the effective sum total of these motivations that they judge*...Being a proper name the word "art" is a blank.....[so] with the word "art" you are pointing a finger at all the things that make up your critical collection, your personal imaginary museum. In calling *this* thing art, you are not giving out its meaning; you are relating it to everything else you call art....(our emphases).
>
> This is why aesthetic judgements are always comparative, even though it would be useless to try to say precisely what they compare.[12]

We have a long way to travel with de Duve yet, but it is worth pointing out the first indication of a different course and intent. We applaud the inclusiveness of: 'but it is with the effective sum total of these motivations that they judge...' Similarly, 'in calling *this* thing art, you are not giving out its meaning; you are relating it to everything else you call art...' in short the entire 'proper name' thesis, as we read it, *forbids* the kind of paradigmatic exclusions that allow forms of essentialism to pass for adequate reasoning. Remember our requirement was to construct an inclusive theory of patterned complexity *in the face of* so-called essentialist theories which really operate as theories of *correction*; that is, they exclude every instance that does not concur with the paradigm as *false* phenomena. Essentialist corrections *require* falsehood and crimes to justify the narrowness of their view. They *need* the field of investigation (let us call it Being) to be comprised of authentic and inauthentic elements (lets us call them beings).

It is crucial to see that our rejection of the schema of authentic/inauthentic and de Duve's implicit support by virtue of his inclusive, proper name thesis - does not result for him or for us in descriptions of chaos and the suspension of critical judgement. That is rather the extension of the charge of *in*authenticity to the whole sphere of social phenomena, including and *especially* 'judgement'. That the refusal to judge is a *postmodern* characteristic simply underscores the unity of postmodern, modern and *ancient* essentialism: they share the same crime-obsessed paradigm. Instead we explicitly propose - with de Duve's implicit support - that beings (small b) are not 'guilty' but qualitatively differentiated; not guilty of contradicting the category (say 'art' or 'social phenomena') by virtue of their difference but exhibit *necessary* differentiation and complexity. That is not a model of chaos nor the suspension of judgement. It is to say that such structures (as, say, art) and judgements about them stand in autopoietic and ecological relationships.

In this sense, we argue, it is not the essentialists (Plato, Kant, religious fundamantalists, modernists) or the post-essentialists (postmoderns, post-structuralism, deconstruction) that can ground judgement but the structural inclusivity essayed in this text, in de Duve and above all in Durkheim with the idea that structural constraint is inauguary, positive and constructive. The entire movement of essentialism, then, from ancient to Enlightenment to Modern to Postmodern can be seen as the mutation of the decision, authentic or inauthentic (Plato) to the vexed question of as*certain*ability or necessity (in Kant, in Modernism) to the abandonment of the judgement (postmodernism). But the abandonment of one paradigm is by no means the same thing as the construction of another. More of that later. For the moment we formulate Socrates and Kant as lawgivers and their descendents as good (modern) or bad (postmodern) administrators. That is not to say the modernism is in any way better then postmodernism but that the modernist was a better and certainly more naïve policing regime. But policemen are not moral philosophers nor do they become moral philosophers through losing faith in the law. They usually become corrupt.

But on the other hand, de Duve betrays the categorial imperative, suspiciously active. This is not surprising given the importance he attaches to Kant. It takes, for example, this form: 'with the word "art" you are pointing a finger at all the things that make up your critical collection, your personal imaginary museum.' (op. cit) Or: 'This is why aesthetic judgements are always comparative, even though it would be useless to try to say precisely what they compare.' (op.cit.) Notice the shudder? The first indication of the loss of faith: 'it would be *useless to try* to say precisely what they compare.' We see this 'shudder' as a vacillation between the claim of the proper noun against the common noun; the contradiction between the uncategorial *naming* 'Art' and the *comparative* col-lection of the category 'art' masquerading as 'your personal imaginary museum' What a telling phrase! To find 'art' (small a and therefore category *and* definition) pop along to the *museum* - even it is your imaginary one. And then there's the suspiciously titled *paradigm* case of art: the pisspot again.

It's not that the pisspot isn't *a* paradigm case; it's being *the* paradigm case bothers us. We know his reasons: 'inasmuch as it begs you to call it art and nothing else'. Can we propose some 'co-paradigm' *cases*? - as befits a theory of patterned complexity and for that matter the concept: 'art was a proper name.' Let's begin with the kind of art that lies outside museums and does *not* 'beg you to call it art and nothing else.' Why *a priori* should that exclusion mark the paradigm? Suppose we take children's' drawings - are they to be excluded by Duchamp's pisspot? Suppose we take instances of 'folk' art (we apologise for the patronising term but its irony serves us here). Images of ritual dances and masks spring to mind, but so too do make-up and high-heel shoes; so too do the funeral paraphernalia of Ancient Egypt - the endless models of everyday life from the baker's to the butcher's work; the vast collections of small mummies from fish to cats to snakes to birds. But the instance *we choose* (of 'folk' art) actually is in museums and dates from the mid-twentieth century. It is 'folk' and by implication not a part of the (proper) historicity of (the proper name) Modernism because its values and purpose lie elsewhere. It is largely forgotten and often weak on the quality side. It is gathered in several museums in Germany, Austria and Israel and in a sombre, cheap and awesome book titled, *The Art of the Holocaust.*[13] And we pronounce the sentence 'this is art' despite the splash of Duchamp's pisspot. However, that generality, *Art of the Holocaust,* is not sufficiently specific for either de Duve or us. In the book there are several instances of obviously 'professional' and accomplished work, done in extreme adversity - usually, then, drawings - by artists who later perished in the camps. However great their claim - and it is arguably tantamount to a 'proper' alternative, anti-formalist 'Modernism' - we choose a ragged, crude and decidedly *un*accomplished and child-like piece scrawled in pencil and crayon By Ludwig Surokowski [14] and titled *Memories of Torture of New Arrivals in Gross-Rosen* (this is *written* boldly across the bottom of the drawing). It depicts a scene, reading left to right, of 'established' prisoners in prison clothes seated at large tables. In the centre new arrivals are shown naked, crouching on a bench with some on the floor undergoing various forms of beating. To the left, five new arrivals, also naked, are spread in cruciform positions, face up on the floor. One is being stamped on. It is not clear whether they are being 'washed' but one of the guards has a bucket.

Remember: 'Art lovers....may have many motivations, some cultural and learned, others emotional and sensual, still others intellectual and even moral; *but it is with the effective sum total of these motivations that they judge.'* (op.cit.). This thing is certainly art but it is not *loved.* It is respected. Goya's *Disasters of War* is certainly art, certainly greater art than this; greater also than Monet's charming pictures - but not *loved* in the way they are. The description art *lovers* is the problem: it won't allow those other motivations their full scope. Tacitly, it undermines the diversity of art as proper name and art as autopoietic phenomena by requiring, or just suggesting, it is recognisable on account of the love it invokes. This is tacit essentialism, tacit correction.

What does *New Arrivals* propose that the pisspot does not? In the first place, despite being in a real museum it blows apart the 'imaginary museum' by citing its origin in the furtive actions of prisoners in a concentration camp. De Duve's 'museum' does not actually suggest - but becomes perilously close - that art like *New Arrivals* becomes art only as it enters the museum. That implies it was a matter of *choice* and indeed *partly aesthetic* choice when it is perfectly clear that the first making *and* the subsequent museum-collecting of *New Arrivals* was a matter of compulsion: first as an act of showing and second as an act of remembrance and respect. We do not imply that either compulsion - let us call them compulsive preservation - are necessary in any mechanical, Kantian or absolute sense. Both *need* not have happened and in the deepest sense *should* not have happened - but given the circumstances they are both vital to human memory, morality, narrative and iconography. It is vital to see that this is not simply a *modern* cultural act, like the pisspot, but a compulsion central to our modernity, our postmodernity and our prehistory. In other words as Ellen Dissanayake argues[15] art is not an ethnological but an *ethological* phenomenon - a fundamentally necessary *behaviour*; a behaviour *for* the human community and *in the face of* the terror that surrounds it. But Duchamp's *Fountain* is just an inverted pisspot.

Of course, that is somewhat unfair: it is a uniquely active, inverted pisspot. Proposing it as the paradigm case of art is the real problem: it is tacit essentialism which tries to nail autopoiesis to one significant event. Of course, autopoiesis has events - but not one that determines the rest. Of course, the urinal makes a series of proposals which *rightly* question art. 'Rightly' in that Duchamp has the *right* and art the autonomy to place itself in question. But to propose that or something like it as the paradigm case is to lose sight of the complexity by suggesting, like Socrates, that the majority of (art) events can be safely ignored. But unless de Duve has his own Oracle or is some kind of religious fundamentalist (which he *should* tell us about) he cannot possibly hold that position because it is staggeringly irrational.

This brings us back to de Duve's self-contradiction: 'Among certitudes of this sort, the particularly fragile and totally unjustifiable feeling that Duchamp's urinal "contained" a theory of art...'(op. cit.). We can now argue that Duchamp's urinal does not contain a theory of art but that numerous theories of art - de Duve's included, ours included - contain the possibility of someone like Duchamp and something like the urinal. The 'misreading': Duchamp's urinal 'contained' a theory of art, is invited by de Duve precisely because of the imaginary 'museum' and the paradigm case. That point is not so much important as the contrast it throws up: an *autopoietic* theory of art is radically, objectionably and immorally inclusive. Nevertheless, in contrast to the theorist's amorphous and imaginary museum the artist *must* begin from one place. It may belong to the totality of a network or tree of possibilities but *it will be a point*. That (dis)juncture is the event of naming, not simply baptism but birth. Our objection to de Duve is not that his event consists in a col-lection (hidden as imaginary museum) but that it does not collect very much: not quite essentialist, not quite corrective but certainly not reasonable. His branch/birth is finally and narrowly categorical: art, not Art and therefore not naming. In other words his collection is not theoretic, not reasonable but idiomatic – like Kant. Reason should describe the tree whilst *idiom* is confined to a branch. It may be that reason has little to say except to deny the claims of idiomatic branches to represent the tree. More positively, it may begin to describe the relationships and position of an idiom vis à vis the tree. Reason's elusive goal is not 'reasonableness' in the sense of acceptable, pleasant, morally fair but, far more dangerous: to seek and try to describe the structures that shape and the energy that drives the growth of the tree.

Our hunch here is that 'taste' is implicated – but as *drive* – and belongs to a wider ecology of the will to live. That and its concomitants - the organisations and devices that protect survival and those that threaten it - is the stuff of the paradigm case: including the pisspot, including *New Arrivals*; including even the ghastly aesthetics of the regime that forced those new arrivals. And so: back to the pisspot.

'....this object is the most exemplary, the most paradigmatic of all works of art, inasmuch as it begs you to call it art *and nothing else.*' (op. cit.) On the face of it then, a reduction; or, perhaps, a correction? Place it in context: this is a response (Duchamp's response) to the unparalleled complexity of Cezanne. Painting has its subjects in the traditional sense. In Cezanne it has also rectangularity, flatness, a new synthesis of colour and implied space, new methods of composition and drawing, new perspective, new viewpoints, its primitivism and its sophistications. In Duchamp it 'has'- it *is* - the unassisted ready-made. Or perhaps the response is to Manet's sheer nerve in treating Modernity as a spectacle that his class and gender may savour. We know, however, that Duchamp's preference was Seurat. De Duve says: 'What Duchamp admired in Seurat was the "scientific spirit"...'[16] Then he cites Duchamp directly:

> There was no essential satisfaction for me in painting ever, And then, of course, I just wanted to react against what the others were doing, Matisse and all the rest, all that work of the hand. In French there is an old expression, *la patte,* meaning the artists touch his personal style, his 'paw'. I wanted to get away from *la patte* and all that retinal painting.[17]

Now de Duve, wearing his different hat, has much to say in this context about the diminution of the 'craft' of painting through the twin influences of the invention of photography and oil paint 'ready made' in *tubes.* The shift away from 'handwork' is a well-aired modernist preoccupation and de Duve's comments here dovetail nicely; but they need not concern us. Now amount of unassisted ready-made *paint* can determine the shift to the unassisted ready-made *pisspot* - or snowshovel or whatever. But - 'no satisfaction in painting, *ever'* and '..of course, I just wanted to react *against*...Matisse and *all the rest'* and '*I wanted to get away'* - certainly *do* determine a course of action that is '*not*-painting'.

150

We cannot speculate on Duchamp's motives but it does seem truly strange to begin from painting, its 'retinality' and *la patte* if that is precisely where you do *not* want to be. All right, let us concede that this beginning was only a matter of circumstance - and having found himself there and formulating his distaste he *'wanted to get away'*. But that negation (let us say it frankly) that *loathing* of painting, will not sit with the imaginary museum. Or conversely: Duchamp's hatred - remember his taunt: 'as stupid as a painter' - is compromised and betrayed at every instance of the museum, imaginary or not, that also contains 'Matisse and all the rest.' Add to this clear sentiment a seasoning of moral authority that put the critical artist - very fancifully - in the *avant-garde* of socialism and the duty to deconstruct bourgeois taste and you have a rather potent mixture. The complexity that links Manet with Goya, Cezanne with Poussin, Seurat with Cézanne or his drawings with Millet's - the 'love' with the perceived requirement and the determination to make reforms - is set against a terribly simplistic requirement to 'react against'. The problem: What is it to paint modernity? - has decayed into the simplistic form of presenting 'not-painting' - preferably in a gallery where the rejection would be more explicit than 'not-painting' by *instead* being an insurance agent or a doctor or mathematician. The potency consists in the ease with which one can 'not-paint' as opposed to doing something else, painting included. So easy, so potent, so labour-saving as to be genuinely modern and egalitarian, the cult of not-painting, and not anything else either, especially not-*ruling,* is born. And because it is the easiest, most labour saving and most thought-saving of all rules it is destined to become the dominant cult of modernity. Of course, when you have 'notted' enough and there is still no result other than having to choose something in an embarrassment of positivity, then you are on the threshold of postmodernity. At last! - but not quite. We *dare* not choose; dare not choose reason over religiosity or even democracy over 'other political systems'; dare not choose painting over not-painting and at last throw the pisspot back into the lavatory; dare not until recently even educate our own children for fear of undervaluing their infant experience and contribution. So we are stuck, as it were, firmly *between* modernity and postmodernity (and have the gall to call it pluralism) because something like Duchampian 'deconstruction' still calls all the shots in so many cultural, political and especially academic spheres. And that, as we have seen, is authoritarian. Modernist and contradictory. Above all, it is stuck, rigid and dead.

The Duchampian gesture has grown old, no doubt but in its day - and its day is not so much over as in twilight - it paraded as ironic, carefree and mocking. Rather different from the compulsive, outraged representation of *New Arrivals*, then. Not so much a branch of the tree of re-presentation but a detached assessment of its habit of mimesis? We want to argue that this is a most fundamental misreading. There are two related concepts that can help us here. The first, following Derrida, is *iterability*; the second, following Dawkins is the notion of *memes*. (The conventional reader will find these very strange bedfellows).

Derrida says

> The possibility of repeating, and therefore identifying, marks is implied in every code, making of it a communicable, transmittable and decipherable grid that is iterable for a third party....[18]

Crowther's simpler defintion is:

> the iterability of of a sign or group of signs is their capacity to be recognised and repeated across many different contexts of use. Iterability is that *stable* dimension of meaning....*independent* of any one specific context of employment.'[19]

Earlier Crowther argues [this definition] 'is actually partly destructive of poststructuralism'. It certainly is! - so far as poststructuralism is characterised by 'scepticism about the fixity of meaning, categories and, indeed, the stability of the self.'[20] (ibid) But look at the wording that forces itself on Crowther: de*structive* of *post*structuralism! One begins to smell a rat - or better, a place in which language can be forced to whisper absurdities but actually shouts out the incommensurability of the paradigm. So, as a provisional position, let us say that a re-iterable meaning or cluster or pattern is presupposed. Let us refrain from any spurious measure of its (in)stability but insist that it takes place within a social setting and not in an abstract or formal intellectual space or idiom in which the Kantian or neoKantian 'subject' might exist. Then it easy to see that the relative (in)stability is radically undecidable and the expectation of a general measure of (in)stability is only a persistent idiomatic trait. Actual (in)stability would rest on such 'unsubjective' issue as access, the ability to read, experience in playing the game, motive, talent, circumstance. Remember this cuts both ways: it will not decide between stability and instability; it simply reinforces the possibility of circumstantial continuities and discontinuities. In sum 'iterability' seems to be presupposed but problematic. Let us now turn to memes.

The term was coined by Richard Dawkins [21] an arch neo-Darwinist and, it is argued, one of the popularisers of genetic determinism. Some of his wordings are polemical or plain misleading. The classic case is the 'selfish' gene, but this one really hits the jackpot. It is intended to provide a parallel to the 'gene' but in the sphere of (especially) human culture. Rather like the 'iterable unit' it is presupposed but - through its relationship on the one hand to the stabilities of the gene or the French *meme* and on the other to shifting phenomenology of members, membership, memory, re-membering - it soon takes on a life of its own that challenges all definition. Rather like de Duve's proper name and our preferred 'autopoiesis' it existence rests on members' *judgement* that 'it' - a meme - exists. It is, then, at its loosest, the ability to assert *patterned* complexity and have the asserted pattern re-cognised by another member. We have a fine state of affairs now: Dawkins the disciple of Darwin is radically less deterministic than Derrida.

We hesitate to complicate matters further but it is probably necessary at this stage; we can simplify later. It will be our intention to emphasise that iterabitiy (the identification and transmission of memes) takes place between *members* - not subjects - and as such has an essential *historicity* (to use de Duve's word) or is characterised by *situated evolution*. The complication then arises in the form of prehistories, or more properly, previous evolutionary events and their ecologies. In that sense, it can be argued that 'memes' are not the simple *cultural* phenomena that Dawkins perhaps intended them to be. Taken instead as identifiable, repeatable units - however accurately or inaccurately - memes provide simply another name for self-replicators in the most general sense. In principle, then, the memetic, self-replicative and indeed the iterable do not presuppose a human social origin or even a biological one. It is rather that the iterability and the memes we recognise as 'human' belongs to a vast ontology and chronology of 'replication' that reaches into the depths of Being. It is only on the basis of this evolved ecology that anything like 'memes' in the cultural sense is conceivable. That is to say (and this firmly rejects both Plato and Kant) that autopoiesis belongs to Being and not to some segment of beings. In other words, the apparent closure that *seems* to allow one subsystem (such as human society) to *appear* 'closed' - its autopoiesis processes being only *self*-referential - is a closure that has either been *achieved* at some previous evolutionary juncture, or is not a closure at all, but an active relationship we have failed to grasp. We shall pursue that later and elsewhere. We include the sketch here because it illuminates the scale of paradigm change that is at stake. We may now narrow and so hopefully simplify the picture once again.

We said: we cannot speculate on Duchamp's motives but it does seem truly strange to *begin from* painting, its 'retinality' and *la patte* if that is precisely where you do *not* want to be. We conceded that his position was possibly circumstantial, that he had little choice and that the distaste for painting came upon him, so to speak. After all, we have all made mistakes! This apparent small anomaly now becomes rather important. In the first place it shows that Duchamp *was a painter*, this was the structure that in some sense contained him; in some sense it constituted his primary field of iteration; it was at least one of the dominant components of his membership of society. Several memes are identified here with greater or lesser precision: painting, retinality, *la patte,* Matisse 'and all the others.' The memetic complexity immediately strikes us and it doesn't matter *at all* whether you begin from a Crowtheran position of 'relatively stable iteration' or a postsructuralist caricature of instability. Duchamp knows *exactly* what he means by 'all the others' - and so do we. And it doesn't matter *at all* who they are. No relation of correspondence is even faintly implied and so no stability or instability. Is the case of the meme 'Matisse' any different? Is Duchamp an expert on 'Matisse' who will give a scholarly - and stable - account or a bit of a maverick who doesn't know that much about 'Matisse' and anyway appears to have little sympathy with his work and is likely to generate mistakes, instabilities, lose significant information? Of course it simply doesn't matter. In the world of memes those questions are utterly irrelevant. Let us examine why this must be the case.

Duchamp was a painter. That claim is conceded; he may iterate within that field. His iteration takes the form of a pisspot and several other unassisted ready-mades and a series of statements. That is his right on the basis that iteration is as open as 'the ability to assert *patterned* complexity'. The pattern is: retinality, *la patte,* Matisse and all the others; I want to get away from 'this'. This is a meme and a memetic judgement. Now everything turns on whether 'we' accept the invitation to recognise - retinality, *la patte,* Matisse and all the others - as something we also want to get away from. The crucial judgement is: shall we allow the pisspot into the museum? If we *do* then we choose not to think Duchamp is mad, and Duchamp – *the painter* - has remodelled the meme. We may not agree that we also 'want to get away' but we cannot assert the non-existence of the question. It is now a meme we must handle *very carefully*. Because once the pisspot's inclusion into the museum has allowed the crudity of 'Matisse and all the others' - once the museum, that is, has concurred with the violence of the formulation - the pisspot is now the refined object in and as the discourse it engenders - *against* the retinality and *la patte* of Matisse and all the others. It is of course, extremely harsh and authoritarian but that *is* the memetics of membership; that's how autopoiesis works: structure despite structure. It may be that two mutually inimical structures can find sufficient ecological space to live alongside, even feed off one another. It is not *guaranteed* - but we think something of the kind happened to Duchamp or that the pisspot got incorporated in the rebuilding of painting. One thinks especially of Jasper Johns here. However, we are not yet ready for the later course of Modernism. Let us say instead that talk of stable or unstable iteration is quite beside the point. We are speaking exclusively of the *vitality* of memes.

How is Duchamp's memetic negation more, less, or as vital as painting in the traditional sense? Surely not-painting is inherently a more sickly animal than painting? Who would want to be a not-painter? Even Duchamp turned to chess. We have several suggestions here but let's first discount the re-absorption of Duchamp *into* painting. He gets *eaten* here and since there's no such thing as a free lunch the best he can claim is going dutch. The first is the alarming possibility that not-painting or 'hating painting' belongs to that class of bigotries whose vitality is based on their simplicity - they are easily repeated. They also bring social advantage in that they place the bigot above the object of bigotry. This would make Duchamp the Hitler of painting and not the ironic darling of the avant-garde. More credibly Duchamp's negation appeals to that tendency of verbal representing that asks, what essentially *is* painting? He is seen then as the one who suspends belief, brackets, puts into question. That is, he appeals to Platonic idioms within ostensibly modern usage, since the question 'What is painting?' cannot be answered at any level other than: it is a memetic complex. By 'ostensibly modern usage' we mean of course, post-Darwinian. That is not to say that one accepts Darwin *carte blanche* - it would be impossible and ridiculous to say so. It *is* however to place evolutionary history, autopoiesis and patterned complexity in the first rank and to consign theories of creation, essentialism, formal conceptions of subjecthood and random plurality into the same dustbin as astrology and religious fundamentalism.

It is with hesitation that we return the related questions of crime and jurisprudence; hesitation - because as our last sentence showed we are inevitably drawn into the conflict traditionally put forward as reason *versus* superstition. Pluralist versions of poststructuralism tend to see reason (western reason) as the colonial power and are therefore apt to concede at least equal status to alternative (such as religious) worldviews. The term 'superstition' would be thought appalling. But as we have seen, that pluralism cannot avoid its own authoritarian requirements. Rather than seeing this as a question of good guys and bad guys let us stick to ontology. In simple terms, postmodern pluralism requires *you* to be like *it*. Rushdie is still paying the price for not understanding and not predicting that this is *offensive*.

Pluralist tendencies within poststructuralism think that Duchamp is 'preferable' to the *discipline* of painting. The evidence is everywhere but de Duve's fascination is enough for now and better than most accounts. But it is also clear that Duchamp cannot fit the pluralist agenda either. For in 'not-painting', which appears to be an open space, there is a jurisprudential record at stake and in the making. In the permanent court of appeal 'retinality' has been allowed in the face of the difference between Michelangelo's, Goya's, Rembrandt's, Turner's, Pollock's, Richter's (now called) 'versions'. 'Retinality' has entered the jurisprudential record as *sufficient ground* to ignore the ramifications of these differences. Read the same for *la patte* (we may safely ignore the difference between Rembrandt's 'paw' and Vermeer's) - and for 'Matisse and all the others'. It is *ruled* in the preference for Duchamp entered in the jurisprudential record and with the vital piece of evidence - the pisspot - held in the museum of henceforward legality that these terms are sufficient as descriptions, sufficient grounds for new action and sufficient grounds for ignorance. Of course that could be de-ruled. That's what we are about. But for the moment 'we' can safely ignore all these instances collected under retinality, *la patte* and Matisse and all the rest; an ignorance of the mundane 'all the rest' uncannily like the practiced ignorance of Socrates. An essentialism of the 'paradigm case' that matches perfectly. We now only need the next step: to grasp painting *qua* discipline as crime and expel it from the Republic. Conversely we exalt not-painting or not-anything or *de-construction* as the moral life. Socrates, of course, called it irony but it did the same political job. Before we leave this section let's just sketch the remit of that political requirement: it is to put 'theory' reduced to deconstruction above 'practice' as its rightly subjected matter. That is the objectionable face of the old paradigm now reasonably exposed. We must reply that theory reduced to deconstruction is not theory at all but a limited ritual with no rational basis. And second: since its subject matter - very like the Kantian 'subject' has been reduced to a formal category whose apparent complexities are insignificant - *theory as deconstruction has no subject matter*.

That of course was Socrates' claim: 'Human Wisdom is worth little or nothing... he amongst you is the wisest who, like Socrates, knows that this wisdom is worth nothing at all....His wisdom is the knowledge of the negativity of all finite content.'(op. cit.)

We have then, a truly strange situation. The same memetic complex (let us call it practiced negativity) at once belongs to Socrates and to Duchamp. It is apparently shared by Christianity and poststructuralism, by art history and by an alternative path grounded in the critique of Hegelian philosophy. It will reappear in many other guises. How can this be?

The first conclusion we can draw is that this memetic complex is not really any kind of property or paradigm that belongs to specific worldviews but is a constant possibility grounded at least in language-as-usage and arguably more deeply in the processes and imaginative possibilities that make language possible. Note that the preoccupation 'knowledge-as-power' is irrelevant here. This is not a power-group's property but a memetic recurrence. Humanist perspectives whether based on 'the subject' or power-sharers miss that point. The upshot of that point will become dramatic in later chapters.

The second we formulated in a preliminary way above: the alarming possibility that not-painting or 'hating painting' belongs to that class of bigotries whose vitality is based on their simplicity - they are easily repeated. We can now generalise that preliminary in this form: The widespread vitality of the memetic form 'practiced negativity' is based upon the simplicity of its iteration. As such it has the potential to define what counts as 'critical theorising' because it is easy to recognise when it is going on. It is a relatively easy practice. The downside of course is limitation: it defines and delimits what members do when they theorise: they negate. The same applies, in principle, to painting and to politics. What first appears as irony and a foible, then, becomes first cultural impoverishment and then political impotence.

It is crucial to see that from the *images* we have so far presented show that painting does not necessarily share this memetic propensity but on the contrary tends to break it. Until Duchamp, that is; the pisspot is the symbol of the proposed injection of painting with the memetic propensity of self-negation. Crucially, this is not to be understood as an act or event or even as a simple characteristic possibility - but as an instruction to replicate: a drive, a compulsion, a memetic dynamic. This why the *memes* presented by Socratic irony and the pisspot are 'central' and not peripheral concerns - or for Plato and de Duve, 'paradigmatic' - because they insist on their essential nature as instructions to recognise and replicate. Otherwise the memes 'Socrates/Duchamp' would be as dead as the dust that remains of the so-called 'realities' - when, of course, they remain 'vital' in every sense.

Notes

1.   de Duve included.
2.   A recent show of Picasso's use of photography was held at the Barbican. Degas, Nash, and Bacon certainly used photographs (and many more). Both the use of photographs and the quality of the their work *as paintings* indicates that such artists have always seen that there are components in photography that can be re-presented in the altogether different discipline of painting. This is not to say that bad painters do not produce 'copies' of photographs or that the relationships between the disciplines cannot be creatively blurred, as in Warhol.
3.   de Duve, T. (1996) p.77.
4.   ibid. pp.77-8.
5.   ibid. p.78.
6.   ibid.
7.   ibid. see p.52.
8.   ibid.
9.   ibid. pp.52-3.
10.   ibid. p.53.
11.   ibid.
12.   ibid. pp.58-9.
13.   *Art of the Holocaust* (1982).
14.   ibid. p.175.
15.   Dissanayeke, H. (1992) espec. pp. 9-13.
16.   de Duve, T. (1996) p.175.
17.   ibid.
18.   Crowther, P. (1997) p.10.
19.   ibid.
20.   ibid.
21.   Dawkins, R. (1989) espec. pp.189-201.

8 Greenberg's Notion of Competence

Crowther writes:

> Iterability presupposes a relation between sign and field of signification which is one of reciprocal dependence. And that dependence is one manifestation of a broader functional unity which stabilises the whole sphere of human existence. Consciousness can only identify some item by subsuming it under a more general form - such as a group, a class, a kind, ... a series....; but, reciprocally, it can only operate with such general forms in so far as it can comprehend them as functions of their individual instances. And this is not a passive correlation. Each encounter with a new instance of a general form modifies our sense of that form and through this enrichment our subsequent comprehension of its individual instances is, in turn, modified.[1]

This is public text; the position of a *writer* who knows he has a truly vicious problem but is determined to set it out calmly, without panic. In person, he has the habit of isolating some of the more awkward bits of artistic practice by drawing scare quotes in the air and saying 'cree-ay-div' in an American accent. The person - as opposed to the writer - if odder, is the more genuine. 'This cognitive competence, the principle of reciprocity both grows from and refines something much more basic - the direct correlation of the human body with its surrounding world.' (ibid.) Fair enough - but the formulation is just too tame. When Duchamp places the general form of art in question, the thing he does *not* do is stabilise, enrich, refine or 'follow principles of reciprocity'. His action is more like a *coup d'etat* which, in its aftermath sends all kinds of previously established institutions - for example, this 'group, or class, or kind or series' - in search of the precise terms of the altered status, function and justification. No doubt some groups, or classes or kinds, or series, or 'heads' - will roll. Of course, Crowther doesn't intend to be taken that way and he will not deny the radicalism of Duchamp's 'reciprocity'. Our point is that the calm formulation is academically customary when perhaps alarm would be more humanly prudent - especially when we realise that iteration is not primarily a matter for the human body and 'its' world - as an individual - but for the social body which never even faintly approaches the condition of one's property. Not even for Duchamp, though 'he' proposes a whole new jurisprudence and a whole new regime.

Accounts of iteration and memetics rarely grasp the implications of this idea; indeed they rarely pass first base. A recent edition of *New Scientist*, for example carried a main article on Memes by Susan Blackmore[2] but the editorial comment contained this priceless misunderstanding:

> Memetics have nothing equivalent [to identifying evolutionary physical relationships] to fall back on. Any taxonomy of cultural trends is bound to be *subjective.*' (our emphases).

But such taxonomy is bound to be 'subjective' only in the context of a paradigm - like Kant's - in which the *subject* is dominating and self-constituting pivot of the universe of all possible phenomena. Obviously, *we* must argue that any taxonomy of cultural trends cannot be other than *memetic*. The entire principle could be summed up by saying that *memetically* there is only *identity* and difference *from* - and nothing else. There is no formal 'other' space in which the ostensible 'subject' is free to perform - infinitely, randomly and according to self-constituting whim. Instead, the social space of memetics presumes a structured *range* - not of caprice but of *intelligibility-for-mem(e)bers*. The rules of 'identity' or of recognition are in a sense known -if only as the presupposed ability to act as members. It is presumed in the socio-ontology of the species, to the extent that any series deviation form that norm instantly attracts the status of pathological.

If the rules for indentity and recognition are presupposed as 'known' and we mean in the 'fuzzy', interactive sense that invites praise or censure or (in)comprehension - what is it that governs the rules of difference? The number of units or memes that can be identified within a meme-complex that are capable of variation without sundering the *range* of an identity. Art as common noun and as proper name are in that sense both arguable; that is why the pisspot can assume the mantle of paradigm case because it threatens to abolish the range of art's identity. It had to be an object that would shatter these boundaries and it did so by appearing to be capricious when it was, of course, a member's calculated move, with entirely predictable outcomes: as art, the pisspot abolishes the range of art's identity; as not-art it abolishes itself. After Duchamp's pisspot, as 'arguably-art' every artistic practice *has* to negotiate between these extremes. There is nothing subjective about this; it is absolutely memetic.

Another way to grasp this idea is to say that *naming* is both memetic and plastic. Taking naming in the sense argued by Wittgenstein [3] it is the

160

fundamental origin of what he called the 'elementary particles' of language. Two consequences follow: it is impossible to specify the number or type of names that can be established; the elementary particles of language are, or assert that - the named entity exists in a certain state of affairs.

This notion of naming as both memetic and plastic - in common sense terms, not unlike mimicry and variation - heals at least part of the division between paradigms as diverse as poststructuralism's linguistic instabilities, the early Wittgenstein's stable picture-language and the neuroscience's current interest in the unique extent of post-natal plasticity in the human brain. But in no sense should plasticity be seen as a mysterious, occult freedom. Instead, the *plasticity* of naming, precisely *as* naming, is routinely exercised entirely because of the *memetic* structure of what we presuppose and call 'naming'. In other words we know what it is 'to name'. On that stable but open knowing - on that meme-complex - rests the entire iterability and plasticity of the naming process. What Duchamp does, essentially, is to pit the plasticity of the process against its own stability. In this sense (despite de Duve) proper names and common nouns are not the decisive points of reference: it is naming itself that is disrupted or put in question. On the other hand this is a *pretence*: naming is not really questioned at all, since the ostensible 'question' requires that we understand (and condone) naming in order to (pretend to) put it in question. That circularity is as tedious as trying to put it into words. And this is why Duchamp does not and cannot really name another kind of 'doing' art so much as to propose negation - endlessly, tediously. Whilst another naming - cubism, expressionism or indeed the reabsorption of Duchamp *in* 'art' - *cannot* violate the schematism of naming as memetic plasticity.

Our proposal for this section is, then, that from Duchamp onwards, any artistic claim must confront the possibility of being lumped (and abolished) *with Matisse and all the others*. In simple terms, it must show that the sentence that applies to *all the others* does not apply to *it*. After the supposedly capricious Duchamp, then, art becomes embroiled in competition for legitimacy. That is not to say that this struggle did not exist before: it manifestly did and Duchamp is only important because he was (judged) part of that struggle. It does mean, however, an intensification, and more importantly, a distinct narrowing so that the different qualities shown by this art or that tend to be drowned in claims of superiority.

We do not propose to be drawn into the ridiculous rhetorics that surround various artists' claims to reflect progressive socialism (and their opponents are of course fascists) nor the specious aspirations to purity associated with such as Mondrian (also invoking Plato). Their histories are well-documented elsewhere.[4] Our interest, and opposition, is with Greenberg, partly because he explicitly cites Kant, partly because his intervention occurs so close to both the highpoint of modernism's insularity and its point of collapse but finally because of that dreadful concept 'competence'. This does not, of course, assert that Greenberg's position was not politicised - quite the contrary. His own politics were quite clear, if simplistic, but that affected us all. Nor can the new ascendancy of American-type art be disentangled from the political aftermath of World War Two. That also is well-documented elsewhere and does not require our summary.[5] It is crucial to understand, however, that whilst the determinist might see causal relations or 'reflections' and their more sophisticated counterparts see ideological continuity, or 'political' focus is no less explicit but quite different. We are less interested in the ostensible policy but in the memetic materials that make that ideology and policy constructible and intelligible. To say 'memetic material' implies concrete starting points and possibly, specific limits; not a free-for-all. We shall focus, then, on the memetic limits and constraints that arguably, and ironically, link the Platonic Republic, Greenberg's salon communism and Post-War American, 'colonial' liberalism. That focus aims not to ignore, but to influence or to alter the basic materials of cultural politics.

Greenberg writes:

> I identify Modernism with the intensification, almost the exacerbation, of this self-critical tendency that began with the philosopher Kant. Because he was the first to criticise the means itself of criticism, I conceive of Kant as the first real Modernist.

> The essence of Modernism lies as I see it in the use of the characteristic methods of a discipline to criticise the discipline itself - not in order to subvert it, but to entrench it more firmly in its area of competence.[6]

It is difficult on close reading to square an 'exacerbated tendency to self-criticism' with Duchamp's ironic, even comical beginnings. And yet we have seen how Duchamp's apparent carefreeness swiftly assumes authoritarian implications. Something of the process of this change is exhibited in the stages of Greenberg's reasoning. He is keen to establish its legitimacy, especially in the form of continuity: Kant was the first, *real* modernist. This is a decisive blow against the view of Modernism as 'riding with the times' or as an aesthetic ideology of 'progressive' change, or as the visual counterpart to an emerging capitalist ideology. But, moreover, the continuity is not simply over time; it is the affirmative reapplication of method in two forms: the reaffirmation of criticism as the very (critical) means of self-limitation; the reaffirmation of the characteristic methods of the discipline as the means by which the discipline secures greater critical competence. This is massively memetic and in two senses: it is grounded in the priority of replication and is committed to rearing the best replicative complex: the most competent, the fittest.

Notice the *urgency* of the task: 'Modernism...includes almost the whole of what is truly alive in our culture.' (ibid.). Or: 'A more rational justification had begun to be demanded of every formal social activity; and Kantian self-criticism was called on eventually to meet and interpret this demand...'[7] Notice the imperious form of ' more rational justification *had begun to be demanded'* - presumably by rational*ism.* (The italics are intended to draw attention to the idiomatic form we have discussed above). As idiom or as convenient cultural peg, 'rationality' justifies the urge and the demand, but it is by no means clear whether this explains or instead covers a massive autopoietic demand whose 'desire' to replicate is constantly avoided or regarded with great suspicion. The interests of power groups, the tendency to homeostasis, normalcy, discipline, the people, Enlightenment *et al* are marshalled time and again to explain this. We remain unconvinced by either interest groups or other 'human' or subjective purposes. For the moment let us think this urgent dynamic as the memetic field in which membership is enacted. Several points follow. First, we reiterate there is no separate space outside the complexity of social memes in which free or formal or arbitrary or asocial subjects roam. In terms used earlier, the memetic and the plastic are presupposed in and as naming. In the terms now in use: member and discipline presuppose each other. There is no different, 'other' sphere in which membership is *un*disciplined. But neither, if we look at the wider picture, is this a consequence of any localised humanism - be it power interests, rationality, metanarratives *et al.* Rather the vitality of the meme-complexes that exist from time to time in societies is ecologically determined. Or again: the vitality of this or that memetic complex is decided by its ability to 'iterate' in a context of other replicative systems in the widest possible sense. This has very little to do with rational *justifications* which, if anything, only serve to confuse the ontological with the moral. It is clear then, that the foundations of Greenberg's enterprise stand upon an ever-widening contradiction - almost the converse of Duchamp's position - in which the memetic form called 'the discipline' is to be preserved in its 'competence' by destroying its plasticity:

163

What had to be exhibited and made explicit was that which was unique and irreducible not only in art in general, but also in each particular art. Each art had to determine. Through the operations peculiar to itself the effects peculiar and exclusive to itself. By doing this each art would, to be sure, narrow its area of competence, but at the same time it would make its possession of this area all the more secure.

It quickly turned out that the unique and proper area of competence of each art coincided with all that was unique to the nature of its medium. [8]

You bet it did! - in social time almost instantly. One is tempted to ask here: what is it that makes 'painting', reduced to its re-presentative media, 'rational'? Nothing. And so Greenberg is bound to fail precisely at the borderline between painting and art-in-general and social phenomena in general and so on *ad absurdum*. Why did he choose Kant and rationality when it was so utterly inappropriate? The answer must be: because it was *customary*. And in that sense it is not so much Greenberg's problem but a structural deficit of our own memetic *habitus*. Now let's rework the position memetically.

Our first position must be to repudiate entirely the reference to Kant. There is no *necessity*, in the Kantian sense, attached to painting. 'Painting' is not a subdivision of the *a priori*. This might seem like a charge of poor scholarship against Greenberg; in many ways that is justified but petty and beside the point. It is far more important that 'we' - Greenberg and Kant included - conceded that our 'subjecticity', for us, our membership, is already a patterned complexity and a dynamic in which we are already complicit. It is our immediate *habitus* but also our responsibility to mediate. This is where the crucial schism takes place. It is customary to reflect upon that *habitus* and ask: What is necessary? Kant asks that question of reason; Greenberg of painting. For them the answers take the form of essentials, corrections, limitations. For us, the *complexity* is necessary; the necessary condition of memesis.

Evelyn Waugh makes this point with customary wit:

> The whole argument about significant form stands or falls by volume. If you allow Cezanne to represent a third dimension on his two-dimensional canvas, then you must allow Landseer his gleam of loyalty in the spaniel's eye. [9]

Both are precisely-identified memetic devices but Greenberg, of course, can allow neither:

Cezanne sacrificed verisimilitude, or correctness, in order to fit drawing and design more explicitly to the rectangular shape of the canvas. It was..., however, the ineluctable flatness of the support that remained most fundamental....under Modernism . Flatness, two-dimensionality was the only condition painting shared with no other art and so Modernist painting oriented itself to flatness as it did to nothing else.[10]

What is at work when certain memetic possibilities (such as those advanced by Waugh) *must* be ignored when certain others (painting's flatness) *must* be observed? A compulsion; there is no laxity in either course. This is memetic compulsion at work, driving Greenberg's membership forward; he is *immediately* bound by it. What then of the *mediate* plasticity and so responsibility that resides in the member? This too is structured: it is plasticity and not chaos. Greenberg can't cook Modernism, can't sing Modernism, can't pretend doing a Landseer (or a Cezanne) is all right, can't leave it to the gods or somebody else, can't confess it to a priest, can't wait till it blows over, can't write with a novelist's wit or freedom and can't *paint*. What's left? Art-critical *writing*; an idiom that has come to regard itself as analytic, legitimising, discriminatory. He *writes* Modernism; he shows by the idioms of art-critical *writing* how modernism constructs his membership. In this he has no choice - apparently. And so he happens upon a definition, a wording that will serve 'his' purposes; remember: as a member who inscribes his right to that title in *words*.

Remember Crowther's understatement of the principle of reciprocity? The general form and the instance respond to and determine each other - apparently. But Greenberg's memetic task - the *critical writing* of Modernism - is received as the necessity to construct a 'competent' general definition that will include *all* instances. Otherwise we shall be back in the proper names game and this time for real - not inside de Duve's imaginary museum. The so-called principle of reciprocity *demands* that every instance is contained within the general form or it cannot 'stabilise' signification, or anything else. It is otherwise known as the categorial imperative. Then Greenberg's memetic imperatives boil down to a choice: either he can act so as to guarantee the stability of the category by making a concrete stipulation and excluding everything else; or: he can admit no common property, no basis of stability, no rational justification, not even a principle of non-contradiction. Clearly he chooses the former: the most binding category but also *and of necessity* the simplest and apparently least controversial. With immense care and knowledge of his responsibilities, he takes proper account of custom: he picks up a *dictionary* and finds that a

165

painting is a two-dimensional art form! Armed with that consensus he can set to work. Greenberg - aided and abetted by the categorial imperative - hiding in ordinary usage - has made the habitual, destructive error of confusing the essential with the simple (and its converse, confusing complexity with *unnecessary* elaboration). Policing then begins with a catalogue of demons and proscribed practices.

His most ludicrous demonology states: 'The limitations that constitute the medium of painting - the flat surface, the shape of the support, the properties of pigment - were treated by the Old Masters as negative factors that could be acknowledged only implicitly or indirectly.'[11] It is a fine art critic who has forgotten the shaped, gilded, patterned 'flatness' of the early Italian Renaissance, or the brushwork of Velasquez, the uses of pigment in Rembrandt or the attention to medium in Turner. They will of course be re-conceptualised as 'forerunners' of Modernism but, presumably, less competent. The policing is little better and invites transgression:

> Three-dimensionality is the province of sculpture, [How the dictionary helps an honest copper!] and for the sake of its own autonomy has had above all to divest itself of everything it might share with sculpture [except, paradoxically the shape of the support - painting's *most* sculptural property]. And it is in the course of its effort to do so this, and not so much..... to exclude the representational or the 'literary' that painting has made itself abstract.[12]

That does not so much invite as demand Judd's counter-claim: 'Half or more of the best new work in the last few years has been neither painting nor sculpture.'[13] It is only surprising that it took from 1961 to 1965 to get there. But then we are speaking of memetic process and not the apparent freedoms of a pure logic.

If Greenberg had been looking for memetic 'vitality' rather then necessities and certainties and competences in the essentialist sense, he might have been struck by contradictions we have already noted in his writing - but perhaps more so by this strange wording: 'Cezanne sacrificed *verisimilitude*, or *correctness*, in order to fit drawing and design more explicitly to the rectangular shape of the canvas.' (op. cit. our emphases.) What can this mean? Probably little more than a just-so story in which dear old duffer Cezanne nearly gets to be a cubist. But if wordings can betray, and they betray Greenberg absolutely - they can also illuminate.

On the face of it we have a very naïve argument about 'verisimilitude' (Derrida would have nothing to do with it; he would call painting a kind of sign). On the other, this 'correctness' (in the memetic sense) - is superseded by the 'more correct' demands of the rectangle. But this is not just a re-run of specific memetic prohibitions and affirmations. It is rather an admission that painting can, or *could*, toy around with something that could just about, in a weak moment, be called 'verisimilitude'. Summers[14], drawing on Mitchell teases this as far as distinguishing between the written sign, or its arbitrariness, and the visual 'sign' which has to be 'appropriate'. Whilst promising this does not quite go far enough.

For example, one might argue that Rembrandt's late self-portraits are so movingly 'appropriate' as to reduce one to tears. Yet Picasso's figures 'appropriate' their subjects in a much more violent sense. So do Goya's *Disasters* or, rather differently, Turner's dissolution of subject matter. Let's just say that 'appropriation' cuts both ways. That, if anything, is what Greenberg indicates in the accusation that the Old Masters 'hid' or dissembled the (violent) action of their medium. The key point for us is this. *If* painting is a kind of sign, it is not a sign in the Derridean sense, like *writing*, but a sign that is open to the question of its appropriateness and its appropriations. Unlike meaning's iterability, which is relatively stable and because of that open to modification, painting has no such fixity. Hence the emphasis on style, individuality genius and so on. Differently put, if one chooses a simple or a complex common noun - say, 'dog' or 'painting' - the iterable meaning allows a series of grammatic qualifications that open the general to the particular circumstance, *but the general has to be first presumed*. Most of the time that is not only harmless but fruitful - one cannot deny the centrality of the iterable written and spoken word to *every* social phenomenon. But in the service of what seems an innocent project of re-justification and re-grounding - such as Greenberg's - the presumption of a prior generality can be vastly destructive - not simply in reducing the claims of the varied and specific to legitimacy of 'competence' but, more importantly, in obscuring the crucial understanding that 'painting' - imagery, iconography - presents a different set of memetic structures, openings and possibilities from those offered by wording. Put differently, forms of essentialism are deeply grounded in wording. However, they contribute both to its efficacy and its blindness.

'Three-dimensionality is the province of sculpture, *and for the sake of its own autonomy painting has had......*'(op. cit., our emphases). Greenberg betrayed again: one could not imagine a more memetic statement. Sculpture does *this*, painting does *that*. One what ground? Habit, dressed up a little as tradition. If habit is all, why is change proposed? Because of the ' exacerbation of the critical tendency that began with the philosopher Kant'. But we have seen this is at best an irrelevant and at worst a nonsensical relationship. Our key point is that this remained concealed not simply to Greenberg but to all of those who supported him and, like Judd, to all of those who founded themselves on something like Greenbergian critique and took it further, elsewhere, or (like us) as *one* of the bases of paradigm-reform. Strictly speaking, we need not have gone from Greenberg to Judd's more radical position, nor need we be seeking a differently-constituted relationship for the visual. We might have turned to chess or cooking, or war or suicide instead. But then we are not 'strictly' speaking if that means everything is open and undifferentiated. We are not speaking 'strictly' in that sense at all but with the quite different 'strictures' of memetics: patterned complexity, patterned structural opportunity. Echoing Durkheim, what is revealed or concealed is not right or wrong or 'free' - but *normative*. Crucially, it is on the basis of the normative - and not ostensibly free spirit - that actual criticism gets done. Contrary then to the habitually-proposed *uncritical* form of the normal, we can reword our last point as: criticism is actually done by members. And again, the idea of the normative should not connote mechanical resemblances (to use Durkheim's notions again) but structured (or organic) approximations, perceptions, experiments, estimates, 'mistakes' in a multi-information network. Perhaps, in that sense, our objections to Greenberg might be understood as an argument against a kind of serial processing in which verbal definitions set out what painting (for example) is allowed to be - and for a sort of parallel processing in which many qualitatively-different processes shape a number of possible outcomes. This is what we understand by de Duve's, 'Art lovers....may have many motivations, some cultural and learned, others emotional and sensual, still others intellectual and even moral; *but it is with the effective sum total of these motivations that they judge...*' (op. cit. our emphases) except that 'art lovers' may now be read as 'members' - so long as we remember that membership is no less compulsive than loving.

So far we have suggested several candidates for establishing the urgency of Greenberg's memetic actions (or, more simply, the drives, not 'toward' but embedded in, membership. We cited 'rationalism' as idiom, the seductive charm of essentialism that promises on the one hand superiority and on the other a sort of congruence with the categorial forms of wording - in short it is easily intelligible; we cited the desire toward demonstrable competence and the 'promise' of continuing fitness (in Greenberg, 'secure possession'). Most importantly we cited the co-phenomena, meme and member, as the site of iteration and variation and we thought each of these as imperatives. We predicted that Greenberg would fall on the distinction between the specific - the convention of painting - and the generic: the memetic possibilities of *art*. More of that in a moment; there is one more area of compulsion to attend to first: pleasure, taste, the desire for aesthetic satisfaction.

Economics provides us with an autopoetic model - the market - on the assumption of 'goods' taken in the literal and generic sense. Only on the basis of this 'good-ness', which in itself formulates the constant pressures of desire can the autopoietic processes of the market acquire the energy of existence. Differently put, 'good-ness' is the indication that their existence is in any way possible. Relative 'elasticities' are not important here but are at least indicative that we are already in a structured field. Thus the demand for salt is after a certain point *in*elastic because the desire - the goodness - is already quantified. Demand for other goods may be highly elastic because, despite Marxism, because the goodness *cannot* be quantified; there is no clear point at which 'more' becomes unnecessary, where demand is satisfied. Placing this in the context of Greenberg in dictionary-land, he will be eventually forced to concede that 'any painting is a painting' - if it obeys the rule of flatness, supports and so on. Soon the monochrome or blank canvas will confront him. What response has he? All right it's a painting - necessarily- but not necessarily a *good* one. Therefore:

> *It remains*: that when no aesthetic value judgement, no verdict of taste, is there then art isn't there either...It's as simple as that.[15] Or:

> Aesthetic value is affect;...*compelling* you... You no more choose to like or not like a given item of art than you choose to see the sun as bright or the night as dark. [16]

We can safely say it's not as simple as that for sociology; but neither is the characteristically sociological counter-proposal: Greenberg (as cultural dope) confuses social habit with 'innate' imperatives. In that sense his references to the sun and the night would be seen as rhetorics: sincerely felt but intellectually inauthentic: sophistry again - or at least a failing the sociologist must *explain*. It would be his (Platonic) duty. We can also safely say, then, that both approaches are inadequate: the one model insists that you ignore the evidence presented by the other. How can both be accommodated reasonably?

Greenberg's analytic problem: 'Aesthetic value is affect; compelling *you*' - is the tacit assumption that 'we' share the same compulsion. 'It's as simple as that,' is an assertion premised on all of the dubious grounds that set out to demand something like universal values and so involve judgements about both adequate work and adequate response. That, finally,

169

is to distinguish between adequate and inadequate people - though normally put more positively as talent, greatness or genius. Even if sociology's analytic grounds for rejection are weak and themselves premised on an unsupported notion of equality which, translated, *also* means universal sameness - then one can concede that some unpleasant issues lie buried here and gut-rejection is understandable. On the face of it, then, the notion of culture-specific taste or *liking*, seems slightly less objectionable. But we should remember that this also implies culture-specific sanctions no less forceful than those attached to positions like Greenberg's.[17] Still, it *feels* better to say, 'Do your own thing'. The problem is that we still have two positions insisting that each ignore the other; and both contain an implicit 'universality' argument.

The difficulty might be understood - if not resolved - by admitting a more radical notion of autopoietic difference. So as not to fall into the current, sentimental error of confusing pluralism with extensive tolerance it would be better to begin by examining the downside. Taking the Greenbergian position first, 'Aesthetic value is affect;...compelling *you*' - might then be understood as a viable description from one member to another, inviting a form of memetic solidarity. This is unlike the conventional culture-specific response argument in that it leaves intact - it *must* leave intact - the entire issue of compulsion or necessity. It is not a conscious invitation to shared conventionality but a requirement bound up with the experience of an urge that demands satisfaction and the pleasure - the *affect* - in satisfaction: the *liking* is real and not simply experienced *as* real: 'Aesthetic judgement is not voluntary...' [18]; not unlike one's sexuality.

This is not to say it is accepted blindly, as the descendants of Greenberg show quite adequately, but as the reflexive basis for a manifestly critical notion of membership. But, unless 'aesthetic value is affect;...compelling *you*' - there is no basis for solidarity; or better, no basis for a concerted autopoietic difference. The memetic conditions of its being iterated, sustained or varied would then be absent: 'when no aesthetic value judgement, no verdict of taste, is there then art isn't there either...It's as simple as that.' (op cit). The dimension of *exclusion* is also simple, and enormous, but not primarily on account of the 'aesthetic' requirement but precisely through its incorporation with 'dictionary essentialism'. In other words, the *aesthetic* requirement may or not be open - back to de Duve's permanent court of appeal, the jurisprudential record and so on - but the *worded* definition of what painting *essentially is* (the scope of its category) is a decided constriction whose traditional orientation is to get progressively tighter, or less 'incompetent'. The downside, then, as was most clearly the case when Greenberg was 'in power' - is prohibition. The parallel with sexual morality, or more generally the ethics of pleasure and satisfaction, is again discernable.

There is, however a further twist of the knife which is not normally admitted; it's taboo! We are reasonably sure you agreed that the aesthetic requirement - taste, value judgement, court of appeal - was more open then the formalist aspects of Greenberg's position. Fine, if you have some background in visual study (preferably not of the worded type) or are confident in your taste or your visual talent. If not: who are you trying to kid? You know the *last* thing you want is to be put on the spot about a painting - *without preparation*; or admit what you *really* think about Duchamp, or Pollock, or Hirst - or Tinguely! Admit it, you've never heard of him have you? And you are guaranteed right now that if we show you a little film footage to 'help' your comments - in public, before an audience who will remember - the situation will only get worse. The question is: Did you laugh - or squirm just a little? If the former, you are somewhere on the 'inside' - not necessarily secure but at least more secure than the squirmer. And you (and Squirmer) know perfectly well that you are at least in firmer possession of what is socially at stake; and that he will have to tread a path like yours before he can even begin to claim 'equality' of opinion; and you both know that if that were even faintly possible *it would have been done already*. In case you (or we) are feeling, or can be accused of feeling, smug - the same would apply to *any* discipline. Try running the same reasoning with maths or electrical engineering. Or music; the squirm begins again. Why? Because 'we' as humans are supposed to be able to respond to these 'aesthetic' dimensions. But crucially, it does not follow that all humans can respond in the same way, with the same intensity, indifference, intelligence or belligerence. Nor does it mean that every instance of highly-differentiated art form is grounded, or finally groundable, in the distance of our common humanity. Why stop there? Why not say our common relation to a mammal ancestor or a primeval plant or the synthesis of elements in stars? We do 'in practice' stop at something like our common humanity - but it does not take a re-run of *the trouble with Lyotard* - to see that what we mean is a highly-differentiated group sharing a similar time and a similar discipline. In short, what Greenberg offers is a limited social opportunity, an exploration, possibly with benefits. It is only to be expected that the vast majority of contemporaries - let alone 'humanity' - *will be bound to turn it down*. The analogy with sexuality now collapses in the face of vastly greater complexity: the solidarity that is simply expressed in and by gender is overwhelmingly inadequate to this scale of differentiated possibilities.

That the vast majority of contemporaries, let alone 'humanity', will be bound to turn down Greenberg's social opportunity is not in itself objectionable. It doesn't matter even if Greenberg - with allies - shouts 'incompetence' to the rooftops. It doesn't really matter whether they are more or less correct than the 'incompetent' majority; the issue is quite undecidable. What *is* objectionable and thoroughly unreasonable is that the majority should be so enslaved by the categorial *habit* (note: not 'imperative') as to believe that Greenberg is righter then they are - to the point of self-censure - but more importantly, that they are so bound by their own speech customs that the principle of non-contradiction extends ridiculously to painting. That is, they give greater credence to the ludicrous idea of what painting 'essentially is' than they do to the perfectly reasonable assertion that they are many different kinds. That, in a way, sounds ridiculous; it is also the way we have been invited to think for centuries. Without the persistence in everyday language of such Socratic idioms, Greenberg would not be even faintly memorable.

We can now formulate the downside in its most explicit form. It is not just a question give greater credence to the ludicrous idea of what painting 'essentially is' than to the perfectly reasonable assertion that they are many different kinds - of painting - but that there are huge ranges of other social possibilities. In that sense the majority may well direct their attentions elsewhere. But then what really has Squirmer to say about painting? Nothing. It would not be an exaggeration to say he belongs to a different *social species*. We are well aware of the political memories and implications this invokes - but remember we are writing the downside first.

Now let us turn to the ostensibly more sociological position: taste and value judgement are culture-specific. Not to acknowledge this - especially in relation one's own preferences (especially as white, western male etc.) is also 'incompetent' in exactly the Greenbergian sense and also fascist, sexist, imperialist - even if *you* can't see it. We shall not repeat the arguments of previous chapters, except to say that 'mutually-assured conventionality' is not going to cut much ice outside of the laxity of western mores. Our focus here is rather different, or perhaps it turns rather more on how it excludes *insiders* as well as ordinarily-recognised outsiders. Our model insider, here, is Greenberg.

Clearly, mutually-assured conventionality takes some of the urgency out of his project. Further, it denies him his specific identity in this specific sense. It deprives him of the *drive* - 'it's as simple as that' - which recognises and values the art he desires by converting the involuntary requirement he *feels* into a type of foolishness; an impossible decision to

172

abide by a *habit* as if it were a *calling*. This is supposed to be more 'competent' - ironically, in *exactly* the Greenbergian sense - and with strikingly similar prohibitions: a *conversion* is required on the basis that 'we all know' such drives to be habitual and nothing more. Now the drive is just that: to show *all other* drives as conventional in the sense of, 'could be otherwise'. No 'call' is admissible that could not be equally-well replaced by another. Whereas the essential form of painting was defined by Greenberg not by specific interests but by its general physical definition (give or take implied colour-space), so too the essential form of 'calling' is now wrenched from its specific interests into the general form of the category 'callings'. But *callings* cannot be experienced *or grammatically presented* in the same way as 'I desire...' That is to say, the idiom *callings* already defuses the claim of the particular and requires that we discourse on possibilities. That is not objectionable providing we do not confuse the *desire* to speak of generalities with a *definition* of conventionality, for the first is merely idiomatic and the second, ostensibly necessary. The movement from the first to the second as a matter of course is a ridiculous and grave error. At the risk of repetition, however, it is deeply grounded in ordinary usage and utterly objectionable in the form of the effects and prohibitions it proposes.

We don't yet have Squirmer Two but he would be the speaker who moved from generality as idiom to conventionality as definition. What, then has he to say about the specifics of the drive exhibited by the 'insider' Greenberg? Nothing. He belongs to a different social 'species'.

Let's try to place this slightly differently. The proposition is this: the move from generality as idiom - 'callings'- to conventionality as *definition* - of all 'callings' is not reasonable; it is *ridiculous*. It confuses plurality with excess or spurious differentiation. It cannot grasp that what is necessary for the one and unnecessary for the other does not diminish the original requirement or its claim for satisfaction at all. However, in the *definition* of calling *as* conventional it invites one to take part in a social process where they *are*, for all practical purposes, conventional. The conventional speaker, once the invitation has been accepted and becomes learned in this idiom shows 'competence' through repetition. That is, 'competence' is enacted as the repetition of the error that says callings, requirements, drives are *substitutable* when everyone else knows they're not (including that same speaker when he comes across something he cannot admit on the same level as his own conventionality) such as 'excessive' crime, or religiosity, or a claim to enhanced aesthetic sensitivity. This is not at all a claim to common sense - quite the reverse. It is to say, however, just like in the Greenbergian case, very few people will be in a position to accept this notion of competence as a way of life. Very few will be in any position to take it at all seriously - except in the massively protected domain of something like contemporary academic cultural studies, whose imagination and speech-practices are structured by and so resemble Socratic positions that they cannot hear these errors as they are mouthed. In case the point has been missed, for anyone outside that closed minority, the fact that there are different kinds of drives, requirements, ways of life, art forms and so on does not mean they are substitutable or bear some common equivalence - any more than the preposterous Socratic form of the bed that col-lects all beds has any rational basis; for everyone outside that minority *difference* means just that: there *are* different kinds. *No* principle of col-lection follows. If that still feels odd, it is simply that minority form has disproportionate influence for both historical and structural-categorial reasons in our habitual wordings. In this sense 'different social species' may be seen not as a means of exclusion but as evidence of an evolved social ecology. We are not the first to argue this organically-differentiated model. It is Durkheim's essential postulate in *The Division of Labour* and the basis of his ethics. But it is still, we think, the major sticking point: Darwin is accepted as the basis even for his own critique but it seems that social 'speciation' in Durkheim's sense of organic differentiation is still unacceptable. We still, in speech, yearn for commonality and not *differentiated* images of community.

One more presentation. The difference at stake here is that between the profound reality of pleasure, taste, aesthetic satisfaction (as experienced by Greenberg, or so he says) and the same set of experiences taken *as* (or as *if*) 'real' by the sociology of taste given that the (conventional) sociology of taste begins with its self-evident difference across cultural contexts; what is real for one context is not necessarily real for another). Our aim is to show (a) that the sociology of taste taken in that sense is not an account or an analysis so much as a *substitution* of one kind of taste for another and (b) that the reality perceived in one set of tastes but not in another is completely irrelevant; so that (c) the sociology of taste has fundamentally misunderstood the relationship between tastes or cultures and accounts. [19]

If Greenberg is to be believed he identifies in himself an involuntary drive toward aesthetic value judgement and the ability to recognise when that drive is, or is not, satisfied. Further, he is able to reflect upon and make reasonably coherent critical positions (not without contradictions) on the nature of that drive and its satisfaction as a *social* phenomenon out of which the member-specifications 'artist' and 'critic' are made explicit. Our position so far has been to insist that this should be understood as rooted in some general set of human possibilities but concretely experienced as a highly-differentiated and specific set of social practices. Our first difference from the ordinary sociology of taste is to insist that this specific site points toward the humanly-specialised rather than the general. Hence the problem of social speciation. We may now shed some light on the proposition (a) - 'that the sociology of taste taken in that sense is not an account or an analysis so much as a *substitution* of one kind of taste for another' - by relating Greenberg's 'aesthetic' urge to the more extreme and more general example of physical desire.

We resist the temptation to reduce 'physical desire' to something like sexuality or hunger or even the human range of experience. The key issue is that it is involuntary and however powerful its *affects* it is either inexpressible or converted into some other form of expression: body language, cries, scent emissions. Presumably the neuro-bio-chemistry of the urge to mate or migrate or sleep 'explains' some or even all of the components that make the process 'intelligible' for the individual. But the explanations - say, *of* hunger and its satisfaction as a process - stand alongside the process. They do not substitute for it, nor do they diminish its reality. The explanations, so to speak, must 'respect' the profundity of the urge and its processes - or it is worth nothing as an explanation. Or, in the case of sleep, for example, our meagre understanding holds 'its' phenomenon in awe.

The problem with the sociology of taste is that it is just as meagre and undeveloped as our understanding of sleep. Unfortunately, it has not the same humility. Armed with the colossal insight that taste 'varies' and may be somehow related to the social order (for determinists at least) the sociology of taste struts about as though these minor - and for that matter, finally contradictory - observations, constitute a full-blown moral and political order. From the hard determinst 'left' to the soft-left of 'committed' postmoderns (the contradiction is intended) [20] the sociology of taste operates as exposure and correction; showing that once-perceived creative freedom is 'actually' ideology-in-disguise; and the only 'rational' (competent, acceptable, enlightened) cultural pose is the espousal of an ostensible pluralism on grounds of the authorised disbelief in metanarratives. In this sense *'the trouble with Lyotard'* (for example) is not so much that he has authoritarian tendencies but that a programme of cultural cleansing is also proposed. In this process, the profundity of the 'drive to...' (think of Greenberg's involuntary aesthetic judgement) is re-converted into 'postmodern' form as merely customary. For re-conversion also read: deconstruction, explanation, exposure, *real*isation. Where any other drive - such as hunger - is *accompanied* by its explanation, the sociology of culture - that is of tastes, committed choice, received disciplines - claims to become the new (post) culture that supersedes the old: hunger *replaced* by its explanation. The fact that *Modernism* is guilty of exactly the same attempted ethnic cleansing points only to the persistence of the problem and the urgency of its alteration. Moreover, it is the same problem that infects the Socratic Republic: the dissolution of every possible and distinct branch of solidarity in the spurious universalism of worded 'analyses'. At the same time it must be understood that the explanation of culture, by culture will always threaten subsumption.

We now turn to proposition (b): the reality perceived in one set of tastes but not in another is *completely irrelevant*. That cultural practice varies is of enormous importance to the sociology of culture. Conventionally, this is taken to imply a kind of inter-changeability so that the 'preference' for one set of practices is seen simply as preference - and not *need*; further, 'preference' is taken as inward-looking, insular and unsophisticated. When addressed by members as *need* it is seen (by postmodern sociologists) as prejudice, in the sense of bigoted self-interest or self-aggrandisement. Again, the comparison with physical 'preference' is instructive.

We do not - by and large - formulate the variation in forms of physical requirement as 'conventional' though - quite clearly - they too 'could have been otherwise'. Perhaps due to less-immediate self-interest we concede normative variation within specific phenomena and concede specific adaptation between phenomena. Though of course any mention of normative variation or specific adaptation applied to human abilities (especially intelligence) or adaptation (especially those related to gender) will immediately get you put on the right wing and in the heat of controversy before you've even mentioned *how* 'x' varies or is specifically adapted. There will be readers right now concluding that *colours have been shown*. It isn't relevant!

We do not particularly wish to argue for normally-distributed human ability or, more contentiously, to assert a high degree of variation. We *do* argue for a high degree of adaptive variation in cultural phenomena, or - as Durkheim argues - for the patterned complexity of organic solidarity. Neither has this a primarily gender-related distribution. Instead, complexity, so to speak, is *its own* consequence; or better, is the consequence of both iteration and plasticity in the memetic process. No doubt some of these differences can be explained by 'hard' adaptation: climate, technology, population density or isolation. Some can be explained by or as experimentation - the modernist avant-garde essayed one version of this. Some can be explained by evolved co-operation or hostilities, admiration or suspicious rejection. Some by opportunity, or the differential distribution of capital or fortunate birthright. But the point is not a rough classification of types. There are two main issues, as we see it. First, in the evidence of complex difference *nothing* suggests conventionality in the sense of substitutability. Second, it is only by postulating a sort of hierarchy that the conventionality of *lower* forms is also postulated. Typically, this takes place in the Academy or in the more general forms of 'high' Western culture: literature and the arts. In that sense, the ostensible substituable-pluralism of postmodern liberalism is nothing more than old colonialism in disguise. Or, put conversely, there is nothing to suggest that your 'lower' form of adaptation (try Greenberg's aesthetic imperative here, or, Catholicism) is *essentially* conventional, except postmodern liberalism itself. For everyone else, providing we resist cultural imperialism or decline to become academics, adaptation is not grasped *as* authentic but *is* authentic. And to this authenticity the doctrine of pluralism through mutually-assured conventionality has absolutely nothing to say. Indeed it cannot even conceive it. Outside, then, of mutually-assured conventionality - that one experiences one's life as an artist and another as a writer, or politician, or scientist, or sportsman, or heterosexual or as homosexual or someone for whom literature is fascinating or for whom reading is a problem, or who takes delight in ethnic variation or as one who feels threatened by it, or as one who can live comfortably from this social order or one who detests it in every waking moment - is just not an issue. Social experience remains complex, differentiated but *authentic* - and rarely conventional so far as one's greatest interests are concerned. This is why Greenberg, Catholicism (or what you will) continue to assert the involuntary nature of their central phenomena - to the complete bafflement of academic and high-culture postmodern*ism*. (The italics again emphasise *idiom*; you will not be surprised to find that postmodern culture hardly exists outside of the realms already specifically colonised by postmodernism. For example, postmodernists rarely visit postmodern dentists - they much prefer the old, metanarrative-scientific sort of dentist with proper qualifications.)

The bafflement that surrounds postmodern*ism* in the face of different kinds of commitment is also, of course, analytically identical to the Socratic practice of ignorance and grounded in the same blind arrogance: anything felt by others and not Socrates, anything known by others and not Socrates, any wisdom other than Socrates', every type of representation that does not coincide with Socrates' is inauthentic. In this sense, Greenberg's involuntarist aestheticism plays the analytic counterpart to Michelangelo's fascination with the body. Crucially, both aesthetes are driven to renounce themselves in the wordings of Modernism and Neoclassicism; the aesthetic imperative throttled by the categorial imperative. *Every* analyst faces the same risk. We repeat: the risk is the grave error of translating the observable variety of culture and taste - and so the reasonable wish to speak of these phenomena 'in general' - into the unreasonable proposition that they are conventional or substitutable. Conversely, it is the non-substitutability and therefore finally the *non-coventionality* of those such as Michelangelo, and indeed Greenberg, that makes them proper 'subject matter' (not subject-ed matter) for the sociology of culture.

We now turn to proposition (c) 'the sociology of taste has fundamentally misunderstood the relationship between tastes or cultures and accounts.' Our position is of course shaped by our previous sentence: the sociology of taste has misunderstood, specifically, the non-conventionality of its subject matter; it has instead treated it as conventional and therefore not only substitutable but incorporatable into its own higher idioms. But strictly speaking there are no 'higher' idioms; therefore both the sociology of culture and its subject matter are reduced to arbitrary contingencies. In order to counteract this, the converse must be proposed: that the differences between cultures, and further, the difference between cultures and the sociology of culture is (or ought to be) fundamental, non-conventional and authentic. This is not just a matter of saying 'all right' but rather a question of realising that the current paradigm stands in fundamental opposition to that proposal and is indeed grounded in the converse. Simply put, in current practice these differences *cannot be* authentic - or, as we said earlier *cannot be conceived* as such.

This is no easy theoretic move, then, but one which will inevitably provoke a backlash of protest from the previous paradigm; in several senses with good reason. For what the proposition of authenticity implicitly asserts is extreme. First it implies that something akin to social speciation must be taken seriously; that is potentially divisive enough, as we know from recent history, and is quite capable of providing the most vicious ideological weaponry in the wrong hands. From this an even less palatable consequence follows: the sociology of culture-speciation cannot be simply *another* species but must genuinely be an explanatory form. We resist the notion of a *higher* explanatory form - and we have already decisively rejected the paradigm of substitution - but to frame *any* charge akin to 'ideology in the wrong hands' is to distinguish between authentic and inauthentic explanations. Granted, the distinctions will be provisional and subject to de Duve's salient metaphor: the permanent court of appeal. Nevertheless, we submit we have demonstrated that 'mutually-assured conventionality' fails to meet the jurisprudential requirements and, on the evidence, it should be abandoned.

Notes

1.   Crowther, P. (1997) p.11.
2.   *New Scientist* 13ᵗʰ March 1999.
3.   Wittgenstein, L. (1974) espec. 4.21 'The simplest kind of proposition states the existence of states of affairs.' 4.22 'An elementary proposition consists of names. It is a nexus. a concatenation of names.' See Smith, J.A. in Jenks (1995) pp. 239-45. See also Mitchell (1886) pp.5-46 which argues that the connection of name and image in the early Wittgenstein is not incompatible with, or superseded by, the later writing. The contrary, of course, is the more usual 'conventionalist' position of contemporary sociology. We place our arguments against that at the close of this chapter.
4.   see Cheetham, M. (1991).
5.   see Frascina. F. (1985).
6.   Harrison & Wood (1993) p.755.
7.   ibid.
8.   ibid.
9.   He puts these words into the mouth of Collins, 'an embryo don', in the opening chapter of *Brideshead Revisited.*
10.   Harrison & Wood (1993) p.756.
11.   ibid. p.755.
12.   ibid. p.756.
13.   ibid.p.809.
14.   Summers, D. in Bryson et al (eds.) (1992).
15.   de Duve (1996) p.212 our emphases.
16.   ibid. pp. 213-4 our emphases.
17.   see *The Trouble with Loytard* (above).
18.   de Duve p.213.
19.   This is *not* a substitution of indexical expressions by (ostensibly) objective ones, in the sense of Garfinkel's *Ethnomethodology.* But, if the reader is persuaded by that assumption (or something like it) for the moment, tread carefully: the eventual twist in the tale is radically different.
20.   O' Neill, J. in Silverman, H. (ed.) (1990) provides an example. 'Postmodernism celebrates the neutralisation of all commitment from which even mimicry derives.' p. 70. Following our analysis of Lyotard we might ask: What are the tacit exclusions? How is O'Neill so easily classifiable? (One would only need this quote to place his profession, the likely department, the likely date.) Let's just say the mimicry and so the commitment are completely obvious. One could even predict something of his style of clothing and (speaking of clothing) how rapidly the postmodern hat would disappear in maters as diverse as insurance, food hygiene or the need for an accurate bank statement. Perhaps what he *meant* to say, and forgot, was: postmodernism celebrates the neutralisation of *some* commitments.

9　Lucien Freud's Figuration

In the last chapter we first attacked Greenberg then tried to protect him from the radicalisation of his own paradigm. This is not unlike the situation in which Socrates' followers found themselves: in the perfectly consistent 'reasoning' that led to his suicide, their attempts to dissuade him amount to a doctrinal betrayal. To make him the subject of Plato's drama is a further act of betrayal. This is easily enough seen: Plato is manifestly *caught* by the contradictions of Platonism. But so too is Socrates: his only correct position in being unable to choose between life and death is to suspend himself somewhere between. In a sense, that is *exactly* what has happened to him in that he 'becomes' one of the origins of philosophy. But that is only to argue that Socrates suspended between life and death or a philosophy of similar origin is manifestly irrelevant to the truth of human life *or* death. The tides of fate flow. Socrates was never in a position to *choose*, only to be swept along by the strongest current. That is to say that Socrates (or philosophy) misunderstands the ecology of 'choice'. That is not an argument for submission[1] but for a better understanding. Here is Greenberg's hemlock:

> since even an unpainted canvas now stated itself as a picture, the borderline between art and non-art *had* to be sought in the three-dimensional.. [2]

For the 'borderline between art and non-art' read: the difference between competence and incompetence. Greenberg (the policeman) is clearly saying, 'I got it - the law - wrong.' We would of course say that jurisprudence has moved on and on the basis of his own judgements, Greenberg cannot oppose it. This, again, is not an argument for acquiescence. It is to say, however, that Greenberg misunderstood the ecology of aesthetic judgement and in particular, he allied it to a 'critical' doctrine that was *duty* bound to supersede his aesthetics. Had he valued his aesthetic judgement as a surer foundation than his so-called critical reasoning, that particular death might also have been avoided. We are speaking, of course, of the death of painting. But memes, like genes, are not quite mortal and in due course we shall examine a newer generation. Two points first. The striking parallels between Socrates and Greenberg should alert us to the fact that this is not primarily a doctrinal issue but one rooted in human praxis - especially in language. Second, if we are to sidestep this propensity, it is not the case that regenerated painting, or drama, or new thinking, or new appetites must justify themselves before what passes for critical reason. On the contrary it is critical reason that must understand, justify and finally ground itself in the existential fact of regenerative re-occurrence. In other words, autopoiesis is not the subject matter of reasoning but its *cause*. Similarly, critical reason and its moral ambitions are not the court of judgement before which autopoietic phenomena appear. On the contrary, they are precisely criticisms, evaluations, ambitions - in short, *informed strategies*, of no particular greater rank than other 'informed strategies' - such as flying, swimming, hunting, defence of young, participation in a market, religious ceremony, sexual intercourse.

> A doctor is looking to make the person better, weller. Whereas the painter looking at the person is looking to get anything from that person to strengthen the picture, which is still an invention, however modified, however near he steers to the person. I mean, however he inhibits himself - perhaps through excessive naturalism or whatever - he's still looking at the person for the picture's sake and not for the person's. [3]

According to Greenberg's 'critical' reasoning Freud is an incompetent painter. As befits a policing regime based on the dictionary, Greenberg's position is fundamentally literal. We open this section with an analysis of what that might mean, drawing upon some of our earlier terminology, especially the notion of representation. Our primary aim is to distance ourselves from Greenberg's error and to show that it is an error, not a difference of convention. This is not intended to challenge the aesthetic conventions we call 'Modernism', though it certainly needs a different name. Our analysis is not, then, directed against the painting-idioms of Pollock or Rothko or Newmann. We shall return to that in our next chapter on Richter.

Greenberg's notion of incompetence turns on a spurious grasp of facticity: the physically-ascertainable components of 'painting' – the support, the canvas, the materials – are elevated, for no good reason, over those aspects associated with selection, process, intention, representation and finally (in the blank canvas) with judgement itself. It is strikingly odd (remember Greenberg represented our culture) that we should approach the critique of a re-presentative tradition by denying, as incompetent, representation itself. For Greenberg's reforms are inconceivable unless we first concede the memetics of representation as at least one of painting's major functions – but then argue for its abolition. Take another example. If we agree that astrology no longer has credibility we can hardly insist that astronomy must adhere to its 'characteristic methods'. Similarly, in announcing our secularity we should not be expected to abide by the disciplines of Christian religious observance. But this is what Greenberg (we) wanted. 'Our' culture wanted to do this. We did not say 'painting is over' in the same way as 'god is dead'. We required instead that its social functions - selection, process, intention, representation - be removed but, somehow, we should carry on with the material husk. Apparently, it did not occur, at the time, that there was a deep, indeed unbreakable, continuity between the evolved materials and their social functions. It did not occur at the time (despite the fact that we already knew it) that these two ostensibly separate classes of phenomena were systematically related. It was simply assumed that the ascertainable physical bits could be severed from the social bits; the former preserved, the latter discarded.

If we had approached any other social species in this way – severing the material of the wasp or the ant from its social ecology – we should not expect the individual to function as before. We should not expect it to function at all. Neither is it idle to ask what might happen to the 'information' coded in, and the insect's brain: Where do hardware and software separate? But humans, of course, are not primarily members of a species (and therefore structured) but 'subjects' (and so not structured) – or so the story used to go, not very long ago. That position ostensibly allows us to discount the entire information-structure of the most information-saturated species (ourselves) as an ecological irrelevance – because in the old language, it is subjective. In the new language it is memetic and ecologically vital. Stated in terms of painting: the field we understand by that term is a plastic meme-complex coded in the social ecology of our species. However, painting is a plastic, not a compulsive or involuntary behaviour and therefore parts (or all) of the meme are, by definition, malleable or expendable. Those possibilities are also coded in our social ecology. Simply put: no subject, no a priori 'bits'. Another way to say this is: painting is a *possibility*. It is remarkable that our species, uniquely characterised by its post-natal plasticity, should want to burden itself with irrelevant 'necessities'. One can see why: 'subjective' suggests restricted views and consequent errors. But it does not follow that phenomena characterised by plastic possibility, like painting, have lurking within them a leaden nugget of essence concealed by the manifold forms of appearance. Greenberg's error, Socrates' error, *our* error is the simple confusion of what can be specifically defined – a discrete object – with a class of memetic possibilities whose relationships are also memetically-decided. We submit that as a reasonable 'in place of a definition' for a secular and evolutionary-autopoietic worldview.

In this sense, Freud offers a rather better understanding of painting than Greenberg. That is not particularly strange but his regularly claimed uniqueness in keeping alive genuine figurative painting suggests also that generally, our culture has a poor understanding of its functional possibilities. At the same time, 'uniqueness' is a most non-memetic concept and should be treated with extreme care. First, it is nonsensical to cite 'uniqueness' in Freud's early work. He clearly belongs to a group including Minton, Bacon, Auerbach and was taught by Cedric Morriss If anything his early work also shows rather hackneyed reference to surrealism. But he is – and remains – 'special' for the oldest and most routine reasons: name and fortune.

Leaving Germany in 1933 - as Hitler became Chancellor - the Freuds took a flat in Clarges Street, off Piccadilly, opposite Green Park and the brothers including Lucian were sent to Dartington Hall - which 'had offered Ernst [the father] specially low terms on account of his name.' [4] He stayed there a short time before moving on - regularly - on account of his disruptive behaviour. [5] It is idle to speculate whether his social status helped to insulate Freud from the more ordinary course of Modernism. Or, whether his economic position and his father's good sense meant that the Freuds were 'refugees' in a very special sense. What is manifestly clear, however, that – if insulated, or capable of making more choices than most, – it was only to the extent that another memetic requirement was able to assert itself, namely, the discipline of figurative or 'representational' painting. Moreover, all his work, not least the early work, demonstrates the violence of this process: the doubled re-presentation of the 'actual' subject and the subversion of the painting's 'actual' material as an image.

Early work such as *The Refugees* [6] or *Evacuee Boy* [7] demonstrates the memetics of reduction, the plasticities of *signs-for* threatening to become convention (like the Ancient Egyptian drawing-writing system) But always plying convention against convention, meaning against dissolution, image as also object, sign as material. *The Refugees* - a family with interlinked arms demonstrates exceptionally conventional idioms from 20th Century figuration in the handling and distortion of the limbs, hands, faces and eyes; the latter to evolve into the intensified trademark of his work, only gradually disappearing in the mid to late fifties. Similarly the rejection of perspective - or its compression by 'stacking'- and the abbreviation/absence of modelling are easily-read idiomatic repetitions. The *Evacuee Boy* similarly asserts a violence in the nakedness and in the handling and in the deliberate emphasis of *paint* 'replacing' the body which can be traced to any number of orthodox 'Modernist' sources from Soutine to Cezanne or 'pre-modern' sources - irony intended - in Goya or Rembrandt or Titian, or early human art or, for that matter, Freud's childhood drawings. The point is: this is nothing especially *new* but a set of emphases and idioms from an ancient and modern set of possibilities in a persistent memetic field. The textured brown pigment 'stands for', stands instead, *re-presents* the jacket; the heavily-worked yellows and pinks and greys 'render' the naked body in a manner not particularly dissimilar from pictures thousands of years old. But they are not wordings nor have they been wordings for the same stretch of time. They have another, long social history; they belong to (an)other public traditions(s).

Freud's extraordinary distinction between the doctor who makes you 'weller' and the artist who *uses* you to make a picture displays the residual guilt of this historical separation. Doctor as good guy makes you 'weller' (a while back it would have been the philosopher who made you 'better') while the wicked artist turns you into commodified raw material "for the picture's sake and not for the person's". What a moral dilemma! But - what does the doctor do? He remedies a *defect*. This is not a moral action but a pragmatic one and based on the supposition that it is 'right' to cure humans. This is a practical act of species solidarity, not a moral act and one might postulate many species from corals to fish to fleas to cattle who might benefit were the human species not so damned good at getting 'weller'.

The remedial role of the philosopher (Platonist, Modernist or Postmodernist) is only slightly less species-centred but finally more *sinister*. Each seeks to distinguish between the enlightened and entrenched whether entrenchment is enacted by appearances as opposed to essence, superfluity as opposed to necessary form, or excessive ethnological commitment as opposed to ostensible detachment. But again, the first two claim on ontological grounds to be 'above' questions of morality whilst the third announces an amorality that is finally incoherent. Might it be that the painter is the moral figure rather than the doctor? Well - not quite - or not at least on the basis of the earlier work's re-presentative action.

The later work is quite different, however. For us, the key changes begin in the portraits of 1954-8 [8] and by the early sixties it is decisive. It would be absurd to call it 'complete' since the phenomena in question are not classifiable objects or discrete beings. The change is in part stylistic or methodic: the brushes are larger, the paint more pronounced, the line less defined, the handling more rhythmic. The space is also beginning to shift toward the more elevated and tightly-focused viewpoint of the late work.

Described mundane surroundings - the studio - become more pictorially important. These changes are crucial: we will not trounce them with a 'yet more so' move. Freud remains a painter; he still uses people to make pictures. But there is a distinct shift bound up with all of these changes in which the possibilities of painting expand. Freud seems to us to have re-discovered without compromising his 'contemporary' status that the violence of re-presentation towards its subjects, also turns upon itself: in claiming the person as its raw material painting also, potentially, opens up a new 'inhibitition' (as Freud puts it) though we would call it discipline or memetic field. In Freud's work, not uniquely but certainly impressively, the memetic possibilities of 'subjecting' people to painting is re-established as an inquestive field. We do not - or not necessarily - imply that the inquiry aligns itself with notions of science or critical theory, but that it does imply that (Freud's amongst others') painting becomes an occasion in which the contemplation of the body is sanctioned. But even that is too much like neutral or value- free inquiry. Rather the occasion is double-edged: Painting is certainly *valued* but as a place in which seeing and the object seen are placed into question. Not a general or a verbal questioning but the kind of inquiry that painting, human sight and the human body *between themselves* both permit and delimit. This is why the philosopher's remedial essentialism or the postmodern's de-entrenchment are finally sinister: they would forbid the coalition and the enquiry as incompetent or over-committed; that is, as a type of bigotry. That is not to say that the inquiry itself is, in a way, innocent; nor, conversely, that when visual assertion intercedes over visual inquiry that the process suddenly gets 'wrong'.

Pictures like *Man in a Mackintosh* and *A Young Painter* both from 1957-8 or *A Woman Painter* from 1954 [9] are amongst the earliest to demonstrate a pictorial 'regime' that is more adapted to the scrutiny of the human face than to the idioms of modernist-ic figuration. We repeat: this is not a moral argument. It is not somehow better to efface oneself or one's preferred conventions by copying the sitter's likeness - in one's preferred medium. Or to use Freud's words, 'inhibiting' oneself through 'excessive naturalism' is not a moral postulate. Nor is his ostensible realism any more socially correct or normatively 'accessible' to a public tired of the avant-garde. Think of an office or public building faced with a choice between Freud's paintings of Leigh Bowery or his vast *Benefit Supervisor* series and a Pollock or a Richter 'abstract'.

Derrida's re-invocation of *ergon* and *parergon* - main and subsidiary work - is perhaps closer to the mark. The *ergon* as Freud immediately and candidly admits is painting - and nothing like the doctor's 'restoration'. The sitter 'being examined' is undeniably parergon. But for Derrida, the former is inevitably parasitized by the latter.

> But that is what an idiom (painting) is.... It does not merely fix the economic propriety of a "focus" but regulates the possibility of play, of divergences, of the equivocal -a whole economy, precisely, of the trait. This economy parasitizes itself. [10]

Or, as Jay summarises:

> Arguing against the integrity of the work of art (the *ergon*) he [Derrida] showed that it is always polluted by its framing contexts (the *parergon*), so that any purely aesthetic discourse cannot itself avoid intermingling with those it tries to exclude - ethical, cognitive, or whatever.... [Cezanne s pledge.... is, doomed to be betrayed.] For what is inside and outside a picture is undecidable. [11]

These insights are interesting but compromised with, at best, a post-structuralist agenda and, at worst, an intellectual fashion for emphasising the chaotic. Simply insert 'finally' into Jay: what is inside and outside a picture is finally undecidable and the proper response is clear: We are not speaking 'finally'. Or, to put it another way, despite the ingrained idioms of philosophers, the absence of finalities, of any kind, does not prevent us formulating the current ecology of a set of phenomena. To Jay, the complete response is, then, what is inside and outside a picture is precisely *decidable*. That is, the key dimension is the social decision or action in the specific instance, along with the energies and structures that energise it, and not, ever, painting-in-general which is *a priori* undecidable (or non-specific) and irrelevant. Put simply 'painting in general' is even less conceptually useful to a socio-ecology as 'non-specific organism' is to a general ecology. Derrida's only advantage over Jay is that, at least, 'parasitization' has an active, organic ring - but of course he didn't mean that; he meant to invoke decay and degradation. We are instead concerned with the living act in Freud's painting; and even its projected 'death' does not invoke 'the way of all flesh and of all human construction' in the obsessive Biblical or philosophical sense of 'deconstruction' but the complexities of autopoietic change.

Freud, as a painter, decides what is inside and outside the picture. It is key to our position that no decision of any kind is feasible outside membership and that the decision therefore has normative or memetic components. Moreover, the decision is made for the sake of painting. This is not an act of selflessness but of membership: a place where Freud *can* decide. But on account of being part of *painting* which is of itself for the sake of others' membership, that decision will be open to others' responses, interpretations, ignorance, indifference, hostility. Where Freud can decide so can others. But this does not mean that the decisions are 'open'. We are again speaking of replication and plasticity in a meme-complex. To use a simple analogy: you *may* compare Freud's painting to Duchamp's pisspot but you *may not* hang it in a public urinal. The 'absolute' reasons for the *may* and the *may not* will not be answered because there is no relevant authority. Or: those sort of reasons have no further part in rationalism.

Freud, as a painter, decides what is inside and outside the picture. But reciprocally, his being a painter, announces an enormous concession. Perhaps at other times he will decide on other forms but, as a painter, he has yielded the total scope of his action to pictorial possibility. This is the key delimitation of 'parasitization' or of what is 'inside and outside'. In *Man in a Mackintosh* and *A Young Painter* and *A Woman Painter* there are specific exclusions of his earlier idioms. The eyes do not form the twin spherical centres of attention. Their oval presentation is stressed along with a somewhat flatter but somewhat more authentic space. The colours and the brushwork are more broken. They no longer subordinate themselves to a two-dimensional pictorial geometry but rather suggest the mass as the outcome of patches, rhythms and broad lines of colour painted each for itself and each, seemingly, of equal weight and intensity. The scale is somewhat larger and confined to the head and shoulders. Clothes - often complex in structure and monumental, simplified backgrounds assume greater importance. In pictorial terms they become the 'equal' of the sitters features. In sum, the pictorial system as idiom is radically open to the sitter's features and their description but is quite as radically closed as a *painted picture*. This economy is not 'parasitized' nor subject to gradual de-construction but is a most *determined* site of social action. If anything - as we clearly know - both Freud and the sitter are parasitized for the sake of painting. Unlike Derrida, where idiom and economy are *bound to be* parasitized, the precedence of painting takes rank over both previous idioms and subject matter. Nor is this an economy in which the goodness of the goods sets forward the drive to appropriation or satisfaction; it is instead a quest, an open exploration whose outcome is not known and is constantly in contention. There are few who dare risk this openness and even fewer, like Freud, who having risked everything can command our attention to the outcome.

Risk is perhaps the crucial notion here but it is also essential to see that it is not the notion of risk that informs Duchamp nor someone like John

Cage. It is not that their risk is any less extreme in its consequences but rather that its destructive or random quality is virtually guaranteed. (We specifically exclude painters such as Pollock and Richter here. See next chapter). In *Standing by the Rags* [12] something of the difference is exposed. First, the pile of rags as subject matter can stand comparison with anything Duchamp presented and offers unavoidable iconic reference to the re-absorption of Duchamp in artists as diverse as Pollock, Rauschenberg or Robert Morris. The rags are, beyond question, a reference to the themes of deconstruction, chance and visual complexity that characterise Modernism. But they are also painted, that is to say, re-presented in paint - with something akin to the complexity and dedication afforded to the nude figure. Again, painting as 'open' exploration seems to have levelled every other rank below its own priority. How is the risk different from Duchamp's and his descendents?

Here we may agree with Lyotard. Modernism's risk-aesthetic is a nostalgic one; it offers the solace of good forms. More sharply, for us, the rhetoric of deconstruction, whether in Derrida's wordings or Duchamp's unassisted ready-mades, 'represents' but no longer *takes* risks. This is why, Modernism culminates in the blank canvas or the hubris of whatever *I* say is art *is* art. Freud risk is not autodestructive; it is autopoietic - which is to say that he is not wholly in control and is certainly not the controlling centre. First he is constrained by the discipline of painting - as we have already explored - and this demands the kind of attention he must pay to his icon of randomness: the rags. There is an element of duty and ritual and repetition here that exposes the unassisted ready-made as most competent labour-saving device. Perhaps Greenberg is right: Freud is an interesting painter but definitely 'incompetent', economically-speaking.

Then again there is the vexed matter of the nude. She is deliberately placed against the spectacle of the rags; it is bigger than her; she is subject to it. But Freud is also subject; he loses his control and authority the moment he has set the spectacle before him and renounced himself to the necessity of painting; not photography, not a kind of performance. She and he will be bound to that repetition; to the monocular viewpoint, to the aching return to the pose, to the painstaking mapping of colour and shape, to the endless effect of new mark upon old, to difficult decisions in the face of necessary approximations, to the brutality of the representation in all of its demands. This is not to say that he is out of control of the painting and of course he was *already* painting when he engineered the spectacle. The risk lies in the submission to paint and that the submission was unnecessary or futile but will certainly happen again and again. It is already thousands of years old. What is at work: fascination, compulsion, habit?

Our answer must be: exposure. What is exhibited, or better, what *this* painting exhibits is the exposure to the phenomena of vision that painting requires of its maker if it is to be at all successful. This is not to argue for its purity; plenty of tricks abound and are *necessary* - like Duchamp's detested *patte*. The whole edifice is marked with *la patte*. How could it be otherwise? But *la patte* and its co-phenomena, the brushes, the paint, the canvas are also unparalleled in requiring the utmost discipline of the eye. Nowhere is the eye more exposed to the questions of seeing than through the traditions of painting. Painting is seeing wrenched from its customary, practical instrumentality and initiated into the intoxication of self-absorption, performance and acclaim or censure.

We may now formulate the notion of exposure a little more precisely. It is essentially a phenomenon of transition: from the necessary functionalism of the innate faculty to the memetic plasticity of the 'invented' world of disciplines, styles, self-reflection and justifications. Exposure is one and the same as re-presentation, the socialisation of the *given* - in which it loses its previous innocence. No doubt there are plenty of occasions when this happens to human sight. We are citing painting as one of the most developed and most important, where innocence is absolutely lost. In this sense the interplay of exposure and what is exposed take on an existential dimension. It is there is Rembrandt; it is there in many of the images we have cited; it is there in this painting. We formulate it as the fundamental beauty of futility, whether as the human body or as the pile of rags or as the painter's work or as their archaic interplay.

We now turn especially to the painting of the body in this picture; first the question of the pose. Taken as a whole it is singularly hard for viewers to place themselves in an appropriate spatial position. The viewpoint seems excessively high (this is of course characteristic of many works - especially the pictures of Leigh Bowery) in the sense that it won't quite 'read' with the floor, where the viewpoint feels lower. Nor will it quite read with the title *Standing by the Rags:* she might be lying down or leaning. Are the rags are piled vertically or scattered horizontally? How can she 'stand' at such an angle? Might a concealed, half-implied corner 'explain' the setup? Perhaps it would; but then, on that 'extra' demand, are we not threatening (literally) to quit the painting, made *for the sake of the picture*, for the sake of some other information requirement about 'the setup'? If so, let us say then, that the condition of the painting, *for the painting's sake* is the ambiguity itself, not explained. We enter its 'odd space' for its sake - or not at all: the picture as an information-system or re-presentation imposes that closure upon us. Take it or leave it.

Then the positioning of the arms: the left by its angle and its relation to the head resonates with many painted Crucifixions. The right, part forced behind the hip, suggests forced restraint. Placed between the two and impossible to align with 'standing' the head appears to rest in compelled passivity, dropping back and to the left, completely without resistance. A kind of suspension suggests itself.

Now the legs, again like many Crucifixions, they appear to stand whilst the upper body is inactively propped, rested, nailed, half-seated. They also have colossal weight culminating in the vast, flatfish feet; and yet even feet of this size could not stand a body at that angle. Again: take it or leave it; enter the painting for its sake, or move to any other business. You can take the colossal visual buzz this monumental composition offers (and all of its enigmatic suggestions) or get bothered about the physics.

Now the colour; not that we intend to *separate* it from questions of drawing, form and composition. There are four distinct regions. The smallest being the triangle of light reds and browns that read as 'wall'; then the blue-grey-red band that reads as 'floor.' The two other areas, the nude and the rags, have similar importance to each other. The rags present no particular colour-'surprise' being painted in a mix of near-neutrals though the tonal range is full, the detailing surprising and the rhythms are *breathtaking*. And how they evoke: on the one hand, discontinuity, debris, overpowering scale; and on the other, the painterliness of Velasquez or Manet, the chaotic energy of Pollock.

The rags, for us, are integral to the great spectacle, scale and corporeality of the image – but for those not 'into' painting they may (we suppose) assume the status of background or secondary elaborations. As for the body, however, the audience 'not into painting' is more vocal and less forgiving. For now the charge of *literalism* arises – precisely as the materially-other 'sign' - which we know to be a *painting* - threatens to operate primarily as *image*; that is, to claim the knowledge, the concept, the control if not the very visibility of the thing represented *for itself*.

Those not quite comfortable with painting will object to the effect, – on the *sitter* – of the knobbly textures of the paint, of the livid reds and heightened blues in some of the flesh hues as suggesting putrefaction, of the whole business of subjecting the model to 'his' gaze as an exercise of complex ideology and power that reduces the sitter to a meat-like bulk, a commodity of a certain weight, a usable spectacle. But these *are* consequences of visual inquiry through painting and a mark of its extraordinary power that anyone should consider that the image has some retrospective 'effect' on the being of the sitter. No one would accuse words of the same reduction. When I say 'My granddaughter is 18 months old' –

and offer no other description no one would dream of accusing me of reducing another human to merely age, gender and familial relations. But when the grammar is built not from words but from the materials and conventions of pictorial possibility, that sort of over-literal interpretation is commonplace and at a variety of levels. Indeed it is often invited.

Our counter-argument (developed in more formal terms below) is to propose both the necessity and authenticity of the *mutual* transformations that take place in the relation of painting to its subject (in this case the nude). We need to 'forgive' painting its imagery and perhaps also its excesses for the sake of the picture, for the sake of its memetic possibilities.

We are now in a position to attempt a more formal exposition. Our topic on the one hand is the guilt and ambiguity that surrounds the image - given above in Freud's contrast with the doctor and for the remainder of this chapter in the difference between word and image.

The key notion is again *autopoiesis*. It is of crucial importance to understand that this term is paradigmatically different from the notions of structure that precede it. In general terms, the older notions of structure tend conceive of discrete entities or of dialectically-constituted difference, often with some implied dominant or overdetermining class of phenomena. They have tended to be characterised first in terms of stability, then progressive change, or more recently, as heterogenous, or plural, or chaotic. Moreover, the discussion of such structures has tended to place human interest, description, reason in the central position. As such they may be described as humanistic and are certainly permeated by an interest in moral consequences or more recently by the loss of moral certainty or 'disbelief in metanarrative'.

Autopoietic difference, by contrast, is radically temporal. Its conditions are 'ecological' which is to say that its specific structures are *ecological possibilities*. No metanarrative is possible beyond that statement; no privileged dominance that is other than another ecological *possibility*. If that *is* a metanarrative it is without substantive content except to exclude all other (substantive) notions of difference and to assert that difference in its every instance has had, and will always have, this ecology as its ground. That, nevertheless, is a significant result – for in place of the older paradigm which premised a so clear a distinction between natural and social phenomena that one could entirely separate the latter – an ontology is implicitly or explicitly premised in which social phenomena become an *instance* of autopiesis, not 'unique' and certainly open to the pressures of constitution and extinction that face every other distinct class of phenomena, social or natural.

We should draw attention to two more general consequences before we move to our specific focus: the distinction between words and images. First, we stress the importance of *possibility*. Autopoietic phenomena are the result of many co-active variables producing characteristic patterned complexity: they are homeodynamic. One should not then suppose either a fixed essence or an indeterminate range of contradictory versions; those are the stuff of the older paradigm. The homeodymanic we propose will have its own specific degree of stability of variation determined by the ecology of its ontological 'neighbourhood'; stability and variation are themselves possibilities.

Second, this view is itself taken as an autopoietic consequence. That is to say it fits neither within the claim to absolute truth or within the claims of radical relativism. We argue instead that like all other autopoietic phenomena it is emergent, or formulable, and that its 'truth' is of less consequence than its ecological viability. In this sense we are saying the argument is 'vital' – it has begun *to show itself* – and if it turns out to have ecological viability it will also show itself to be 'vital' in the sense that the older paradigm called 'necessary'. As we shall see, this produces theoretic consequences that are *not* humanistic.

We now turn to our first specific focus namely the distinction between word and image in human culture. If that seems an ironic given the remarks above we shall argue the contrary: that humanism has so occluded the discussion as to be no longer capable of development; it has shown its own redundancy in descriptions of human culture.

How has the distinction between word and image come about? Humanists provide a spectrum of answers which – for our purposes can formulated as the possibilities between two extremes: ethnology and ethology. The former implies a characteristic in human *culture*; the latter in human *behaviour*. If that sounds horribly like nurture versus nature, we aplogise: it goes with the literature. For the moment let us say we need –and indeed will radicalise – these extremes; but 'our' ethnology is not the unstructured opposite of 'behaviour'; nor is our ethology limited to 'what humans do'.

Perhaps the most extreme ethnological position would be to say that the distinction between words and images belongs essentially to the speech-idioms of philosophers and similar analysts of these almost virtual 'phenomena' and has little relevance outside those customs. There is a grain of truth in this as we shall see but in case that truth seems attractive, we should remind ourselves that, if so, those analyses are completely futile as explanations. The counter-extreme – usually deemed to be a possibility since Alberti's invention of perspective – suggests that human intelligence, as a behavioural compulsion, eventually comes up with a system of representation that for all practical purposes is adequate to the task of 'true' or 'natural' representation; in this claim, it surpasses and replaces all previous systems. As Mitchell puts it:

> The best index to the hegemony of artificial perspective is the way it denies its own artificiality and lays claim to being a "natural" representation, "the way things look," "the way we see,".... the way things really are. [13]

Of course, Mitchell cannot accept this sort of uncritical positivism and neither can we, or you: this is *post*modernity, dammit! And so 'we' agree to go along with the compromise:

> ...there is no neutral, univocal "visible world".....if vision itself is product of experience and acculturation .... then what we are matching against pictorial representations is not any sort of naked reality but a world already clothed within our systems of representation. [14]

That *seems* reasonable: it could pass as a substitute for the Kantian distinction between 'appearance' and 'thing in itself'; for Kuhn's or Feyerabend's versions of 'critical' science; for the problem of the implicated observer in critical sociology; for an illustration of the connection between knowledge and power in Foucault – and so on. At the same time, also reasonably, Mitchell will not concede what he calls the 'linguistic imperialism' of treating images as variants of text: 'Derrida's answer to the question, "What is an image?" would undoubtedly be: Nothing but another kind of writing...' [15] Can we agree to this compromise?

Have you ever met anyone who has *confused* a picture (with or without perspective) with the 'naked reality' – except in very contrived context? Of course not. And yet, this confused being pops up all over the philosophy of art. At the same time, remember, both Freud and Manet attracted the kind of literal criticism of the image that accused it of 'abusing' its subject matter What of Mitchell's 'compromise'? Note the wording: '[no] sort of naked reality but a world already clothed within our systems of representation.'(op. cit.) Isn't it just a *little* ungrateful? Apart from pursuing the metaphor of clothes and nakedness (any half-decent critic could have a field day with which of those told 'the truth') there also seems to be steeped in some rather more ancient and unconscious metaphors: essence and appearance, the deceptions of the mundane, the inauthenticity of representation. This wording could have come out of a fundamental Platonism or Christianity. Nevertheless it did *seem* reasonable, did it not?

Mitchell, sensing correctly that we are *all* caught up in this contradiction but don't feel compelled towards Derrida's 'final solution' turns to Goodman; not without reservations.

> Realism is relative, determined by the system of representation standard for a given culture or person at a different time. Newer or older or alien systems are counted artificial or unskilled. For a Fifth-Dynasty Egyptian the straightforward way of representing something is not the same as for an eighteenth-century Japanese; and neither way is the same for an early twentieth-century Englishman. We usually think of paintings as literal or realistic if they are in a traditional European style of representation.[16]

As we said, Mitchell has reservations but before we turn to his criticisms, let us say why we find this inclusion quite staggering in its absurdity and why we cannot agree with Mitchell that 'it does not lead....to any serious or damaging objections to his [Goodman's] system.'[17]

First, it contains more of those virtual, confused beings so dear to philosophers of art. There are at least three here and various more, readers and so on, implied off stage. We are invited to believe in this nice, straightforward Egyptian who having being thoroughly but straightforwardly schooled in the *correct* way to describe such 'natural' phenomena as the Gods and the divine Pharaoh would, naturally, do them that way. You know: humans with lion heads and hawk heads and that little scarab beetle rolling the sun on its way. And when it came to a little pornography – yes, they were into that too!– well, they didn't show the couple having it off in the 'natural' way we should. No, of course it would come out looking, well, 'Egyptian'. If you'd like to check it out it's titled *Erotic Scene* c. 1305-1080 B.C.[18] and apart from looking a bit too accomplished it could have come from any modern lavatory wall. Nevertheless it did *seem* reasonable.

Then we have Modern Bloke. Do you know that European painting only looks natural to him because of acculturation? "Well blow me down with a Rembrandt! Why didn't *I* know that?" says Modern Bloke. "Some smart guy that Goodman." Mr. Bloke sits down and scratches his head for a while. "Speaking of Rembrandt, Mr. Goodman," says Bloke. "Why do I think of him more realistic than Manet?"

"Well," says Goodman, "he's still quite new you know and so he still looks a little artificial." Then turning towards his fellow philosophers of art – he winks and says, "It's the way we tell 'em." Nevertheless it did *seem* reasonable. It just shows you the power of acculturation. Mitchell's more succinct critique is this:

> The problem with this equation of realism with the familiar ....the 'standard'... is that it fails to take into account the prior question of what values underlie the standard. It is entirely possible for some style to become familiar, standard.... without its ever laying claim to realism.[19]

In short, Mitchell's notion of the image seems to be in the same sort of trouble that image-theory has had for as long as philosophy can remember. He turns to Gombrich, to Lessing and finally to Burke for help. The first two are not particularly relevant to our purposes and we shall return to the Burke shortly. Let us agree, however, with Mitchell's earlier and provisional formulation:

> Perhaps the redemption of the imagination lies in accepting the fact that we create much of our world out of the dialogue between verbal and pictorial representations, and that our task is not to renounce this dialogue in favour of a direct assault on nature but to see that nature already informs both sides of the dialogue.[20]

So far as text is concerned we note a touch of bias in Mitchell towards its ostensible richness compared with images; hardly surprising in a writer when the images he chooses are often impoverished. However, he draws on a number of French sources whose preoccupations are so anti-visual that they provoke the title *Downcast Eyes: the Denigration of Vision in French Twentieth Century Thought* in Jay's major study. More of Jay shortly; we shall argue that Mitchell's proposed dialogue between verbal and visual seems to us impossible on these foundations.

Mitchell shares the basic and arguably most influential characteristic of current notions of language informed by French thought: the arbitrary nature of the signifier. We are not arguing the contrary though an engaging critique emphasising onomatopoeic *origins* is proposed by Dissanayake.[21] The *emphasis* on the arbitrary, however, seems to us overdone and profoundly ideological. If anti-Hegelian or anti-'totality' or even anti-imperialist in its first origins it seems to operate primarily as the key to the conventionality of language and the deconstruction of *every* sign-regime, as 'kinds' of language, including those that draw on visual images. It is the very source of what Mitchell calls linguistic imperialism. Therein lies our objection: not to the notion of the arbitrary sign per se but to its *categorial* extension in the supposition that *all* signs have this proto-linguistic character. This is not an argument for 'naturalness' versus conventionality but rather to say that the nature of the categorial 'regime' itself passes more or less unnoticed.

Even when Mitchell cites Burke the effect on his own writing remains unseen:

> Language, precisely because of its arbitrary nature moderates everything that it mediates so that it can provide even the most painful and disgusting images of sense with the required "distancing" required for delight and sublimity: '....affections of the smell and taste, when they are in their full force and lean upon the sensory are simply painful; ....but when they are moderated in description or narrative, they become sources of the sublime as genuine as any other, and upon the very same principle of moderated pain.'[22]

The key point, for us, is the notion of 'distancing' or 'moderated pain'. Unlike the usual claims of theoreticians to produce 'higher' abstractions or the tendency toward what passes for formalism, the effect of words as distancing or moderating is quite simply *reduction*. And despite Mitchell's slightly more careful wordings – 'images of sense' – we know perfectly well what is moderated: 'raw' reality. This is an exceptionally difficult position for a theorist who tends toward semiotics. Mitchell *shouldn't* have Burke's pre-Derridean innocence; but it's there and in full measure. For us, what Mitchell admits – implicitly, but nevertheless as the instinctive ground of his ability in language – is that words intervene so as to manage the relation between reality and the speaker's sensibility; and that the relation is reductive. His innocence 'betrays' his complicity: in being a user of verbal language: he *knows* this as the very condition of usage. This resonates very closely with the impossibility, without contrivance, of mistaking the image for the real.

This principle, in more formal elaboration, will shortly assume great importance in the paradigm of autopoiesis. For the moment, let us stay with the more concrete effects on Mitchell's writing. The relation is curious: on the one hand his sense of being enmeshed in a chain of representations is haunted by a persistent 'raw' reality that keeps popping up, live and kicking, just when you thought reason had 'proved' the counter-argument. But then 'Pop!' – it's just as quickly gone; we are back in the endless chain of signifiers until the ghost haunts again. It looks as though Mitchell's redemption of the imagination through the dialogue of visual and verbal 'informed by nature' on both sides hides a more radical and problematic 'nature' philosophy than Mitchell would care to admit.

Yet there remains that 'reduction', which is perhaps too weak a term, premised in the very distinction between words-in-general and images-in-general. Our positioning is utterly different. The terms 'image' or 'text' have no substantive meaning in our paradigm. If they 'mean' anything they signify the reduction itself. This somewhat counter-intuitive notion is crucial to what follows, so let us prepare it another way. Mitchell, you, or we, can *say* that a painting contains an image; we can say a photograph contains an image. We might engineer a situation in which the same object or sitter has an image in a painting and an image in a photograph; and we might strive to make sure these two images are as similar as we can make them. But there is no continuing reality between the two that one could call 'image' per se. Rather an image is differently realised in each case by virtue of photographic and pictorial possibility. The image lives or 'lies' in the stabilities and instabilities of these media in relation to *concerted* perception; that is, they exist in that we have evolved means for 'realising' images that have a level of social stability or viability. But there is no underlying image – even of an identical subject – that links the two. It is rather a verbal construct and not a particularly abstract one at that.

Demystified, the *verbal* notion of image that ostensibly underlies the painting and the photograph is no more fundamental than the decision to place them both in the same display or storage bin or file or predicate. Most fundamentally the verbal 'image' is the sound of profound neglect. No photographer or painter could *work* that way. This is not a distinction between theory and practice, then, but between indifference and action. In other words, in speaking of images-in-general (or texts for that matter) the reduction is so great that the ghost of reality is *completely* exorcised. The reduction is so great that the arbitrariness of the signifier can no longer be discerned: it has not re-presented the signified but effaced it; there is no standard by which its arbitrary character could be discerned or have meaning. The matter could be placed entirely algebraically:

Mitchell: Suppose I is not T.
Derrida: But I may be T apart from the supposition.
Arbiter: I is or is not T

No wonder reality's ghost is re-invoked. Those of Derridean persuasion could re-run the tedious exercise with the painted or photographic image in place of text and we should then be able to revel in an even more nauseating fall into the abyss of signification, until boredom

198

or hostilities or hunger or the possibility of sex intervened. For us, it is time to quit that paradigm altogether.

If language, text, image, representation are to be saved from reversion into algebra we must accept that categorical over-reduction is one of their real or 'structural' possibilities. It is not simply a Platonic, Christian, Derridean or Mitchellian caprice: the phenomenon has been around far too long for that dismal dismissal. In short, it must have a functional origin in the ecological sense and by implication, a point at which it becomes dysfunctional. This is not an appeal to avoid excess or identify 'surplus' in the marxian or protestant or humanist senses. Both function and dysfunction are taken as autopoietic: the dysfunction has declared itself in the form of a loss of vitality.

It is ironic that philosophers should be so concerned with what amounts to the limits or the critique of the correspondence theory of truth because this is precisely what autopoiesis prevents in the very act of distinguishing between organism and environment. Moreover this is not, not even primarily, a 'human' problem: *every* organism is distinguished from its environment and consequently 'correspondence' is a fundamental obstacle to any theory of representation. We have already cited the concept of 'bringing forth worlds' as the active 'management' of the relationship between organism and environment. Luhmann provides an alternative, more formal but persuasive formulation.

> There is.....no point for point correspondence between system and environment (such a condition would abolish the difference...). The system's inferiority in complexity must be counter-balanced by strategies of selection......; the order the system chooses in relating its elements results from the difference in complexity between it and its environment.[23]

Knodt's *Foreword* offers this summary:

> In information-theoretical terms, complexity designates a lack of information that prevents a system from completely observing itself or its environment. Complexity enforces selectivity, which in turn leads to a reduction of complexity via systems that are less complex than their environment. This reduction of complexity......is essential. Without it there would be nothing, no world consisting of discrete entities, but only undifferentiated chaos.[24]

Further on in what we take to be a metaphor but rather a good one, she says:

What we call 'madness' is nothing more than the hyper-complexity of psychic systems that can no longer distinguish themselves from their environment. [25]

Loosen the terms 'madness' and 'psychic' and allow 'chaotic,' 'dysfunctional,' 'self-cancelling' paired with 'social,' 'information,' 'representational,' 'cultural,' 'critical' - and you have a most provocative description that *cries out* for its application to Modernism and Postmodernism in everything from the readymade to Greenbergian 'competence' to the monochrome canvas to the postulate of the equality of all values.

To underscore our point specifically: Greenberg's 'competence' *correctly* aligned with Kant and Plato, the 'critical' desire to stifle images in words, and the Duchampian destructive gesture presents an instance in which the necessity of complexity-reduction is pushed to the point of dysfunction; where complexity is so reduced that the barely perceivable difference between specific system – art, painting – and its environment ceases to have viability. It disappears with the readymade and reappears in Kurt Schwitters or Jasper John's reassimilations; it disappears in again in Kosuth's notion of art as tautology, (that is, as *any* tautology); and reappears in the robustness of Freud's figuration or Richter's dialectic of hope and despair in *painting*. Like Mitchell's ghost of reality it haunts in an oscillation of presence and absence.

However, when wordings start to have that 'presence-absence' ring we begin to smell a rat. This is the sound of (post)modern idiom. So let's try to generalise our point by emphasing as firmly as possible that 'reality' is not a ghost, nor a phenomenon, nor a pure beyond of thought – nor even a structural requirement in systems theory. Reduction of complexity – or the *management* of complexity – may be describable in formal terms but it also has a concrete reality. You don't have to 'correspond' with the tiger's teeth to know they mean trouble. A cat does not need a complex ornithology to know that the beat of wings and the movement of the body shape mean 'catch and eat'. No amount of molecular science will assist the shark's ability to detect minute parts per million of animal products in seawater. Birds, houseflies, bees have never 'understood' aerodynamics nor invented the processing-systems they use to fly. It is the central conceit of the human and cultural sciences to fail to see that however much they subsequently wish to understand or to assert their own autonomy, *cultural* orders such as verbal and visual representation *must* evolve from similar functional origins. The alternative is creation *ex nihilo* with or without God's help. In short, we should not oppose or seek to transcend the 'orders of reduction' that language and image imply but to treat them as foundational; to develop them through practice, analysis and mutual dialogue; to recognise that their transcendence or abolition whether in the shattering of Western metaphysics or a more radical disbelief in metanarrative than Lyotard envisaged is to essay the demise of humanity itself. This, then, is the nature philosophy that Mitchell cannot admit, the natural epistemology that 'ghosts of reality' have persistently obscured, the starting point which is both existentially 'vital' and rationally necessary.

Stated generally, then, and without the baggage of traditional negations (so far as we can consciously avoid them) the verbal and the visual are both *necessary* – vital or foundational – 'reductions' that mark the possibility of human representation; that is, *inter*-action with an environment that both sustains and threatens our very existence. It is not, then, rhetorical but *precise* to call them existential conditions; nor is it exaggeration to compare transcendence with extinction. This 'natural' epistemology is also practical – or *ought* to be pragmatic – whilst the reduction to verbal-categorial subsumption or to the image that wholly 'stands-for' is as dangerous as transcendence. Like transcendence, they are too simple. That applies to most of the traditional so called 'critical' idioms from Platonism to poststructuralism: they are too simple; they do not recognise nor confront complexity in anything but a token manner: as conventional, chaotic, inauthentic, ignorable. That is not to exempt the artist or poet as the *alter* to the critic, but to emphasise the inter-penetration of critical and 'assertive' idioms.

Enough, then, of negativity; verbal and visual, *especially* the differences that separate them are the authentic conditions both of humanity in its origins and of its social phenomena. That is to say that the complex natural environment and the complex social environment are distinguished from the species and the member respectively by these representational orders. Or, to place the 'paradox' at its sharpest they are both authentic as 'reductions' and 'virtual' as re-productions. It is still possible to misconceive this necessary structuring along simplistic lines such as social/natural or necessary and surplus. The problem of such distinctions is that they aim, hopelessly, to arrest the homeodynamic at some 'approved' point and therefore convert what is properly understood as *possible* distributions into fixed quotas of 'certain' description. Whereas, the notion of autopoiesis removes 'our' approval as surely as it generated and will presumably also make extinct the species. 'We' do not decide, then, what is truly authentic from what is merely virtual in our representations. At best, we merely contribute to an outcome that is quite beyond human moral or rational control.

This last point is crucial: if the outcomes, say of imagery, are decided autopoietically – as sculpture, as photographs, as paintings, as x-rays, as television pictures, as the discernable figure in the night-sight of a rifle, as the infra-red trace of chemical autograph – then the question, 'What is an image?' is no longer viable. The 'category' has misunderstood or usurped its reductive function *vis à vis* its environment; it has quit a viable ecological position. In short, it has become extinct. What replaces it has meagre points of common origin: some relation to the total possible wavelengths of light – which *must* be counted 'a reality' and some sort of cellular-based responsive structure whether it simply responds to light/dark or approximates to a recognisable 'lens'. Other than that 'images' are as related and distinct as species. The question of common roots or ancestors, then, is not a matter of speculative or formal inquiry but a type of inquiry close to both archaeology and palaeontology. The point we should stress is that the categorial 'reduction' implied a uniform continuum whilst an autopoietic model stresses possibility, disjunctures, opportunities and adaptations. Simply put, there is no ecological-autopioetic reason to assume gradation but every reason to assume discrete types, species and adaptations: many norms but no uniform normality. This is approximately the same proposition as the absence of correspondence and the 'overcoming' of indeterminacy through specific, systematic 'reductions'.

Back to Freud the painter and his hypothetical doctor. We are now in a position to see that this concrete illustration hides the distinction between a doubled reduction – the perceived image and the painting – and an ostensibly 'literal' actor who is, so to speak, invited by the body's illness to remake it well; as it was before; as it *should* be. This somewhat Edenic metaphor is ironic given the actual, that is, reductive, history of medicine, especially when the family name is Freud. Nor does it say anything about the efficacy (or its lack) in the reductions we know as 'medicine' or 'painting'. At the same time practically everyone else would make the same sort of choice if pressed: in absolute terms it doesn't matter but in species terms we may want painters but we need doctors. This serves only to underscore the authenticity of the relation between real environments and 'practical' reductions. But what *need* does Freud's painting serve? Or more precisely: How might we approach that question?

The Platonic answer is clearly, 'none'. Socrates' suicide offers the same verdict on his entire life. Greenberg isn't much better; he has to ditch his own aesthetic in the end. An autopoietic model allows us a different way forward: instead of asking 'what need?' and searching in our own imaginations for a *human* want that painting satisfies we should perhaps reconsider autopoietic 'vitality' as opposed to human necessity. Certainly, this will inter-act with some sense of human need and necessarily also with some notion of human ability but, crucially, in its inception it is a possibility offered by the relation of sensibility to environment – a possibility offered by Being - and not, or not simply, a human invention. Neither of course are humans 'human inventions' *despite* Socrates, Kant, Nietzsche, Derrida....

We distanced ourselves from speaking of 'images-in-general' as a kind of dysfunctional neglect; at the same time we argued for the 'vitality' of 'orders' whose functions reduced complexity. We further postulate that 'images' be understood as such an order – or better as multiple orders – that do not exist 'in general' though they may have shared characteristics but as specific, discrete, ecologically-rooted 'kinds'. One of the characteristics they share – but plainly not in the same way – is to maintain a distance between the boundary of the system (organism etc.) and the environment by providing coded 'visual' information in place of correspondence or 'collision'. *Perspective* – understood as the sub-conscious codification of ordinary vision or as the explicitly-understood system - is such an information-system (or virtual world) that *must* be shared by every species that focuses (and makes use of) the panorama of environmental light-energy on a retina. This 'image-in-general' is not a category but a distribution of situated possibilities; it is not an abstraction but most concrete. It is not an abstraction but a concatenation of mechanisms, information codings and decodings that presuppose each other and their ability to inform other processes – from, for example, locomotion to painting. Images are, then, not categorial, but ecological or autopoietic events. Their 'humanity' is in truth marginal to everyone but ourselves.

That Alberti can 'invent' perspective or that Freud can paint *Standing by the Rags* is no more nor less fundamental than a cat making use of a related image-ecology to catch a bird. They are phenomena of a similar kind. Both are 'vital' to themselves; neither is necessary; both are amoral. We are reminded of Judd/Morris' requirement that a work of art need only be interesting – that is it should engage (humans) in the possibilities it organises. From this 'organisation' it follows that the structure is both ecologically rooted and memetic; *far* from random but capable of plastic reorganisation. Only by forgetting the organisation could that plasticity become infinite; by remembering it, plasticity becomes a matter of function or dysfunction. Painting, finally, is *for* that autopoietic range. As interested parties we no doubt favour function over dysfunction; as analysts let us stress both possibilities.

Freud's painting is not *for painting* or for *art* as an autopoietic range as modernist painting attempted to present itself. Kosuth is typically authoritarian in this respect: 'Johns and Reinhardt are probably the last two painters that were legitimate *artists* as well.'[26] Freud, by contrast, is interested in a distinct set of possibilities; some may call this repetitive, others 'deepening.' For us, the verdict goes either way depending on the painting or even the part of the painting you want to address. Anything else would be 'uninteresting' wording. This is not the place to pursue the point, however. Somewhat higher on the agenda is Kosuth's paradoxical insistence that the total memetic possibility we call 'art' – *legitimate* art – should come to be represented in *two* painters with the latter being one of the most restrictive painters ever. It would be trite to repeat the arguments deployed against Greenberg. Let us instead remind you of an earlier premise: that (following Wittgenstein) the possibilities of naming cannot be decided or restricted in advance. This we presented as the guarantee of plasticity which underlies memetic re-presentation (rather than repetition). Clearly, then, if Freud's restrictions present the possibility of repetitive reduction, this is (or can be) offset by increased internal complexity.

Goodman's distinction between density (of the image) and articulation (of the text) touches on this. As Mitchell explains it:

> The image is syntactically and semantically dense in that no mark may be isolated as a unique, distinctive character (like the letters of an alphabet)... Its meaning depends rather on its relations with all the other marks in a dense continuous field. He cites the "untransferable" spot of paint that can be read as the highlight on the Mona Lisa's nose.[27]

Luhmann is characteristically formal but grasps more of what is at stake. Following the discussion of differential complexity between system and environment he adds:

> a system can become complex only by selecting an order... The premise that for each system the environment is more complex than the system itself does not require a constant difference in the degree of complexity...... [E]volution is only possible only when a sufficient complexity of systems- environments and in this sense evolution is the co-evolution of systems and environments. Greater complexity within systems is possible because the environment does not manifest random distribution but is structured selectively by systems in the environment. Thus one must

interpret the relation of complexity between system and environment as one of intensification..[28]

This is the crucial incommensurability: Luhmann's intensification set against Kosuth's reduction to 'legitimacy', Freud's 'dense' traditionalism against Reinhardt's discontinuous modernism. 'Morphology' - to use Kosuth's term – is the site of contention.

For Freud, several 'morphologies' are at stake and of value: the traditional form 'painting', the discipline of figuration; hence, the attention to the human body and other structured forms (interiors, landscapes); also, then, the idioms and stylistic requirements: the resemblances to tradition and contemporary work, the nude, painterliness. Kosuth's notion of morphology signifies a rejection:

> Painting is a *kind* of art. If you make paintings you are already accepting (not questioning) the nature of art.....[M]orphological notions of art embody an applied *a priori* concept of art's possibilities.... With the unassisted *Readymade* art changed its focus....from a question of morphology to a question of function...from 'appearance' to 'conception'...the beginning of 'conceptual' art.[29]

This is achingly conventional stuff implying: accepting is bad; questioning is good; acceptance *precludes* questioning; possibility is better than actuality; everyone before Duchamp/Kosuth is a cultural dope; you can't return to a previous cultural site of inquiry (good job no-one told Picasso or Manet or Freud). We've been hearing this nonsense since Plato. It is apt - that is, Platonic – for Kosuth to thunder in conclusion: 'Art is the *definition* of art.'[30] (our emphasis) But before we slam the doors of the Republic in the face of the Enemy let us be sure what it is: opposed to 'concept' or 'definition' it is morphology, embodiment, autopoiesis, homeodynamics, finitude, all that lies outside the control of human *wordings*. If one could imagine such a thing within secular culture, this would be blasphemy; it is certainly hubris.

Recall, then, our earlier point, now in slightly different terms: 'art-in-general' is not a category but a distribution of situated possibilities; it is not an abstraction but most concrete. It is not a definition but a series of mechanisms, information, intentions codings and decodings that presuppose each other's viable interaction. Art is not categorial, but ecological: a series of autopoietic events.

Turn now to the face of the nude in *Standing by the Rags*. Set against the arm and showing how limited its physical identity must be – can you deny its tenderness in the face of Kosuth's ranting? Can you deny its place in the reality of human limitation?

Notes

1. The most horrifying form of philosophy's submission is Heidegger's: 'The Fuhrer himself and alone *is* the present and future German reality and its law.' See Rosen, S. (1969) p.123 and Ch. 11 below.
2. de Duve, T. (1996) pp.225-6.
3. *Lucien Freud: Paintings and Etchings* Abott Hall Gallery Catalogue 1996 p.7.
4. Bernard, B. 'Introduction' in *Lucien Freud* (1996) p.9.
5. Bernard offers several tedious accounts of Freud's specialness, ranging from his letters to his extraordinary looks. This is not serious reasoning to say the least but it is a characteristic way to write about artists. Let's just say he ended up at art school.
6. Lucien Freud (1996) pl.19.
7. ibid. pl. 21.
8. ibid. plts. 87-93.
9. ibid. plts. 91, 92 & 85 respectively.
10. Derrida, J. (1987) p.2.
11. Jay, M. (1996) p.516, see also Smith, J.A. 'The Denigration of Vision and the Renewal of Painting' in Heywood & Sandywell (eds.) (1999).
12. Lucien Freud (1996) pl.251.
13. Mitchell, W.J.T. (1987) p.37.
14. ibid. pp.37-8.
15. ibid. p.30.
16. ibid. p.72.
17. ibid. p.73.
18. Peck, W. (1978) pl.83.
19. ibid. pp.72-3.
20. ibid. p.46.
21. Dissanayake, E. (1992) pp.170-88.
22. Mitchell. W.J.T. (1987) p.138.
23. Luhmann, N. (1995) pp.25-6.
24. ibid. xvii.
25. ibid. xviii.
26. in de Duve (1996) p.246.
27. Mitchell. W.J.T. (1987) p.67.
28. Luhmann, N. (1995) p.26.
29. Kosuth, J. in Harrison & Wood (eds.) (1992) p.844.
30. ibid. p.849.

10 Gerhardt Richter

This chapter concerns Gerhardt Richter and in particular the contradictions in his work, if they are contradictions, that allow Kuspit to title a chapter *Gerhardt Richter's Doubt and Hope* [1] or Heywood to call a self-proclaimed inarticulate's work *An Art of Scholars*. [2] The latter is Henrich's phrase and is drawn from *The Contemporary Relevance of Hegel's Aesthetics*. [3] Our position is quite the contrary: we are well aware of the continuing importance of Hegel and indeed Plato to contemporary 'aesthetics'. For us, that implies joint irrelevance insofar as that aesthetic paradigm is no longer vital or reasonable. That argues, if implicitly, that aesthetics and reasonable, or vital, knowledge have (long ago) parted company and that the persistence of 'aesthetics' in its conventional state rests on an interest in the antique and surpassed or on academic failing Both, of course, may be the same thing. Heywood summarises then cites Hegel:

Culture, then, originally a vehicle for individual and collective liberation from nature..... is essentially an activity of making or self-formation...[H]owever culture comes into conflict *with itself* (our emphasis) because the untheorised actualities, the existing particulars of which it consists.... are an obstacle to the task of abstraction. The unstoppable relentless drive of the abstracting and reductive theorising which characterises this culture inaugurates.....cultural *terror* whose currency is *death*... :

'The sole work and deed of universal freedom is therefore *death*, a death too which has no inner significance or filling, for what is negated is the empty point of the absolutely free self. It is thus the coldest and meanest of all deaths with no more significance than cutting off a head of cabbage or swallowing a mouthful of water.'[4]

You can see already where the story is going to go: Richter's 'scholarly' art is to be so infected with this concoction of abstraction and ostensible enlightenment as to 'cause' its self-effacing conventions. Ryman is offered as the counter-movement: 'context specific norms...natural constraint...*labour*.' These are the commitments of the experimentalism of 'classical modernism'. [5]

It's not too bad as a just-so story; the trouble is: it's the *same* rotten, old story. It's saving grace or self-ridicule, according to your choice, is that staggering term: 'classical modernism' – which betrays itself quite simply as the preferred taste of a very English, very meagre elite (if that is the right word) which still draws university salaries but knows itself to be surpassed, ridiculous and waiting for retirement. If you are unlucky enough to fetch up in a department or other academic context in which 'classical modernism' holds sway you will quickly sense that your freedom of speech is curtailed, various lines of inquiry and various authors are strictly taboo and any attempt to *think* is taken as an attack upon the god of 'practice' – in Heywood, 'labour'. When outsiders arrive – such as external examiners or even (God help them) candidates for lectureships or postgraduate studentships – one notices their bemusement as they first sense the internal orthodoxy. Many bowels have shrivelled at the announcement of the drone-in-charge (not Heywood): 'We are all Modernists here!' Fictitious 'practitioner-led' alliances are postulated in defence against The Enemy which, ludicrously, is characterised as 'Leeds-type theorising' by which they mean T.J.Clark and G. Pollock. More ambitious theorising 'cannot' exist or is dismissed as barmy. By the way, 'practitioner' is classical-modernist speak for 'artist' – and that means *painters*.

Death by abstraction? Who is Hegel tying to kid? Heywood for one. This is the *same* Hegel who can argue:

Christianity says: God has revealed himself through Christ... Ordinary thinking straightaway interprets this to mean that Christ is only the organ of the revelation...But..this statement properly means that God has revealed that his nature consists in having a Son...so that the Son is not the mere organ.... but the content of the revelation. [6]

Reinterpreted outside the 'figuration' of Christianity, this passage asserts the 'belonging-together' (to use Heidegger's words in a most un-Heideggerian sentiment) of finite and infinite or of beings and Being. This is Hegel at his most affirmative and inclusive, where the specific finally has its own meaning and significance. But 'death by intellectual abstraction' is Hegel wearing Socrates' absurd, suicidal hat. We do not deny that the vast panoply of Hegelian dialectics is schizophrenic but: which one would *you* choose? Conventional aesthetics – here as Heywood-Richter-Henrich – allows itself that archaic, narcissistic and self-indulgent scenario of the philospher's imagination: that reflexivity can be carried to the point of self-annihilation; that thinking can kill its host. For everyone else, killing generally requires third-party intervention and suicide is not the norm. Even suicide needs an instrument.

Contrast this nonsense with Maturana and Varela's definition of cognition as 'embodied action.' (op. cit.) Stated in simple terms, modernists – classical or not – are pre-Darwinian humanists. They have no conception of evolution or autpoiesis and so will inevitably draw from an otherwise-positive Hegel the false lesson of unfettered regression. They do not see – despite their desperately good taste – that they *require* an autopoietic principle to ground it. Without that, 'good taste' is merely a species of elitism whose God is known to be dead. With autopoiesis, however, these entrenched scholars are cynically 'reasonable' enough to know they would have to fight their corner in a more hostile environment - and realise that asserting their good taste will at least inhibit local opposition so long as they hold academic tenure. And that will do *for now*. This is not analytically viable nor has it any significance; 'classical modernism' denotes merely a skirmish in English middle-class good manners and academic self-interest.

Heywood, like Hegel, is also a schizophrene. How could he not be? They are part of the same memetic trait. Here is Heywood's lyric side:

Particularity means ...not just factual uniqueness, but the significance in our lives of things, people and events for which neither substitutions or reproductions are possible. Particularity in this sense defines an important aspect of embodied, temporal experience. [7]

Abstract painting [touches particularity] by the ways in which the precise qualities of the painted mark are assembled and made to matter.....Particularlity is not just an intellectual idea; it refers to an important aspect of experience in which the specific, unique qualities of phenomena are at the centre of attention, and the general or abstract aspects are of secondary importance.' [8]

Notice the completely antithetical meanings of 'abstract' paintings and 'general or abstract aspects'. Moreover, the 'unique qualities of *phenomena*' – 'for which neither substitutions or reproductions are possible' - begins to look like semantic chaos or the kind of impossible claim that Merleau-Ponty makes for art and primordial realities. [9] Suffice to say that the lyricism and the analytics are magnificently at odds. Perhaps, after all, it *is* a decent description of the incommensurability that confounds postmodern culture in its lyric and theoretic modes.

Heywood dislikes Richter's 'mechanism' or 'simple systems' as opposed to Ryman's careful receptivity. He cites: '...all the colour patches were joined up and merged into one grey. I just stopped when this was done.' [10] But not all of Richter's work is like this; neither, for that matter, is Ryman's receptivity particularly consistent. Kuspit is a little more Richter-friendly. He insists – along with Richter and against the 'hilarious' misunderstandings of Buchloh [11] – that Richter's work has emotional 'content': 'What content is it that the Abstract Expressionists are supposed to have in contrast to me?' Richter cries. It is left aside that no-one has established *any* such content (Richter and Kuspit included) that is not definable under the will to unintelligibility, self-effacement or some other act of negation (of 'content'). It seems that Richter-friendly and unfriendly positions produce remarkably similar results. But Kuspit has one interesting dialectic in reserve which resonates with Heywood's particularity; he frames it instead in terms of shame and the lack of shame.

The poles of Richter's ambivalence are what I would call a mood of deprivation and asceticism – a sense of shyness, even involution – and a mood of unashamedness.....which Richter found so fascinating in the work of Pollock and Fontana. [12]

The first mood can be explicitly identified with the involution or 'death by abstraction' of Heywood's scholar-artist. The latter cannot. Moreover, the original interview (with Buchloh) contains this exchange:

B: Can you remember what particularly interested you about the work of Pollock and Fontana?
R: The sheer brazenness of it! That really fascinated me and impressed me. I might almost say these paintings were the real reason why I left the GDR. I realised there was something wrong with my whole way of thinking.
B: Can you enlarge on this word 'brazenness'? It has connotations of morality; surely that's not what you mean?
R: But that is what I mean...... I realised above all that those slashes and blots were not a formalist gag but grim truth and liberation... [13]

At odds as ever – and with more obstruction than help from Richter – Buchloh loses the track at this point and reverts to a formalist-modernist set of questions. For us, the crucial points are these: involution, the scholar's way, is not inevitable; it can (like the GDR) be left behind. Moreover, for Richter, it is *false*: the blots and slashes are the alternative *grim truth* and liberation. As he constantly insists to Buchloh, this is not scholarship nor inhibition but 'grim truth': existential necessity and *certainly not* 'classical modernism'. Of course, no 'classical modernist' ascribes 'classical modernism' to Richter but, even more perversely, they *do* consider him to be a kind of failed or inhibited modernist; or at best as one who demonstrates the impossibility of that 'return' to an aesthetic centre (and so a sort of enemy). Nothing could be further from the truth. He loathes that 'formalist gag' – that limit – as surely as Duchamp detests *la patte*. But he *is* a painter and like Duchamp is beset, therefore, by structural contradictions.

Richter is 'modernistic' in several crucial respects. Perhaps the most obvious of these is the scale of his pictures and – despite protestations about the greater significance of 'content' or 'mood'- there is an obsessive concern with materials, actions, implements, the surface-format, in short, particularity. He also professes a perverse sort of avant-gardism, an anti-traditionalism: 'That's why I painted from photographs, just in order to have nothing to do with the art of 'peinture' which makes any kind of contemporary statement impossible.' [14] The anti-aesthetics of Warhol and Fluxus are also quoted with approval. Also, ironically: 'I thought [Ryman's painting] was very good...because for the first time it showed *nothing*. It was closer to my own situation.' [15] Then comes the decisive contradiction:

R: ...painting ought to have more effect.
B: So you would reject the accusation that is often levelled at you, of cynical complicity with painting's lack of effect?
R: Yes...because.... painting is not without an effect. I just want it to have more of one....
B: So....you don't see yourself as the heir to...a state of fragmentation in which no strategy is really valid?
R: And I do see myself as heir to a vast, great, rich culture of painting...which we have lost...but which places obligations upon us. [16]

There follows a series of minor elaborations on the cause of this loss –such as photographic depiction but these are taken as only contributors:

R: ......I see the basic fact as the loss of the Centre.
B: In Sedlmayr's sense? You can't be serious? [17]

But of course, Richter *is* serious – the problem is only that Buchloh can't believe him – and, unlike Sedlmayr, Richter has no desire to reconstruct the Centre: it is *irrevocably* lost.

Given that Richter elsewhere says: 'Art is the highest form of hope'[18]– you can see why his interlocutors eventually lose patience. For Heywood his 'chief virtue' lies in being 'insufficiently theoretical' – or in the idioms we might invent for classical modernism – 'nearly a painter'. For Kuspit: 'Richter's illusionlessness is responsible for his art's apparent lack of pathos; which is exactly why it ultimately seems so full of pathos.'[19]

Sorry but that's one contradiction too many for credibility. Back to the drawing board! We can all agree (not least Richter) that he is a *painter* and let us leave aside for a moment, what kind and how successful. A theorist he isn't (even Heywood agrees) and the neoHegelian framework of art-scholars is distinctly archaic and unconvincing. Perhaps the problem lies, then, in what Richter says or what he says he does or what we understand by what he says. Recall he 'just stopped' when he had produced an overall grey. This might be understood differently from how it was presented above. Take out the 'just' and the implication that 'stopping there' was as meaningless or meaningful as anywhere else and we might – just *might* – read a different *proposal*. This process, as it were, is *put forward* to see if the result carries any effect – or not. This would not then necessarily contradict all those other occasions in the abstract paintings – not to mention the colour charts – where Richter emphasises the lengths he took to make them 'work'. The difference, in other words, is procedural, not logical and therefore not contradictory. Nor is the 'grey' proposal, then, a sealed-and-settled 'simple' nihilism – though it may be, or may become, a mistake. In this sense, the grey 'proposal' set against Ryman's control, or his own control at other times, or the dreadful orthodoxy of 'classical modernism' may be better understood as *risk*. That chimes rather more with the lost Centre, the obligations of painting's culture, the response to the contemporary and the disaffection with 'peinture'. Conversely, it is not convincing evidence of 'scholarly' reduction.

Moreover, it would tie up rather more plausibly with Richter's approval of the 'brazenness' of Pollock, another chancer, certainly no 'scholar.' This point is crucial because it opens the difference that pictorial resemblance generates when words would broker a stalemate. The relationship Richter-Pollock *worded* after the event of the loss of belief in Abstract Expressionism and more convinced of Richter's nihilism than his hope would inevitably re-conceptualise Pollock as a forerunner: a sort of naïve or proto-Richterian nihilist. But remember Richter on this subject: Pollock's slashes and blots are 'grim reality', the truth not naivety. Taken in that sense, the pictorial resemblances, which we may codify as 'assisted chance', assert a quite different reality. If haunted by the 'loss of Centre' they are the visible ruin; if haunted by the negations of the intellect, they are the raw stuff of positivity; if haunted by the modernist desire for human control and mastery they represent the unquenchable challenge. All of these, of course, reduced to a rhetoric of painting – but then we have seen the necessity of reduction (the system's order *vis à vis* its environment) and how powerfully 'real' are its virtual mediations.

Let us try to approach this point in a different way. We spoke of the 'schizophrenic' character of Hegelian dialectics: that revelation was able to show itself in the fullness of finite determinations, or, as and in the 'fate' of beings; but at the same time, the power of abstracting-theorising was unlimited: it was literally the power of life and death. If taken somewhat too far, this metaphor is still not a foible. As we said elsewhere it is too deep-seated and archaic for that kind of dismissal. Rather, it is a fundamental structural possibility of abstracting-theorising in *words*. Death through abstracting-theorising *can* be imagined; it is the counterpart to the categorial: no *thing* can resist col-lection in this way. At the same time however it is 'only' a mark of the order of verbal language. As we argued in the previous chapter, this ordered reduction is an essential characteristic of systems in relation to their environments; 'only' an order, then, designates an evolved ecological complexity. But it is still possible for such an order to prove dysfunctional or excessive in its reductions. In this case, abstracting-theorising crosses the threshold of dysfunction when it proposes (confuses) the order of signification with the order signified: when phenomena are *equivalent* to words or when, to use a previous term: there is no 'outside-text'. This is not primarily a moral, analytic or philosophical postulate it is a *practical* one: if words do not 'know' their limit at every moment of use, they have ceased to have any ecological function. We do not propose a repetition of the previous chapter, which described this limit or difference as an existential condition of the relation between humans and their environment. In that chapter, we were primarily concerned with excessive *reduction* and, so far, in this chapter our focus has been similar - but it is now time to explore the converse: transcendence, exposure. Previously we equated transcendence with extinction. That has not changed: we are not exposing representation to correspondential compliance with the environment: that would be as ridiculous as exposing the 'true' body by stripping away the skin. It is the managed inter-action that is ecologically interesting.

It seems to us that there comes a point in Modernism which is as easily recognisable as it is difficult to understand. It begins to occur with Pollock and Newman and Rothko – when either the number of elements in the pictorial order is reduced; or when the level of complexity remains high but the degree of pictorial control is reduced. This is not an exclusively modernistic phenomenon; you can find it in Rembrandt, Velasquez, Richter, Carl Andre, Richter, Ryman, et al. In the case of Pollock, the work of both hand and mouth are supposedly given up to extra-normal influence: for the hand it is 'action' that paints; for the mouth it is the unconscious that 'speaks'. What is 'authored' in the work, ostensibly, is not what Jackson Pollock (and all of his training) can do – but what Being can do, despite or through him. This is not a ready-made nor is it really openness to chance. An assisted ready made? Not quite; assisted autopoiesis. Richter does *exactly* the same thing. Both believe strongly in the 'content' that ensues. Both are able to criticise similar attempts when the results lack existential weight.[20]

In Rothko's case – or indeed Morris' – the elements are so reduced to specific colours and materials, they cannot be *mistaken* for anything else. They are 'specific objects'. The result: a field of presence exerting its specific influence on the spectator, ostensibly unmediated by convention. We know this is *not* the case. We *also* know that 'minimalism' in this sense is not just another attempt to be, so to speak, 'decorative'. Richter does *exactly* the same thing; he also despises decoration: it also lacks existential weight. Are Rothko's rectangles or Morris's cuboids 'ready-mades'? Not quite; assisted autopoiesis of a slightly different kind.

Is this a case of mutually-assured gullibility (as the popular press would undoubtedly say) or something more worthy of consideration? If the latter, let's resist the temptation to praise it to the skies. We are dealing with a deeply-felt but certainly *only human* consideration. Richter certainly *feels for* what we call 'assisted autopoiesis' or what he might call chance and openness. Having established, reasonably, that he is not a scholar in the sense we are essaying and that his 'authority' consists in knowing the processes of his own paintings and knowing his 'own' vocabulary, we want to insist that 'assisted autopoieis' is the more authentic term.

B: What part does chance play in your painting?
R: An essential one. It always has. There have been times when this has worried me a great deal and I've seen this reliance on chance as a shortcoming on my part.
B: Is this chance different from chance in Pollock or Surrealist automatism?
R: Yes it certainly is different. Above all it's never blind chance: it's a chance that always planned, but is also always surprising. And I need it in order to carry on, in order to eradicate my mistakes, to destroy what I've worked out wrong, to introduce something new and disruptive. I'm often astonished to find out how much better chance is than I am.
B: So this is the level on which openness is still thinkable and credible in real terms? Chance?
R: It introduces objectivity so perhaps it's no longer chance at all. But in the way it destroys and is simultaneously constructive, it creates something I would have been glad to do and work out for myself. [21]

Claiming for ourselves the scholar's position, we find this exchange is interesting but badly flawed. Let's try first, then, to rid ourselves of the more blatant contradictions: first of all 'chance' and whether Richter's 'version' is any different from Pollock's. The implication of Richter's response is that there is 'blind' chance in Pollock whereas Richter 'plans'. This is, of course, nonsense. Both painters 'plan' and make use of what they call 'chance' – except of course that the elements that are permitted to 'take chances' are, more or less, the traditional components of painting with a few added utensils, media, strategies designed to limit 'traditional' levels of control and to 'provoke' if not traditional then certainly memetically-intelligible patterns of 'freedom'.

But this is not a game played, so to speak, in bad faith: the failing lies with the words and not the paintings. It is not chance at work here in any real sense but two accomplished painters allowing the sheer beauty of combined pigments to show itself. In short, this is *provoked* autopoieis where the components and their interaction are known and desired. It has, if anything less to do with any scholastic, abstracting or reductive intent but with a very real sense of care - not unlike guiding, shepherding, cultivating, with all of their moral and quasi-religious connotations. Like cultivation and husbandry, it too has its savage side: it makes Richter 'glad', this 'grim truth'.

Then there is the question of 'objectivity, so perhaps it's no longer chance at all'. (op. cit.) Given in response to Buchloh's asking is what sense is openness thinkable and credible, this is an odd statement. It's also characteristic: 'Sacrifice oneself to objectivity. I have always loathed subjectivity' [22] What can he mean? The notion of sacrifice is important: certain kinds of control and intention are no longer feasible: 'Be a reaction machine, unstable, indiscriminate, dependent.' [23] Again the wording hinders as much as it helps. We suggest that its resolution consists (in Richter's words) 'to accept this willingly'. [24] For what is gained in the concession of 'purpose' is the ability to re-act in the face of what 'chance' provides: grim truth and gift. This is nothing other than a redefinition of the function of the painter as a co-actor in the ecology of the work. This does nothing to diminish, or reduce, or abstract, the cultural or ecological position of the painter; it rather shows *privilege* – not wholly unlike the notion of 'grace.' He and we are the recipients of both the destruction and the construction. We might rephrase: 'I'm often astonished to find out how much better chance is than I am' – by simply adding the word 'alone'. The artist now works 'in community'.

'Art is the highest form of hope' at the same time as 'painting is total idiocy'. Of course, it always *was*. This is what we intended by saying this conundrum was 'only human'; in other words, through something as 'idiotic' as re-presentation humans can hope to survive in an environment that alternates between succour and hostility. We also share similar 'functional idiocies' with every other species: from birdsong to the sense of smell. Sated in more formal terms the 'closure' is *necessary*. The system can only 'open' itself to the complexities of the environment by adaptive selection of its own 'orders of complexity'. This dialectic of closure and openness is essentially similar for all painters: for Rembrandt's simplifying devices and his intimate verisimilitude; for Richter's chance-aiding implements and his determination to 'get things right'; from gladness to terror in the face of grim truth; from *Crucifixion* to *Autumn Rhythm*. But also: for the cellular boundary of the simplest organism in its 'idiotic' drive to live; in the risk of ingesting the body of another in the idiotic drive to stave off one's own entropy; the idiotic risk of the mother in bearing the child. Without God, autopoiesis has the first the last, and every 'word'.

Notes

1. Kuspit, D. (1995) pp.237-46.
2. in Jenks, C. ed. (1995).
3. Heinrich, D. (1985).
4. Jenks, C. ed. (1995) p.127.
5. ibid. p.138.
6. Hegel, W.(1971) p.17.
7. Jenks, C. (1995) p.133.
8. ibid. pp.133-4.
9. see Merleau-Ponty, M. (1964) 'Cezanne's Doubt' and Jay, M. (1993) pp.157-60.
10. Jenks, C. ed. (1995) p.135.
11. 'Interview with Benjamin H.D. Buchloh, 1986' in Richter, G. (1995) pp.132-66.
12. Kuspit, D. (1995) p.242.
13. Richter, G. (1995) pp.132-3.
14. ibid. p.139.
15. ibid. p.142.
16. ibid. p.148.
17. ibid. p.149. The reference is to Sedlmayr's *Art in Crisis:the Lost Centre*.
18. ibid. p.237 see also Text for catalogue of *Documenta 7 Kassel 1982* in Richter, G. (1995) p.100.
19. Kuspit, D. (1995) p.245.
20. Richter, G. (1995) p.133.
21. ibid. p.159.
22. ibid. p.78.
23. ibid.
24. ibid.

11 After Heidegger: Notes Toward a Unified Ontology

We now propose to link our opinion of the outcomes of our text with the more generalised issues outlined in our opening chapters. We have presented at length the contradictions of postmodernity's apparent pluralism and need not repeat or summarise the arguments here. Our earlier requirement is, however, crucial. We contrasted the limited, hoped-for, but finally unintended pluralism with a theory of patterned complexity that, we argue, demonstrates its own necessity. Chapter one concluded with this formulation, which we will shortly modify:

> Perhaps the desire for heterotopia is well-founded; a good instinct, so to speak. Given our analysis above, if heterogeny is anything but an illusion founded in a second-order morality with virtually no authority - then heterogeny and its desirability must arise out of (our) interaction with Being itself. Heterogeny - if at all authentic - must be understood as an ontological *requirement* and not as a second-order ethical *preference*.

For us the foregoing has been an extended tautology whose root, branch and entire possibility is the concept 'autopoiesis'. We propose below to disentangle the concept from its applications, illustrations, our interests and prejudices – so far as possible. What follows, then, is an attempt to provide a formal summary of an autopoietic ontology. However formal the intent, it will be, by default, geared by our interests and ignorance and therefore 'toward' the socio-philosophical. There should be no doubt, however, that we intend (at least to contribute to) a *unified* ontology. That is to say that an autopoietic ontology is radically inclusive. It grounds 'phenomena in general' and explicitly rejects special ontologies for sub-classes just as it rejects all of those that might contradict it. Consequently, whatever libertarian impulses inform our everyday lives, any ontology per se is a precise act of inclusion and exclusion; it must articulate its own tolerance and intolerance. Only on that basis is a subsequent morality a human possibility

Our summary will take the form of a contrast between two kinds of images of community. One is the 'belonging-together' of Being and beings essayed in Heidegger. The other is a series of autopoietic proposals that follow from 'Darwin's dangerous idea', systems-theory and theories of consciousness that stress the relationship of system or organism to environment rather than the assumed priority of the human or social in thinking ontologically.

Every ontology is faced with the task of explaining evident, patterned complexity and in particular the contradictions that occur at the manifold levels of appearance, perception, understanding and communication. We have explicitly rejected those ontologies that begin by discounting some or all of what is evident by distinguishing between authentic and inauthentic phenomena. This distinction has nothing to do with epistemology or the capacity for error. It is essentially an *a priori* decision that some of Being 'counts' and some does not. Often what 'counts' is decided by implicit human interest. To place our objection simply and in more modern 'Kuhnian' terms: it is not a convincing strategy for a paradigm to assume that incommensurate phenomena can be discounted as inauthentic or as aberrations.

Such ontologies must include a point of disjuncture through which, so to speak, inauthenticity can flow and present itself to consciousness *as* inauthentic. Unconvincingly, Socrates offers *anamnesis*. More effectively, Christianity offers 'original sin' and so lets in the distinction between the graced and the non-graced, which is relentlessly exploited by those seeking more mundane authority or advantage. If its older form is genius, its modern manifestation is the expert.

Crucially, where modernity credits the experts, postmodernity (literally) discredits them. An autopoietic ontology insists on a quite different requirement: advantage, effectivity, power, inequality are homeodynamic, structural possibilities and opportunities. Given this emphasis it is clear that postmodernity's too-easy discreditation of authority-in-general – disbelief in metanarratives – rests on an underlying and implicit concept of inauthenticity carried over from ancient usage. Predating both modernity's expert and renaissance 'grace' postmodernity's underclothes are distinctly medieval.

More conventionally stated, postmodernity's easy shift from one convention (expertise) to *any* other (Nazism, liberalism although you are not supposed to notice the impolite possibilities) rest on the presumption of conventionality in the strictest sense of 'could have been otherwise' and therefore on randomness. An important point, if not an easy one, follows. Randomness cannot genuinely operate as partial or even as widespread but only as totality. Otherwise it would simply be a kind of fall out from, or beside, a non-random structure. Hegel makes much the same point about infinity: it cannot be 'beyond' but must *include* the finite. Nor, then, can the ontological 'universe of possibility' be random – or if it once was, it has surpassed that state in, so to speak, a non-random 'singularity' or special event. Put more plainly an autopoietic ontology has to assume non-random agents such as forces, processes, tendencies as the origin of its own possibility and of the phenomena it seeks to formulate. Therefore, autopoiesis proposes distinctions of the type: possible/impossible, viable/nonviable, and their consequent processes and structures.

The tendency to count and discount certain classes of incommensurate phenomena is parallel to and compounded by the tendency to formulate different origins for different classes of phenomena. The key example in this context is social as opposed to natural phenomena. This produces the ludicrous proposition of a series of incommensurate ontologies whose institutionalised form is rigid separation (and mutual farcical caricatures) of 'hard' and 'soft' academic disciplines. An autopoietic 'reform' would stress the unity of origin and the consequent re-production of *differentiated orders*. This proposal, discussed above in relation to Luhmann, also asserts that without differentiated but mutually self-constituting orders there could be nothing but random 'noise'. In this sense, an ontology of autopoetic heterogeny is demanded by heterogeny itself and is not any sort of preferred option. We shall open that tautology in due course.

Before moving on it is appropriate to note Hegel's re-appearance and to discuss again his influence on (especially French) 20th Century thought. Rosen accuses Hegel of discrediting Reason by claiming too much on its behalf. Similarly, the reaction against Hegel in France associates him with unacceptable claims to the supremacy of European thought, politics and ethics and so with actual or intellectual imperialism.[1] However well-founded these claims and however repulsive the manifestation of supremacist policies, there are nevertheless unintended and counter-productive philosophical consequences. The proposition that Reason as a European idiom is grounded in the nature of and so 'belongs to' Being - and on that ground has a claim to supremacy - is correctly seen as offensive both by Europeans and by those of different worldviews. But the proposition that (re)cognition belongs to Being, where cognition is understood as a widespread, ecologically-organised response to an environment and not simply as a human faculty is a quite different and *necessary* proposition. We realise that a cultural-supremacy theory can be re-read into that position but we argue that is not sufficient grounds to forbid its analysis.

If French thought considered the risk too great or too distasteful – for whatever good reason – the effect is to cut Hegel out of the proper ancestry and to promote Kant as the founder of modern philosophy and in particular of its phenomenological and liberal tendencies. We have made our arguments against Kant already: the formal 'transcendental' subject cannot evolve into the 'member' (except by making membership its whim). We argued instead that the precursor of the viable member is the viable species and the precursor of the species is another viable species where viability understood in the strictly temporal and ecological sense. There is however, a further consequence. Where Hegel apparently discredited the relationship of Being and thinking, by (so to speak) 'concretising' it in the politics of European Enlightenment, the renewed influence of Kant operates so as to underscore a fundamental *separation* of Being and thinking 'in' the formal subject. Then Heidegger - because, unlike Hegel, he apparently claims so little for everyday reason - becomes *the* fundamental ontologist; the model for re-thinking the 'belonging-together' of Being and beings (the very term is his) and in particular the belonging-together of Being and Thinking (in the Heideggerian sense). This is, for us a grave error with grave consequences most essentially because his version of that relationship – the 'belonging together' is anything but a small claim and is very tightly structured.

Heidegger characterises Western thought – Western *metaphysics* – as 'representational thinking'. We considered this matter above; for the moment we require only the following contrast. For Heidegger, representational thinking is bound up with the human enterprise of exerting control over Being and is the ground of modern technology. Heidegger's thinking – which he also characterises as 'thanking' – attempts to re-call or remember Being by various strategies – leaps backward, overcoming metaphysics, silencing, or 'shattering' ordinary speech and (so) listening to what Being 'says'.[2] For us, whatever strengths there are in his argument it contains a sort of reverse humanism. Human instrumental control is stressed along with its negative consequences (it is both the root and 'route' of manifest inauthenticity). So arises the project of 'overcoming' this negation or abandonment or 'concealing' of Being. Given the distaste for Hegelian totality and the collapse of credibility in Marx's essentially humanistic-technological project, and contemporary disquiet as to the costs of technology, this begins to look very attractive. Where Marx allegedly combined an ontological and a moral project in the totalising concept of dialectical materialism, and modern technicism is amoral, Heidegger appears to offer a fundamental ontology requiring moral repentance. We shall shortly argue that this is a fundamental error but for the moment let us underline the widespread proposition that something akin to Heidegger's 'thinking as thanking' is absolutely necessary to 'save' the West from nihilism, the will to power and the guilt of its political past or its technological present. The Heidegger-influenced critic performs the priestly function of exorcism and provides the model for good conduct. Without wishing to demean but rather to be more accurate 'good conduct' is better understood as good manners. Hence the extraordinarily, respectable popularity of *de*construction when its doctrines are so relentlessly negative.

Whatever humans and their technology are guilty of, we would instead stress (following Luhmann) that the maintenance of a specific, distinct order is a condition of the existence of every phenomenon and especially cognition – human or not. In Heidegger's world these conditions – which we agree are components of control, but not necessarily human – are inauthentic in a sense close to that argued by Socrates and Augustine. Heidegger would, of course, fundamentally disagree with that presentation. Plato is seen as at least one of the points of origin of metaphysics. Nevertheless you will scan Heidegger in vain for any positive or even interested formulation of mundane socio-political life.

If that is not always quite true it is because of an extra spin that Heidegger puts on his concept of Being. Heidegger(ians) will hotly disagree with that. According to him/them, a *concept* of Being is the last thing intended; that would be metaphysics. But we insist that Heidegger *has* a concept of Being and that concept is finally humanistic.

Any number of grounds might be cited but the fundamental one is his 'framing' (we choose the word carefully; it is close to Heidegger's own 'enframing' and means to assert conceptual control) of the very relationship of Being and beings – those precise linguistic terms coloured by 'belonging together' and the conviction that representational thinking has violated or lost sight of the essence of belonging. The language – the belonging together of Being and beings – asserts Being as the *origin* of beings and not (as metaphysics would have it) as the most abstract or general class or category of beings, that is, something generated by human, linguistic *positing*. Recall Heidegger's rage at Kant: 'In Kant Being is merely the positing of the copula between the subject and the object.' (op. cit.). And yet what is the term 'beings' (small b) but a similar class? No doubt Heidegger is constrained by some of the disciplines or idioms of metaphysics – a position he concedes at times.[3] It appears then that however close Being comes to the poetic evocation of Origin or Divinity it remains the destiny of this particular God to beget 'beings' in the sense of category and thus metaphysics too. Heidegger, again, will half-admit this:

> Metaphysically represented man is constituted with faculties as a being among others....[but] confined to what is metaphysical man is caught in

the difference of beings and Being which he never experiences....Metaphysics belongs to the nature of man. But what is this nature itself? What is metaphysics itself? Who is man himself within this natural metaphysics?[4]

We might construe this in the sense Heidegger (we think) intends: that everyday humanity is oblivious to the difference but that, properly understood and re-directed, philosophy may bring itself to attend to the difference as such. In this interpretation there appears a philosophically-attractive duty to remedy a real and profound neglect in an almost religious sense.

> Metaphysics closes itself to the simple essential fact that man essentially occurs only in is essence where he is claimed by Being. Only from that claim [has] he found that wherein his essence dwells.....Such standing in the clearing of Being I call the ek-sistence of man. This way of Being is proper only to man.[5]

Or more simply and echoing the more disturbing bond between overcoming metaphysics and passivity:

> Before he speaks man must let himself be claimed by Being, taking the risk that under this claim he will seldom have much to say.[6]

Equally disturbing, the editor's explanatory footnote reads:

> ...man stands out into the truth of Being and so is exceptional among beings that are at hand *only* as beings of nature or human production.[7]

The alternative sense then relentlessly emerges. There is only one duty – to be claimed by Being – and all other duties are at least less-authentic. You may well be able to tease an academic seminar into accepting this – and even into feeling a certain piety about it. But if you go so far as to suggest that the 'duty' is a literary device premised on that old arrogance that man is special amongst beings and the this 'duty' assumes something like a priestly class (a leisured elite) who don't have to mess around with things 'at hand' like tools and washing machines you will suddenly find a very cold shoulder in your face. Your liberal colleagues will become fearsome fundamentalists. They will accuse you of cynicism and nihilism. They will make you a pariah but conveniently not notice nor mention their implicit supremacism (like Hegel) or the clear social hierarchy in which philosophers (like Socrates) are placed above *all* others. Let us at least agree that the old schema of authentic and inauthentic phenomena is at work, together with the privileged status this accords to 'man'. It is truly strange that we cannot immediately see that this is more to do with self-interest than any genuine interest in the ontological ground of the manifold of phenomena. Let's just say that if Heidegger is prepared to 'thank' Being, like Socrates he is remarkably thankless toward beings. Crucially for us, position is both articulated and easily concealed within the linguistic idioms of philosophy. It is essential to see that 'philosophy' is grasped here not as the 'sin' of philosophers (that would be finally trivial) but as a characteristic possibility of human language.

Our position is not cynical not nihilistic: it offers the alternative of autopoiesis. Neither, however is it sentimental: autopoiesis is not necessarily a beneficent or orderly dynamic. Heidegger, however is peppered with sentimental references to Being.

> The unnoticeable law of the Earth preserves the Earth in the sufficiency of the emerging and perishing of all things in the allotted sphere of the possible which everything follows but nothing knows. The birch tree never oversteps its possibility. The colony of bees dwells in its possibility. It is first the will which arranges itself everywhere in technology that devours the Earth in the exhaustion and consumption and change of what is artificial.[8]

It may be apposite to criticise destructive technology, but the answer to that is more likely to come from technology and certainly from the political *will* to make conservation a priority. And prioritisation as we know depends on funding. The birch tree (undiseased) and the bee colony (unaggressive) are of course beautiful images and have an honoured place within the desires and literature of humankind but the literature in question is poetry and certainly not ontology. And there are many Romantic poets or painters who would find the bees and birch just a little too sweet and lacking the terrible force of the sublime. Equally, there are many within the Earth sciences who would discount these images as plain falsehoods in the face of the Earth's convulsive history, designed to comfort rather than enlighten. Moreover, in the desire to avoid assuming control or responsibility, deconstruction appears more morally acceptable than construction and acquiescence in the face of 'fate' seems more acceptable than active politics. That is the best gloss we can place on Heidegger's support of Hitler. The effects, however, remain disastrous, self-deception.

It is time to concede that humanism in its old form and in the decayed reversals of Heidegger-influenced postmodern critical theory has run its course. It no longer commands; its vitality has ceased. Similarly, its own 'enframing', the emphasis on human language, its privileging of 'man' and its the formal-categorial idioms (like 'beings') have been exacerbated to the point of meaninglessness. We repeat: this is not a new situation nor an isolated one. It is at least as old as Socrates and is an entrenched characteristic in the way human language often 'works'.

Compared with the models offered by Darwin, ecology and systems theory the category 'beings' is a deplorable way of 'enframing' the patterned complexity of phenomena. By contrast, Darwin's form of enframing is exemplified in the very title: *The Origin Of Species.* The concept of origin implied here is one to which patterned complexity properly belongs and emphatically is *not* inauthentic nor an easy subject for reduction. We may now re-phrase the requirement of heterogeny. Heterogeny is an ontological requirement because it presents itself (as, for example differentiated orders or species) That is to say that patterned complexity has only *come* to be ignorable through linguistic-categorial reduction which in turn rests on an ontology of guaranteed substitutability. 'God's creatures' or 'randomness' or 'inauthenticity' are the underwriters.

There must be, however, a further twist in the tale. Observed heterogeny –whether we subsequently treat it as authentic or seek to reduce it as merely contingent - is parallel to the requirement that a system selects a differentiated and less-complex order then an environment which then becomes its 'own' complexity. But that complexity has to function effectively to mediate the relations between system and environment. Otherwise extinction is on the horizon. We could place this arrogantly and say that the former, apparent necessity of linguistic-categorial reduction has ceased or been surpassed. But given our modification of the terms 'vital' and 'necessity' along the lines of vitality and viability, it would be more candid to argue that reductive ontologies concede some (or all) of their former vitality to their autopoietic opponents once someone has produced a cogent articulation. That someone was Darwin – however much you dislike the course of neoDarwinism; and ever since heterogeny is ontologically 'vital' (it has vitality) on account of his intellectual descendants. This more complex formulation is not overblown; it is intended to show that cut-and-dried supremacy (in this case of heterogeny over reduction) is just too simple. It is perfectly possible to imagine circumstances in which heterogeny is unacceptable. Hitler proposed 'unacceptable heterogeny' in relation to race and culture. His proposal was literally defeated. More moderately, a version of medicine that allowed both micro-organisms and demons in its explanations offers another unacceptable heterogeny. In our view, the *complexity* itself is vital – or, if you wish, the orthodox metanarrative; but only so far as it is *not* reduced to a cut-and-dried either/or. In other words, heterodoxy and orthodoxy are only viably complex models if they include the possibility of each other.

This means being alive to the inauthentic enframing that Heidegger himself points out but from which he cannot extricate himself. It is precisely the desire to 'settle the question in general' (and the distaste for variables and possibilities) that produces the kind of reductive enframing exemplified in categories like 'beings' or 'phenomena' or formalisms like 'the subject' or 'art'. And quite clearly, they *are* forms of linguistic control. We are not sure that they are controls that ground technology - as Heidegger wants to argue. They are more likely to 'control', that is, *allow* the production of similar memetic processes (conventional philosophy) in specifically-designated habitats (philosophy departments). We see that as both a rational and a predatory statement. Moreover, they are effective instruments of *social* control because the memetic process is made so radically simple that even the dullest participant can tell the good folk from the bad. An index of that dullness is that the only thinker of rank to support Hitler is arguably the most important philosopher for modern *cultural* studies. The irony is overwhelming.

Or again, if we concede to Darwin and his intellectual descendants the recognition of the vitality of heterogeneity, we open ourselves to the charge of an anti-humanism seen from a distinctly humanist perspective. This is why we must insist that humankind is not placed at the centre of the ontological stage whether as genius, expert, in God's image or as the only being that 'dwells in the house of Being'. In this sense, the 'someone' (Darwin) who concedes the vitality of heterogeny might equally be a 'something' once Darwin has exploded the conceit of human centrality. This is why we insisted in our opening chapters that ontology is misunderstood as 'what (human) ontologists do' .[9] An autopoietic ontology insists on the viable status of every practical ontology in every being, however 'primitive'. Or to put it in other words, human and 'other' ontologies are possibilities within what we can only re-present to ourselves as a unified autopoietic ontology. To 'only represent' does not demean but rather insists on autopoietic complexity. It is precisely the requirement of differentiated orders between 'human' and environment. That is why the issue is not simply or only a question of philosophical distortion. We argued above that the issue arose instead out of the structure and possibilities of human language; we can now emphasise that this root is 'necessary' (vital) to the very being of the species but not in anything like the Heideggerian sense. Rather, linguistic 'closure' is *necessary* and is seen as one closure amongst others, each potentially interactive.

It is in this context that we can raise one of the most recent and most objectionable characteristics of 'French' (Heidegger-influenced) 20th Century thought: the denigration of vision. Again the *root* of 'anti-ocular-centrism' is not unreasonable: it argues against the *privileging* of vision in post-Cartesian thought and in science's 'observer paradigm'. But to dispense with one privilege at the price of enacting another – that of language or text seems absurd: a counter-swing of essentially the same pendulum. This pendulum attempts to suppress complexity in the sense of heterogeneity. Of course, that is not to say that Heidegger or Derrida *lack* complexity! It is instead to argue that the complexity that *follows from* the limitation they elect (the supremacism of humans/ language/ text) is unviable – or, if complex, unviably homogenous. Our counter-proposals (essayed in the foregoing) stress the different kinds of order – or 'closures' if you will – in verbal and visual representing operate to both contest and inform one another and not to reinforce the limitations of representation. Put differently: if the limitation we call 're-presentation' is an existential necessity the non-commensurability of its various forms is an ecological advantage where each does not enforce but rather 'exposes' the limits of the other. A word of caution is advisable here: we have *only* thought about (part of) the relationship of visual to verbal in this text.

This is Levin's interpretation of Heidegger.

> What takes place when our visual perception is not yielding, when it is so willful that it cannot give way, and does not visibly give thanks? [10]

> Thinking which merely re-presents..is metaphysical thinking.... Our particular concern is with vision insofar as it either embodies or is capable of *freeing itself* from that body of thinking.....It is important to bear in mind the inherent *aversive and aggressive character* of re-presentation. As the prefix itself informs us, representation is a repetition: a process of delaying, or deferring, that which visibly presences. It is a way of *positing at a distance*, so that vision can 'again' take up what presences - but this time on ego's terms. [11]

Heidegger (and Levin) will elsewhere seek to formulate 'the work of art' as an instance of non-aggressive visual 'representing'. Speaking of Van Gogh's pictures of peasant shoes Heidegger writes:

> Thus it is truth, not merely something true that is at work.... The more simply and essentially the shoes are engrossed in their essence, the more ...do all beings attain a greater degree of being along with them. That is how self-concealing Being is cleared. Light of this kind joins its shining to and into the work. This shining, joined in the work, is the beautiful. *Beauty is one way in which truth essentially occurs as unconcealment.* [12]

The intention, the language, the sentiment is clearly poetic and resistant to 'clarification' or charges of undue obscuration. And it does succeed in depicting a visual ecstasy of the kind often associated with Romanticism but also clearly present in at least the words of artists as diverse as Michelangelo, Cézanne and Barnett Newman – not to mention the words of their more ardent admirers. Who, then, are we to object? Let us be clear: we have no real objection to the poetry –though some sterner artists might find the sentiment, the ecstasy, just a little sickly. But the poetry, the heightening of 'the degree of being' (clearly one of the points at which the poetry falls on its face) always occurs despite the thing depicted whether understood as 'merely' a particular or as an object of use. Art – truth as unconcealment – is always *despite* the truths of appearance and mundane practicality. True, the shoes disclose an 'authentic' relation to a world and the Earth, according to Heidegger – but you can be sure this only belongs to the peasant's shoes and could never apply to a pair of high-heels or in-line skates or top-quality riding boots. No, that would be too 'willful'.

Behind the apparent beauty of the poetry there lurks, then, a colossal level of exclusion – one which excludes all those worlds (except the artist's) that are conventionally ranked above the peasant's wretched but holy will-less-ness. And of course, everything conventionally ranked below the peasant – everything other than humankind just doesn't and cannot figure precisely because it is excluded from artistic or poetic possibility. That peculiar admixture of human exultation and debasement is redolent of Christianity. At the same time the naming of art as 'essential' in the face of the inessential is the most ironic inversion of Marxian notions of surplus value. Put simply, the pious regard in which Heidegger is held by critics of technology-saturated humanism is misplaced because he is a critic founded in and imprisoned by precisely that paradigm. He *cannot* offer an alternative ontology but only an expression of regret. He is actually an apologist.

Vision cannot be characterised through a Cartesian or metaphysical paradigm. For the vast majority of beings (apart from an increasingly isolated subset of academics) it is an active component of the biosphere. Similarly, visual art cannot be 'contained' in verbal definitions, whether ocularcentric or anti-ocularcentric, or in idly-spoken categories that assume some sort of continuum. The problem, then, is to formulate generative principles that ground the most rudimentary ontological requirements whilst also 'allowing' the most complex heterogeny.

The first principles of an inclusive, autopoietic ontology can be stated quite easily: *all* phenomena, the specific and the general, the present and the absent, foreground and environment are autopoietic complexes. There are no special cases, nor middle grounds. That assertion of origin, though simply stated is as radical in its effects as every other Creation theory. In particular it asserts that comparable conditions are at work in determining the probability of *every* phenomenon, living and non-living, natural or social. Crucially, however, this is not to be understood as a reduction of complexity. On the contrary it states that complexity occurs on this ground and no other. Politically, that notion is also radical. It states, for example, that cultural and linguistic complexes based on other notions of Creation are *false*. That simple premise is the ground of the various critiques we outlined above.

How does that differ from Durkheim's notion of social phenomena? First it makes problematic the character of the distinction between social and non-social. We shall return to that several times. For the moment, suffice to say that it places into question his notion of the functions of religion and its role in the organisation of language. Durkheim is actually rather coy on this point. He insists that he does not intend to abolish, rationalise, or 'correct', religion. But that of course is precisely the effect of his writing. More importantly, according to our analyses he cannot admit religion's equal co-existence with his own paradigm. God's creatures and *sui-generic* phenomena cannot inhabit the same culture. One has to go. *So far, in the field of cultural critique that 'one' has been Durkheim* – whilst a degenerated humanism has usurped his radicalism and his political import.

A further principle is co-posited: that structures however simple or complex, however rudimentary or evolved exhibit the capability to replicate themselves to a significant degree. It is absurd to state this degree at the outset. Replication in a crystal structure, an animal species or a social structure is thoroughly differentiated. In all cases, however, the replication must be viable. Put in more statistical terms, the field to be explained is therefore a series of differentiated homeodynamic complexes. There is no reason *a priori* to suppose that every process of replication will be exact. Variation around discrete norms is likely.

Meanwhile we have skipped a requirement: the field to be explained is indeed 'homeodynamic complexes'. That also is not necessarily true: homeostasis (approximate replication) is the precondition of homeodynamics; also homeodynamics may collapse back into homeostasis. This underscores that the context we examine (the field to be explained) is the Earth and its current turbulent phenomena and not some imaginary space where the turbulence (natural, social, living, non-living) has resolved itself in finality. 'Our' world still has opportunities for evolution and extinction. Once again we can underline the difference from Durkheim: his notion of the evolution of the complex from the simple is too linear. Extinctions, transformations, hybridisation, reversals are not even unexpected. Over time they are highly likely.

This brings us the last of the co-posited conditions of autopoiesis – and perhaps also its most fundamental summary. You will see that we have taken care not to limit probability. This akin to our paradigm-requirement that certain phenomena cannot be 'ruled out' as incommensurate. But to stop there would place us akin to post-structuralism and its dependence on notions of randomness. On the contrary possibility (in this paradigm) is *necessarily* limited. But its limits are themselves autopoietic, It is therefore appropriate to indicate the absence of limits at a formal level: probability will not be limited a priori and certainly not by our expectations or preferences. But autopioetic complexity *only* occurs 'in context'. That is to say that the phenomena that occur in any given context (of other phenomena) are those which have a high probability of being established and of sustaining their presence. Again, this is so for the living and non-living, the social and the non-social.

We can call this principle the 'autopoietic economy'. By that we intend to draw attention to several 'economic' characteristics. The first is the simple proposal that any context will contain 'goods' – that is, elements likely to assist or maintain the existence of a given autopioetic phenomenon and conversely, those elements which militate against it. Simply put, it will have a price, affordable or not. Second, we are now able to counter the charge that Darwin's 'survival of the fittest' imposes a metaphor like the market economy on general evolution and by implication on social evolution. It is now clear that this is typically arrogant humanism. The converse is obvious: an autopoietic economy is imposed on everything, including us. 'Our' market is simply an instance. We might sum this principle up by saying that the two terms in 'autopoietic economy' presuppose each other: they epitomise the relation of the particular to the general environment. With either term absent complexity is inconceivable and random noise is the result. The attentive reader will see that this is simply an 'active' (dynamic) presentation of the key formal notion in Luhmann that a system must 'choose' a distinct and simpler order than its environment – in order to be recognisable at all – and on this order it erects its 'own' complexity. We can call this order 'autopoietic' – or, equally well, 'economic'.

It is only on the basis of the ordered difference between the particular (system) and the general environment that representation becomes an issue at all. Otherwise it would be lost in the confusion of presence and absence. But it is also clear that such representations, taken in their most general sense are at least one of the many ways of ordering this difference in a viable manner. 'Sight' then – as a general property of many species is not ontologically reducible to anything simply human and certainly not to Cartesian privileging. Rather it is one of the structures that order the relationship of particular to environment. In contrast to Heidegger's dialectics of revealing/concealing it serves to 'conceal' the particular system – the sighted being – from the potential animosity of its direct environment by providing a relatively sealed boundary with visual analogues to environmental phenomena. Certainly this is an instrument of representation, information and control (it might save you from being eaten or indicate what is available to eat.) It is not, however, a property of the will but an evolved ecological function. That, of course, is why Levin amongst Heidegger's many followers is simply redundant. Again, this is not to preclude of diminish the ecstasy or the poetry that sometimes accompanies human art, but to root it more strongly. Or, to put it another way, sight's representations are as authentic and as virtual as any other faculty whose function is to mitigate the 'reality' of an environment for a specific being – like the bat's sonar or the cat's sense of smell or the pigeon's navigation.

This matter is crucial so we shall present it in another manner. For us, Heidegger's 'shining', 'unconcealedness' etc. are counter-metaphors to something like a fall (in the Biblical sense) into the abyss of representation under the domination of the ego. We instead emphasise that shining/ blinding, unconcealedness/nakedness, openness/vulnerability are rapid ways to extinction. 'Truth' as Heidegger's unconcealment or indeed as the positivists' 'correspondence' is the least likely to permit the vitality of the human species whilst 'representation' is its evolved strategy. The capacity for error, even as the greater proportion of mundane representation does not shake the viability in the least. Or: it is the only economic alternative. Hence the confluence of the virtual with the authentic. And it is only *upon* this root – and not despite it – that anything approaching 'art' is remotely conceivable.

How again does this differ from Durkheim? The solidarity expressed in religion and (whatever he says) ruined in Durkheim is instead expressed in the rootedness of representation. Unlike Baudrillard's tinsel simulacra these representations are, of necessity, both virtual and authentic. Or put, differently, to regret the intervention of representation is analytically similar to the desire to do without one's skin.

These are only 'notes toward' a unified ontology and not a detailed exposition. Having outlined some of the 'root' requirements we propose now to move to the 'higher' levels of complexity – or at least those aspects of human representation that appear furthest from these rudimentaries. The first cause of concern is the wording 'root' which implies a possible determinism – a 'branch'. Perhaps the metaphor of origin and 'history' or 'journey' would be more apt. And we suspect you were already somewhere along the way to preference. *This is the error.* A theory of complexity *cannot* begin with such a choice but rather with the inclusion of the apparent contradiction between determination and plasticity. We could put this cryptically: the question, 'What is the nature of social phenomena?' – or more specifically, 'What is art?' cease to exist in this ontology. Or more simply: there is no *a priori* way to decide between determination and plasticity. The speculation is as ridiculous as an *a priori* definition of the number of species; it is a piece of onto*theo*logy, not ontology. The key, for us, is to recognise that this apparently simple requirement has enormous implications. Before we fill out that formulation let us again note how we differ from Durkheim. We cannot say social phenomena *are* without question *sui generic*, we can only say that, in formal terms, there are probabilities that such phenomena are *sui generic* (though we prefer the terms 'plastic' and 'autopoietic') – but there are also probabilities that they may rest on determining grounds that are not simply or strictly social. The probability rests, of course, on every aspect of the context, including the contexts of formulation. At this point it is paramount to see that no *a priori* designation is possible so that anyone who insists – without contextual evidence – on the primacy of the *sui-generic* vis vis the over-determined, or the reverse, is playing that old game: some phenomena don't count.

The risk we take, then, in addressing complex social phenomena is twofold. One version of 'some phenomena don't count' is *determinism* modelled along the lines of 'real' causes (usually economic or political) and derivative or virtual effects. Its opposite assumes that complex phenomena are free to constitute themselves – something like 'pure' imagination, dreamworlds, fantasms. The first denies the reality of the 'derivative' phenomenon's own ordered complexity. The second denies the reality of the complex orders that constitute an 'environment' – social or not. Autopoietic economy, however, asserts a principle of co-determination. Two consequences follow. It is crucial to see that the *same* economy is at work throughout the spectrum of simple (or rudimentary) to complex. At the same time, however, the evolution of distinct orders and their distinct types of complexity means that the relation of phenomena to their environments is already 'managed' to exclude certain kinds of negative interpenetration and to encourage positive ones. This need for relative closure is manifested in living systems in the form, for example of acquired immunity or in social systems in the type of sanctions we call 'norms', moral codes or 'disciplines' such as painting. But just as AIDS is the acronym for 'acquired immunity deficiency syndrome' and has a specific viral 'cause' – so the immunity that describes the discipline 'painting' is open to memetic 'invasions' that may shape or even destroy its internal cohesion.

At this point we should emphasise again that it is the 'separate' order we call (for example) 'painting' that allows the evolution of its marvellous complexity. And unlike Heidegger's model this complexity is *cannot* be simply open to what we might call (in his fashion) the 'shining', the 'overpowering' or the 'fury' of Being. Instead it is as Luhmann asserts that the *simpler* order that distinguishes the phenomenon from its environment that allows its own internal complexity. With precision, Heideger calls this, correctly, 'representation'. We emphasise *re*-presentation. For Heidegger it's the lock; for us it's the key.

Autopoietic economy assumes viability – or its phenomena would not be open to (re)cognition. If you want to extend the economic metaphor, the costs and benefits *vis a vis* other phenomena means that differentiated phenomena viably 'present' themselves. At this point we leave the level of internally-articulated complexity in distinct phenomena (such as 'art') and begin to consider the co-determined but differentiated complexity of contrasting phenomena: (for example) art differentiated into the orders painting, sculpture and so on. At this point we can clearly see that Greenberg's attempted definition of 'competence' is really quite a natural occurrence. It is more or less 'invited': in order to be a painter or a critic one needs is some sense to know what painting 'is'. The error occurs - and is ironically not quite perpetuated in Duve's 'proper name'- in thinking that what it is, is a noun. Or, to put it another way, of requiring there to be an 'essence' (a competence) rather than a series of possible competences.

Crucially, the former is destructive and exclusive whilst the latter allows distinct 'competences' – which can be easily distinguished from the postulate 'anything goes' by the requirement of viability. Unfortunately postmodernism seems to insist on the 'not-noun' interpretation whilst insisting that 'anything goes' is the *only* viable scenario (and not meaning it at all).

We can return here to our notions of exclusion and criminality. The modern (Greenberg) and the postmodern (Lyotard) mirror each other. The former seeks to exclude every other version of the discipline's competence as somehow criminal. But when a definitive competence refuses to emerge precisely because of the discipline's plasticity, the only ostensibly 'non-criminal' posture is to assume *absolute* plasticity. Hence *post*structuralism – which is not so much a denial of the discipline's recognisable structures (even Lyotard has a notion of the aesthetic) as the refusal to concede that its environment has a bearing on the possibility of its various forms. By contrast, Darwin's notion of species and Durkheim's division of labour stress differentiation and adaptation or co-determination of the specific and its environment. That, reduced to its simplest, says that as soon as plasticity demonstrates *any* kind of stasis, it cannot be absolute. Humanism should remember that humans and their societies are extreme latecomers in the history of plasticity. Despite the arrogance that says human plasticity is the most complex and extreme, then, we should remember that 'our' post-natal and cultural plasticity was simply the one niche that was ecologically available. We had no choice. We *have* no choice but adaptability.

We are now in a position to reformulate Lyotard's distinction between no-longer-credible metanarratives and the pragmatics of performance. Our notion of art connotes plasticity and invention set against Lyotard's simply disruptive practices. 'Our' art is restless, critical and inaugural; what Heidegger would call 'artificial'. For us it is a major function of what in social systems is seen as differentiation and in living systems as speciation. Like Durkheim's division of labour it promotes co-existence through divergence rather than competition for one set of performances. We intend this to read structurally rather than sentimentally. We are not in the business of claiming that difference and speciation do not generate their own kinds of conflict and competition. Understood structurally they, instead promote different kinds of memetic opportunity, alternative adaptation strategies.

Taken in this sense, Lyotard's metanarratives are not so much disbelieved but rather have to collapse in the face of complexity. The crucial point, for us is not the overthrow of those 'wicked' grand narratives; that is just too narrow, parochial, humanistic, too fundamentalist. The 'wicked spirit' then is not the interested narrator, nor the ideological legitimation of a particular political class but the linguistic tendency toward the mis-use of the categorial. Set against visual art's sensitivity to the specific (take again the example of the shoes) verbal categorisation is a blunt and unsubtle instrument that can be carried to habitual or idiomatic extremes. It is not the exalted 'one' place of attention to the impact of Being but a representational programme with distinct limits which it constantly, thoughtlessly, oversteps. Hence the drive in Heidegger toward 'having little to say' or Plato's noisy drive toward silence; not to mention the convolutions of the former's language in the face of the simplicity of the painting of the shoes.

Mis-use and 'idiomatic extremes' tend to suggest human failings: we appear to be back in the business of humanistic criticism. This is not the case. It is better understood as a structural feature of the relationships between verbal language and its 'objects'. Mis-use, dysfunction show themselves as emergent or 'turbulent' properties of the dynamics of linguistic and other forms of representation at work in their environments. Or again, we might conceptualise such turbulence as 'unintended consequences' – much the same as the early Wittgenstein approached the anomalies of philosophy. This would be wrong! First it has little to do with intentionality, but if anything, to do with the structural requirement to think in linguistic-categorial terms. Second – and more importantly – if we focus on the 'unintended' it becomes clear that talk of the will and ego's terms are miles from the mark. Because – even if it seems counter-intuitive – the unintended consequence can only be intelligible as a consequence if it shows itself in the form of an order – however turbulent. The 'turbulent' or anomalous consequence displays *self-similarity*[13] and is therefore neither human nor random in origin – but part of the recognisable dynamics of verbal representation active in an environmental field. It is not, then, primarily philosophical but linguistic. And if you think that is a small point we argue that it is analogous to the structural requirement of perspective in lens-based representation. The difference is that we have yet to fully recognise or take account of linguistic 'perspective'.

It is appropriate to close our text with an image: Rembrandt's portrait of Marguerita Tripp (nee de Geere). We are speaking of the face-on version in the National Gallery. The portrait shows an elderly woman with sunken cheeks, strong eyes and a pinched mouth. She stares straight ahead, clutching a white cloth or handkerchief. She wears a black dress, almost lost in the darkness in which she sits and her head is framed below by a stiff white ruff and above by a black lace cap drawn tightly around the hairline.

Unlike Van Gogh's and Heidegger's wretched, holy peasant, portrayed only as or by his boots, Marguerita Tripp was by all accounts extremely wealthy. She was the wife of Jacob Tripp who made his fortune through mining, metal production - and armaments! Perhaps it would be too unkind to note an identification of aspiration between Rembrandt and his sitter – whilst Van Gogh and Heidegger note with pious regret, they are disinclined to wear peasant shoes. Put bitterly, for both of them, the peasant is of no more consequence than the shoes: both are sentimentalised objects for voyeurs of higher rank. But Tripp and Rembrandt insist that they look into each other's (or our) faces.

Her expression is non-committal. Like *Olympia*, but in different circumstances, she is primarily 'being painted'. Yet despite the elaborately 'period' nature of the costume – and indeed Rembrandt's own style, especially the tonality and colour – she is astoundingly contemporary. But she is visibly aging and will soon die. The effect is to underscore her age, her life and that all that remains of her vividness is the vividness of this canvas-and-paint *thing* that another brilliant but dead human has wrought out of ingenious but simple materials and through a miraculous interrogation of his own perceptions through using those materials. There stands, then, this vividly compelling presence of an old woman 'suspended' in a human practice as archaic as humanity itself: the re-presentation of images. But it cannot be col-lected as an instance of the category 'art' unless you to propose to grant it the minimum of attention (which in other circumstances might be a reasonable or expedient course of action). Nor will de Duve's 'proper name' address it more appropriately. It sticks out as a stubborn refusal to be anything but its unique self and no amount of re-grounding will erase the fact that it is an extraordinary social phenomenon. You need only see its companion piece or any of the Velasquez portraits in a nearby room to see that this extra-ordinariness, whist rare and precious, is not confined to a few sparkling moments in the tradition and the discipline. The gold is there in appropriate measure and, more often than not, it has already been safeguarded for your contemplation. Moreover, these special instances often exclude each other: How do you 'measure' a Turner beside a Rembrandt? They exclude each other in the name and for the sake of heterogeneity. How dry that sounds in words if you can't feel, see, recall the images themselves! And how astounding the experience when you move from the Turners to the Rembrandts, let alone the stupendous difference in (say) the monuments, reliquaries and writing-drawing of old Egypt.

And yet there are points of continuity. The sense of related disciplines remains in the face of the difference. We are surely wise enough to refuse to apply a policing regime of the kind modernism proposed. It is much less clear that we are not tempted by its postmodern counterpart: anything goes. That would of course include the destruction of the Rembrandt 'in principle'. What a delicious irony! What principle? The right of the Rembrandt to survive and be considered rests on no more nor less than its own insistence. An insistence not shouted in the face of nothingness but on the basis of resemblance, tradition, discipline, quality but above all *care*. An insistence that is intelligible, not necessarily to all, but sharable in some important sense. It does not matter if this is elusive.

How does the Rembrandt insist? What does it show? What does it care for? The questions cannot be 'answered' but on the basis of its presence in a social domain, it can at least be commented upon. On another occasion, we might choose differently; again that does not matter in the sense of precluding or prohibition. Here, with Rembrandt, we should like to notice and emphasise the spheres of the eyes and their depth within the sockets, the use and the age that shows itself in those damp orbs. We shall also remark on the illusion of an exchanged gaze, when the trace that remains – and what a trace! – holds something of what he saw, and the gaze they exchanged.

With Rembrandt we shall stare at those sunken lips and the cheeks that stretch and hang over the cheekbones and jawbones and conclude there are few teeth left. We shall also remember the lips and the jaw and the teeth as some of the instruments of her life when she draws energy from the beings she eats to stave off or excrete her own entropy and keep her living system vital. We know that vitality had not long to go and has long ceased. We know that the energy, force and pain in those massive, worn hands has long ceased to grasp food, wealth, status.

And for the moment, though we shall undoubtedly ponder this painting again, we shall also note the decorum that surrounds this spent corporeality, in her clothes and in the rank given to the picture itself. Or, the dignity that we accord 'her' – this image – on the presumption of her conscious being and on the wilful brilliance that Rembrandt achieved through painting 'her'.

Everyone who proposes to think seriously about visual culture or visual art should begin from an understanding that *utterrance* begins with dizzying paradox of insisting that this extraordinary painting (or another *equal* candidate) is at the same time 'just' an instance, an example, a name. Or: every human speaker however young or inexperienced, whether the Rembrandt is known at first hand, or through 'reproduction' or through words or *not at all*, finds 'natural' the conceit that, nevertheless, the Rembrandt justly *belongs* to his idly-spoken category 'art'. And along with that, every such work, seen or not seen, lost or recognised, made long ago or not yet, not perhaps for many years, also can be fittingly col-lected. This conceit is the stuff of Greenberg's policing, of determinism, of Duchamp's pitiful gestures and of postmoderns' pretended tolerance, of Heidegger's 'beings', of Kant's self-creating subject, of Augustine's heaven and earth, of Socrates' corrosive political irony, of language's irrationality. When the eye sees that a mountain viewed from a distance can seem smaller than a fingernail, it knows by experience how to resolve this apparent contradiction. Sight long ago came to terms with its own 'virtual reality', long before humans ever appeared. Our language, however, is young and no doubt also fresh and inventive, but, especially in the field of cultural study, it has yet to distinguish reasonably between the kind of categorical formalism it is free to assert and the manifold of variable phenomena. Like the innocent eye that believes the mountain to be no larger then the fingernail (and is surprised when it 'grows') categorical formalism is surprised and dismayed by variation. It has not come to terms with its own virtual reality, and like the infant feels disappointment and loss when its asserted sense turns out to be nonsense. That is why post-Darwinian cultural theory is so uncomfortable: it is not so much that we lose our privileged connection to God (there has been time to accommodate that) but that our language is beginning to display its own lack of privilege. We define postmodernism as consciousness of that loss of innocence, but also as no more than that: a paradigm imprisoned in mourning its past, however brave a face it pretends to show. But outside of the suffocating confines of humanism and language-centred philosophy or sociology, autopoietic complexity provides a cogent alternative that must be brought to the centre of our disciplines.

The attentive reader will realise we have now reached an impasse – assuming we have understood our argument correctly – namely that the attempt to maintain a paradigm that places ontology first and morality second must eventually confront morality when the guiding principle is the inclusion of complexity. A moral code must surely demand from us at least the same attention as Rembrandt? That is of course much too formal: moral codes can be as important, insignificant, detestable or as valuable as anything else. Let us say, then, that we think we have provided a model of complexity in which – on another occasion – the notion of moral order might be more explicitly re-examined. Suffice to say, a notion of moral possibility is inherent and barely-concealed in the foregoing. Any more explicit analysis will not turn the two fundamentalisms of imperatives and/or their absence.

An ontology that rests on autopoietic economy, must insist that morality, like any other order, is a possible, emergent phenomenon. The problem epitomised by Duchamp's rejections, by the distinction between heaven and Earth, between Being and beings, between authentic and inauthentic is that they suppress the possible structures of autopoietic emergence. They are forms of fundamentalism and as such 'forbid' differentiation. Lyotard's solution – enforced pluralism – would be sentimental if it were not for its intellectual paucity and its concealed intolerances. Moreover, in the context of Durkheim's 'organic' aesthetics where differentiation promotes interaction as opposed to replicated competition for a single, viable social space, so the suppression of difference is also the promotion of perpetual conflicts over one 'authentic' territory. Stated in more general ecological terms, the suppression of difference essays a world populated by one species in permanent internal competition; whereas Lyotard's alternative proposes one species characterised by virtual differentiations, disposable at will. Those, then, who object to something like speciation in the field of social phenomena (on the grounds that it conceals something like our common humanity) had better be clear about the price of fundamentalism.

In a sense, then, we have now provided a material justification for the preference for heterogeny: it works better the homogeny; it is likely to be more vital. This is not, of course, a moral argument. It presumes an autopoietic economy. And its limits will be of the same type: where differing species (animal, moral, cultural) impinge upon each other a settlement will have to be found or the skirmish will continue in its own, costly, hostile way.

Do you recall Lyotard's remark: 'we have paid a high enough price for the nostalgia of the whole and the one' ? (op. cit.) There he was closer to the truth. And for the same reason we cannot permit our test case of 'pure' dissention (the Hitler society on campus): it will cost us so much we shall be forced to destroy it. Our reasoning leads to the conclusion that the price of modern, 'rational' authoritarianism and postmodern anti-structuralism are also too high. Both crush the phenomena they propose to explore; both conceal and suppress the significance of autopoietic economy.

Notes

1. See Pefanis, J. (1992) pp.1-8.
2. Rosen, S. (1969) Chs. 2,3 & 4 remains the most accessible, informative and critical account of Heidegger's project.

3. ibid. p.130.
4. Heidegger, M. (1973) p.87.
5. Heidegger, M. (1978) pp.227-8.
6. ibid. p. 223.
7. ibid. p. 228 our emphases.
8. Heidegger, M. (1973) p. 109.
9. See also Rosen, S.(1969) p.31: 'ontology is much more plainly a speech by certain kinds of beings called 'ontologists' than it is an explanation of the word 'being'.
10. Levin (1988) p. 44.
11. ibid. p. 45.
12. Heidegger, M. (1978) p.181, his emphasis.
13. For an explanation of the formal concept see Gleick, J.(1987) p.103, pp.115-6 & p.162.

Bibliography

Ansell-Pearson, K. 1994 *An Introduction to Nietzsche as Political Thinker*. Cambridge: Cambridge University Press

Baudrillard, J. 1998 *Selected Writings*. Stanford University Press

Benjamin, A. (ed.) 1989 *The Lyotard Reader*. Oxford: Blackwell

Beck, U. 1992 *Risk Society*. London: Sage

Blackmore, S. 1999 *The Meme Machine*. Oxford: Oxford University Press

Botting, F. & Wilson, S. (eds.) 1997 *The Bataille Reader*. Oxford: Blackwell

Boyne, R, 1998 'Postmodernism, the sublime and ethics'. Velody & Still (eds.) *The Politics of Modernity*. Cambridge: Cambridge University Press

Brookner, A. 1980 *Jacques-Louis David*. London: Chatto & Windus

Bryson, N. 1981 *Word and Image: French Painting of the Ancien Regime*. Cambridge: Cambridge University Press

Bryson, N. 1983 *Vision and Painting: The Logic of the Gaze*. London: Macmillan

Bryson, N. 1984 *Tradition and Desire: from David to Delacroix*. Cambridge: Cambridge University Press

Bryson, Holly & Moxey (eds.) 1992 *Visual Theory*. Oxford & Cambridge: Polity & Blackwell

Capra, F. 1996 *The Web of Life*. London: Harper-Collins

Carroll, D. 1989 *Paraesthetics: Foucault, Lyotard, Derrida*. London: Routledge

Cassirer, H. 1968 *Kant's First Critique*. London: George Allen & Unwin

Cheetham, M. A. 1991 *The Rhetoric of Purity: Essentialist Theory and the Advent of Abstract Painting*. Cambridge: Cambridge University Press

Clark, T.J. 1985 The Painting of Modern Life: Paris in the Art of Manet and his Followers. London: Thames & Hudson.

Clark, T.J. 1999 *Farewell to an Idea: Episodes from a History of Modernism*. New Haven & London: Yale University Press.

Connor, S. 1989 *Postmodernist Culture*. Oxford: Blackwell

Crowther, P. 1997 *The Language of Twentieth Century Art: A Conceptual History*. New Haven & London: Yale University Press.

Danto, A. 1985 *The Philosophical Disenfranchisement of Art*. New York & London: Columbia University Press

Danto, A. 1997 *After the End of Art: Contemporary Art ad The Pale of History*. Princeton: Princeton University Press

*David, J-L.

Dawkins, R. 1989 *The Selfish Gene.* Oxford & London: Oxford University Press

Dennett, D. 1993 *Consciousness Explained.* London: Penguin

Dennett, D. 1995 *Darwin's Dangerous Idea: Evolution and the Meanings of Life.* London: Penguin

Dennett, D. 1997 *Kinds of Minds: Towards an Understanding of Consciousness.* London: Phoenix

Derrida, J. 1976 *Of Grammatology.* Spivak (trans.) John Hopkins University Press

Derrida, J. 1981 *Disseminations.* Johnson, B. (trans) London: Athlone Press

Derrida, J. (1987) *The Truth in Painting.* Bennington & McLeod (trans.) Chicago & London: University of Chicago Press.

Dissanayake, E. 1992 *Homo Aestheticus.* New York: Free Press

Durkheim, E. 1964 *The Rules of Sociological Method.* New York: Free Press

Durkheim, E. 1982 *The Elementary Forms of the Religious Life.* London: George Allen & Unwin

Durkheim, E. 1984 *The Division of Labour in Society.* London: Macmillan

Duro, P. 1996 *The Rhetoric of the Frame.* Cambridge: Cambridge University Press

Duve, T.de 1996 *Kant After Duchamp.* London & Cambridge: MIT Press

Eve, R. Horsfall, S, & Lee, M. 1997 *Chaos, Complexity and Sociology.* Thousand Oaks: Sage

Frascina, F. (ed.) 1985 *Pollock and After: The Critical Debate.* London: Harper Row

Freud, L. 1996 *Lucien Freud.* Bernard & Birdsall (eds.) London: Jonathan Cape

Fried, M. 1988 *Absorption and Theatricality: Painting and Beholder in the Age of Diderot.* Chicago & London: University of Chicago Press

Fried, M. 1998 *Art and Objecthood: Essays and Reviews.* Chicago & London: University of Chicago Press

Friedlander, W. 1952 *David to Delacroix.* Harvard University Press

Foucault, M. and Rabinow, P (ed.) 1984 *The Foucault Reader.* London: Random House

Foucault, M. 1992 *The Order of Things.* London: Routledge

Giddens, A. 1992 (ed.) & 'Introduction' *Emile Durkheim: Selected Writings.* Cambridge: Cambridge University Press

Gleick, J. 1993 *Chaos.* London: Abacus

Greenberg, C. 1986 *The Collected Essays and Criticism.* O' Brian, J. (ed.) Chicago & London: Chicago University Press

Hamilton, G.H. 1969 *Manet and his Critics*. New Haven & London: Yale University Press.

Hanson, A. 1977 *Manet and the Modern Tradition*. New Haven & London: Yale University Press

Harrison, C. & Wood, P. (eds.) 1992 *Art in Theory 1900-1990*. Cambridge: Polity

Hayles, N.K. 1999 *How We Became Posthuman: Virtual Bodies in Cybernetics, Literature and Informatics*. University of Chicago Press: Chicago & London

Hegel, G.W.F. 1971 *Philosophy of Mind*. Wallace, W. (trans.) Oxford Clarendon Press

Heidegger, M. 1961 *An Introduction to Metaphysics*. Mannheim, R. (trans.) London: Anchor

Heidegger, M. 1973 *The End of Philosophy*. Stambaugh, J. (trans.) London: Condor

Heidegger, M. 1974 *Identity and Difference*. Stambaugh, J. (trans.) London: Harper Torchbooks

Heidegger, M.1978 'The Question Concerning Technology' in *Basic Writings*. Krell, D. (ed.) London: Routledge

Henrich, D. 1985 'The Contemporary Relevance of Hegel's Aesthetics' in *Hegel* Inwood, M. (ed.) Oxford: Oxford University Press

Heywood, I. and Sandywell, B. (eds.) 1998 *Interpreting Visual Culture: Explorations in the Hermeneutics of the Visual*. London: Routledge

Honour, H. 1984 *Romanticism*. Harmondsworth: Penguin

Karelis, C. 1979 *Hegel's Introduction to Aesthetics*. Oxford: Oxford University Press

Kierkegaard, S. 1965 *The Concept of Irony*. Bloomington and London: Indiana University Press

Jay, M. 1993 *Downcast Eyes: The Denigration of Vision in Twentieth-Century French Thought*. Berkeley & London: University of California Press

Jenks, C. (ed.) 1993 *Cultural Reproduction*. London & New York: Routledge

Jenks, C. (ed.) 1995 *Visual Culture*. London & New York: Routledge

Jenks, C. 1993 *Culture* London: Routledge

Johnson, G.A. and Smith, M.B. (eds.) 1994 *The Merleau-Ponty Aesthetics Reader: Philosophy and Painting*. Northwestern University Press

Kant, E. 1973 *The Critique of Pure Reason*. Kemp Smith (trans.) London: Macmillan

Kosuth, J. 1991 *Art After Philosophy and After*. Cambridge, Mass: MIT Press

Levin, J. M. 1988 *The Opening of Vision: Nihilism and the Postmodern Situation.* New York & London: Routledge

Lovelock, J. 1995 *The Ages of Gaia.* Oxford: Oxford University Press

Luhmann, N. 1995 *Social Systems.* Stanford: Stanford University Press

Lyotard, J-F 1984 *The Postmodern Condition: A Report on Knowledge.* Bennington & Massumi (eds.) Manchester University Press

Lyotard, J-F. 1989 *The Lyotard Reader.* Andrew Benjamin (ed.) Oxford: Blackwell

Maturana, H. & Varela, F. 1980 *Autopoiesis and Cognition.* Dordrecht: D. Reidel.

*Manet, E.

McEvilly, T. 1995 *Art and Discontent: Theory at the Millennium.* New York: Documentext

Michelangelo *Drawings by Michelangelo.* (exhibition catalogue) British Museum Publications 1975

Mitchell, W.J.T. 1986 *Iconology: Image, Text, Ideology.* Chicago & London University of Chicago Press

Plato 1973 *Phaedrus and Letters VII and VIII.* Harmondsworth: Penguin

Plato 1974 *The Republic.* Harmondsworth: Penguin

Plato 1980 *The Trial and Death of Socrates.* Harmondsworth: Penguin

Peck, W. 1978 *Drawings from ancient Egypt.* London: Thames & Hudson

Pefanis, J. 1991 *Heterology and the Postmodern: Bataille, Baudrillard and Lyotard.* Durham & London: Duke University Press

Pinker, S. 1994 *The Language Instinct: The New Science of Language and Mind.* London: Penguin

Richter, G. 1995 *The Daily Practice of Painting: Writings and Interviews 1962-1993.* London: Thames & Hudson

Rose, S. 1997 *Lifelines: Biology, Freedom, Determinism.* London: Allen Lane

Rosen, S 1969 *Nihilism: A Philosophical Essay.* New Haven & London: Yale University Press

Rosen, S. 1974 *G.W.F. Hegel.* New Haven & London: Yale University Press

Rosen, C. and Zerner, H. 1984 *Romanticism and Realism: The Mythology of Nineteenth-Century Art.* London: Faber

Roy Frieden, B. 1999 *Physics from Fisher Information: A Unification.* Cambridge University Press

Runciman, W. (1998) *The Social Animal.* London: Harper Collins

Smith, J.A. 'Manet and Durkheim: Images and Theories of Re-production' in Jenks, C. (ed.) 1993 *Cultural Reproduction.* London: Routledge

Smith, J.A. 'Three Images of the Visual: Empirical, Formal and Normative' in Jenks, C. (ed.) 1995 *Visual Culture.* London: Routledge

Smith, J.A. 'The Denigration of Vision and the Renewal of Painting' in Heywood, I. and Sandywell, B. (eds.) 1998 *Interpreting Visual Culture: Explorations in the Hermeneutics of the Visual*. London: Routledge

Summers, D. 1981 *Michelangelo and the Language of Art*. Princeton University Press

Summers, D. 'Real Metaphor' in Visual Theory (eds.)

The Art of the Holocaust. 1982 London: Pan Books in GB

Vasari, G. 1965 *Lives of the Artists*. Harmondsworth: Penguin

Weinberg, S. (1993) *Dreams of a Final Theory*. London: Random House

Wittgenstein, L. 1974 *Tractatus Logico-Philosophicu.s* London: Routledge

Wittgenstein, L. 1972 *Philosophical Investigations*. Oxford: Blackwell

Wolff, J. *Aesthetics and the Sociology of Art*. Allen & Unwin, London 1983